UFO 1

*A quest to understand one of the
world's greatest mysteries*

AUGUSTUS NICHOLAS

UFO 1: A quest to understand one of the world's greatest mysteries
Augustus Nicholas
First published in 2018
Second Edition published in 2023

Title: UFO 1: A quest to understand one of the world's greatest mysteries
Creator: Nicholas, Augustus (author)
ISBN: 978-1-923156-26-5

All photography © Augustus Nicholas.

Cover design by Gina Walters
Editing by Lisa Lark
Typesetting by Green Hill Publishing
Printed by Lightning Source

Find out more:
WWW.UFOTHEBOOK.COM

UFO The Book Channel

Image attributions
Map of Melbourne by Ilya Shrayber [GFDL (http://www.gnu.org/copyleft/fdl.html) or CC BY-SA 4.0 (https://creativecommons.org/licenses/by-sa/4.0)], via Wikimedia Commons
Map of Glyfada by Pitichinaccio [Public domain], from Wikimedia Commons
Aerial world map by NASA Earth Observatory (NASA Goddard Space Flight Center) [Public domain], via Wikimedia Commons
World Globe by by TUBS [CC BY-SA 3.0 (https://creativecommons.org/licenses/by-sa/3.0) or GFDL (http://www.gnu.org/copyleft/fdl.html)], from Wikimedia Commons

CONTENTS

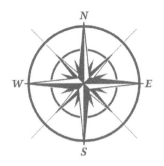

PREFACE

It is with a heavy heart that I write this preface. This is mainly because of my symphony of conflicting thoughts, which flow between religion and the elusive, strange subject of UFOs. The view that UFOs should not exist and the likelihood of ridicule will no doubt lead to the chalking up of further issues and problems in my life.

I have been pulled between the expectations of the religion in which I was brought up, and my efforts to make sense of the unexplained, all the while keeping an open mind where possible, and it has caused me great angst. My science background has tended to be the dominant force in my later years, and sometimes it has challenged my behaviour. At other times I have listened to my inner eagerness for metaphysical enlightenment, or simply collected my inner objections for later verification.

When I was a young child it was explained to me at church that humankind was created "in the image of God", not only in the physical sense but also in terms of self-awareness and a consciousness of "You" and "I". It is well publicised in the media that in recent years far fewer people have been actively religious than were decades ago. And so too have I gently and respectfully set aside the religious feelings and interest that I acquired as a youngster, as my enthusiasm for the sciences and the unknown - in many subjects and topics - gained momentum. My mind had them neatly compiled as I pondered and slept on them like sheets on my bed.

The religious mind has seemed to be the way of intercepting views and search for the reason for our existence. Without an explanation we are left to feel insignificant. We try to have a sense of meaning and purpose in life as we ponder the cycle of birth, work, making money to survive, having children and then dying. Religion teaches us that the way to salvation is by worshipping and obeying God.

The scientific mind also teaches us that we are insignificant when compared to the visible universe, since we live in a galaxy of 100 billion stars, and 100 billion planets revolve around some of them. It has been estimated that there are 100 billion galaxies in the known universe. However, when an article published on the NASA website in 2016 reported that the Hubble space telescope reveals ten times more galaxies in the observable universe than was previously thought, the estimated number of galaxies in the universe was inflated to perhaps a staggering two trillion galaxies.

Because it is inconceivable to think we are alone in this massively sparse universe as we too are infinitesimal, we have relinquished the quest for equivalent significance - although humans have attempted to dominate God by flying to the moon or sending space probes to the inner and outer planets and beyond, and intend to one day travel to Mars.

Many (including former United States Presidents) have referred to the *New World Order*, where hidden agendas of elite globalists in financial power are driving this world towards a *one world government* and aim to reduce the world's population by 90%, and it is slowly coming to fruition. The sole purpose of this movement is to suppress information from the masses and create perpetual calamity in the world via economics and military activity. Many people believe that the technology currently available in science, medicine and defense – for example, military aircraft like the mighty Stealth bomber unveiled in the late 1990s - is somewhat obsolete, having actually been developed decades earlier. Further, it is widely believed that a supposed permanent cure for cancer has been suppressed for many years by the global elite. If it is true, and such technology is never to be revealed to the so-called "useless eaters", then this a crime against humanity.

In most sciences, from high school study of Darwin's theory of evolution to astrophysics studied at university and the Big Bang Theory, it has been a common thread to leave God out of the picture. Of course, there have been distant flickering lights near expressways which inspired a frantic attempt to breach views suggesting religion via physics, which can provide its own answer in the form of algebraic advances. An example of this is Einstein's famous quote that "God does not play dice" in reference to the new (at the time) theory in quantum physics. This was quantum mechanics, which was first developed in the early 1900s, to describe the weird behaviour of tiny subatomic particles. However, years later I found that Einstein's quote did not refer to religion after all; he had just used "God" as a metaphor. Niels Bohr, another famous physicist at the time, replied: "Don't tell God what to do".

How old is the earth according to the Bible? The Bible describes a line of descendants of Adam and Eve, and if we add up their ages, we can estimate the age of the earth to be no more than six thousand years. This is in strong contrast to many scientists' estimates of the age of the earth - a few billion years.

What about dinosaurs? Carbon-14 is considered to be a highly reliable dating technique, but I have learned that carbon dating is only "accurate" to 50,000 years. Perhaps no concept in science is as misunderstood as carbon dating. Almost everyone thinks carbon dating works in terms of millions or billions of years. But it is only useful for once-living things which still contain carbon, like flesh or bone or wood. Therefore we cannot use carbon dating for rocks or fossils, which consist only of inorganic minerals.

With their desire to find meaning in life, many people have turned to supernatural paranormal beliefs of some kind, including belief in psychic power, spiritual energy, and reincarnation. Alongside the desire to find meaning is also the belief in UFOs, alien visitors and so-called abductions. Humans living in this questionable universe have an inherent desire to find the answers to questions that have been asked recently, such as: "Are we living in a computer program?" or "Can we travel through time?"; and questions which have been asked for aeons, such as: "How did we get here?" and "Who created God?". In 2014 Pope Francis even said that he would baptise aliens: "Who are we to close doors?" Misrepresentation of the Pope's message is understandable, but it was meant to demonstrate acceptance and inclusion; at the time Pope Francis referred to a Bible story about the conversion of the first pagans to Christianity.

I hope you will find the sightings I have documented in the following pages as intriguing and mind-blowing as they have been for me. Only two members of my family know about this. When I tested acceptance of my ideas outside my family, by showing a small quantity of my videos and photos to two others, suddenly their attitude towards me changed noticeably and was expressed in their avoidance of me. I subsequently felt that I was seen as a "nutter", or someone who "wears a tin foil hat" - a deceptive term introduced by the powers that be to keep the subject of UFOs in the realm of folklore and pixie dust. I never brought it up again.

It never ceases to amaze me how the very subject of UFOs and aliens in the wider community still meets with the same level of scepticism as in the years after the supposed Roswell UFO crash incident in 1947 and the subsequent Project Blue book that documented and investigated UFO sightings. The many explanations for the "sightings" included: "It was a weather balloon", "It's just Venus", "It was swamp gas"; and the lists go on.

Writing this book took me back in time to my childhood years with all the noise, emotions, thoughts, tastes, and memories of that time, where the predominant factor was the lack of answers to my endless list of questions on subjects that were not widely accepted, including UFOs and aerial anomalies.

I hope this book will find its way around the globe and that, along with my website (www.UFOthebook.com) and the accompanying videos, photos and stills on YouTube, it will enable you to make up your own mind. I know that some of what I have to say is pure speculation and unprovable, and at times it will seem that I am fueling the conspiracy enthusiasts. I can assure you that this is not intentional because all I want are answers to the questions that have plagued me for many years.

I have kept to a minimum any video editing on YouTube, and it is only utilised where I feel it offers comfortable viewing. I know how much we all dislike the grainy, blurry photos and obviously fake shaky videos dumped on the internet as a joke or to misinform. I can assure you that I have not doctored any of my photos or videos apart from the use of features such as cropping, slowing down, or zooming in where necessary. I have just been fortunate enough to be at the right place, at the right time, and you will find that a common thread throughout the sightings is that usually no two sightings are identical.

Remarkably, "ordinary"-looking balloons often seem to follow prominent sightings, as if in some weird way to hide their presence and confuse the situation, causing people to second-guess themselves as witnesses. Correspondingly, in my experience there have been two main types of aerial phenomena: the glowing daytime reflective orb, which I have dubbed High Altitude Quantum Singularity Reactors (HAQSRs), and "vehicles" such as the classic saucer and H-shaped UFO. I will attempt to analyse the difference in the coming chapters.

My ultimate aim is to break the shackles that have enslaved our minds, because the secular mind shines no light on the way out. We live our lives materialistically, trying to outdo each other, and before we know it we are too old to look around and simply live our lives. Prior to death, humans are often known to regret not having stopped to enjoy their lives, and in old age many suddenly realise how short life really is. That is when we start turning to religion again for salvation.

We know about the past, the present and the future, but time inevitably goes in one direction - towards the future. We are so preoccupied with time, always running out of time or rushing to get to somewhere; yet the Theory of Relativity and eastern religions teach us that time does not flow, but **it just is**. Our consciousness is therefore the sole constructor of the illusion of time. It is far easier to say this than to grasp it consciously.

Nevertheless, just as time has been a mystery to us for thousands of years, we have also been obsessed with finding the answers to the mysteries of life. We still do not know how human reproduction occurs at the cellular level, how the blueprint of life dictates that particular cells will develop into eyes, vital internal organs and so on. Mystery is all around us, and the subjects of UFOs and inter-dimensional beings are just a small component of it.

Come along with me on this journey from Adelaide to Melbourne, and Europe. But please keep an open mind as I commission the body of knowledge from various fields of sciences in my attempt to make sense of and explain what I have seen, and to illustrate what I think objects might be and their purpose for being here. Do keep an open mind as we slide throughout my illustrated point of view that, along with the arithmetic, provides the sign that points to the way out of the maze.

INTRODUCTION

Inherent Desire to Understand the Unexplained

I was born in Adelaide, South Australia, in 1961. Throughout my adolescence, I considered Adelaide to be a small country town. You acclimatise yourself to believe this when you constantly hear it. As the saying goes: "If you tell a big enough lie and keep repeating it, people will eventually come to believe it".

Although Adelaide has a quarter to a fifth of the population of Sydney and Melbourne, it has always produced its share of famous and very successful people. Look at actors such as Mel Gibson and Geoffrey Rush, singers such as Bon Scott from ACDC and Jimmy Barnes from Cold Chisel, the esteemed physicists Paul Davies and Sir Mark Oliphant (who had a key role in the development of the atomic bomb). There have also been highly successful business people such as Rupert Murdoch from News Corp and Con Polites the "property king"; famous sportsmen such as cricketer Sir Donald Bradman; and of course, we have had our fair share of famous politicians, but I will not go there.

Comet Ikeya–Seki, 1965, One of the Brightest Comets Seen in the Last Thousand Years

My love for astronomy and science began when I was four years old, when my mother woke me up to share an experience she had witnessed against the dark heavens as she walked out the front gate on her way to catch the first train to the City, where she worked. A massive comet was travelling overhead in an east to west direction. She always got up at 5.00 am to go to work as a cleaner in the City of Adelaide, and she had noticed the comet on the previous few mornings but decided that this time she just had to share it with someone.

As I was sleeping in the same bedroom as my mother, (my father had passed away the previous year), I awoke just as she was walking out the front door. Hearing me, she came back into the bedroom and asked me to come outside and have a look at something in the sky that she could not really explain. I stood there under the front veranda in awe, as I saw high above in front of me the distinct head of a comet with a massive tail trailing behind to the left. I say "trailing", but it actually did not move at all. The whole comet progressively moved a short distance relative to the sky, noticeable over consecutive nights. I cannot remember if I could see it in the daytime.

It was a magnificent sight as it stretched from horizon to horizon, and I will never forget it. It created such an impression on me that to this day I am not sure if it was as big as I remember, but I know for sure that it was huge. I remember being transfixed and unwilling to depart from where I stood. I wanted to stay outside longer and continue observing this heavenly display, but my mother had to leave for work. So with painful dejection, I kissed her goodbye and she took me back inside and locked the door behind her.

I often wonder how I can remember with such detail an event from over 50 years ago, and how I can so vividly recall what it looked like, including the direction it was coming from as I stood in front of our house. I have no idea, except that it was as if my mind's compass prepared itself to cognitively relive the event into my adulthood, revealing itself in my mind's eye when required to.

My mother enrolled me in primary school a year earlier than legally required so she could take on a second job. Years later, I finished high school and was excited about enrolling in university at the age of 16. I went on to do a Science degree majoring in Physics and Physical and Inorganic Chemistry. One of my subjects was Astronomy and Astrophysics, so one day I took the opportunity to ask my Professor what I had seen so many years ago. I knew it was a comet but I just wanted to hear the excitement in someone else's voice as they confirmed that it was no ordinary comet. There was no internet to find the answers back then, and in fact, computers were only in their infancy.

Another subject I studied was Computing and it is true that the early computers occupied one whole room. The computer we had at University was one where we had to enter the FORTRAN and Pascal programs by punching holes in cards via a "type writer", then ensuring that all the cards were in the right order before you gave them to the person behind the desk, who would place them in the computer. Depending on how busy they were, we would return hours later, hoping that we had not made any errors, otherwise we would be required to identify which card had the error, re-type it and hand it back in along with all the others in the correct sequence. When the returned reports were placed in pigeonholes allocated to individual students, the result would be long line-ups at the counter during busy periods.

Accordingly, I was pleased when my Astronomy Lecturer verified that it was **Comet Ikeya–Seki** from September 18, 1965, and it certainly was very bright. He verified that it was visible in the daytime. I finally had a name, and years later after the introduction of the internet, I was able to read up about it. I could have researched it by looking through the archived Australian and world newspapers in a building not far from University, which I sometimes passed on the way to the Museum at lunch times; but I was not sure about the exact date of the encounter so it would have been difficult to narrow the search.

C/1965 S1 (Ikeya–Seki)

Comet Ikeya–Seki, formally designated **C/1965 S1, 1965 VIII**, and **1965f**, was a long-period comet discovered independently by Kaoru Ikeya and Tsutomu Seki. First observed as a faint telescopic object on September 18 1965, the early calculations of its orbit suggested that on October 21, it would pass just 450,000 km above the Sun's surface and would probably become extremely bright.

Comets can defy such predictions, but Ikeya–Seki performed as expected, and was seen shining at magnitude–10 as it approached perihelion, where observers reported that it was clearly visible in the daytime sky next to the Sun. In Japan, it reached perihelion at noon local time. It proved to be one of the brightest comets seen in the last thousand years and is sometimes known as the Great Comet of 1965.

The comet was seen to break into three pieces just before its perihelion passage. The three pieces continued in almost identical orbits, and the comet re-appeared in the morning sky in late October, showing a very bright tail. By early 1966, it faded from view as it receded into the outer solar system.

Ikeya–Seki is a member of the Kreutz sungrazers family of comets, which are thought to be fragments of a large comet which broke up in 1106.

Apollo 11 Moon Landing, 16–24 July 1969

The time of the landing of Apollo 11 on the moon was a very exciting period for me as a young child. We were sent home early from Primary School that day to watch the live broadcast on TV of the landing on the moon. This was the spaceflight that landed the lunar module Eagle, manned by Neil Armstrong and pilot Buzz Aldrin, on the moon on 20 July 1969.

My father had died six years earlier and my mother brought up four children on her own, ensuring to the best of her ability that we did not lack anything. We had a black and white television, and as I watched it I understood that something momentous was developing before our eyes, an event unique in all human history.

I don't remember much about Neil and Buzz walking around the moon. But I do remember when they splashed down safely in the ocean and were picked up and taken aboard a US warship, and then entered a decontamination trailer as we were wondering whether the world would be safe from bacteria or microbes. President Nixon had welcomed them home, talking to them live from outside the trailer.

Years later it became common for the public to debate whether they had actually landed on the moon, or whether it was faked. The movie "Capricorn One" (1977) about a government conspiracy and the landing hoax of astronauts on Mars was partly to blame.

I believe that they did land on the moon, mainly because at least 300,000 people - compartmentalised or not - had some input in the success of this mission, and to this day there has not been any hard evidence submitted by any of them to the contrary. I respect the astronauts who would rather give their lives than allow favourable dissimilar resolution to be a factor present during the mission. The planning to the minutest detail ensured that it was a successful mission, which returned safely to earth.

I am fully aware of the issue regarding the questions about how NASA successfully sent Apollo astronauts through the dangerous Van Allen Belts around earth, the issue around the flapping flag on the moon, and the issue about lack of visible stars in any of the footage. There are many more, such as the theory that the shadows cast by rocks on the moon match the artificial lights in a studio rather than a single one light source (the sun); the lack of evidence of moon dust and debris on the lunar module landing pods; or even the absence of a crater when the module landed on the soft surface of the moon.

Stanley Kubrick's "assignment" to direct the biggest hoax in human history was another favourite amongst the conspiracy theorists. And the list goes on and on, demonstrating a change in the thinking of humankind across our accessible galaxy.

One argument for the authenticity of the moon landings is that the missions were timed so that the Van Allen Belts were at their lowest intensities as they fluctuated with the sun's activity, and combined with the well-insulated spacecraft, proved to be no threat. The flapping flag has been scrutinised in the minutest detail and it has been concluded that the movement of the flag was a natural effect in such a low-gravity environment, as the astronauts disturbed the flag when trying to plant it better in the lunar soil.

What about the fact that we cannot see stars? Apparently, this is also a natural effect with photos in space, because the brightness of the lunar surface drowns out the relatively dim light from stars in the dark sky. This is identical to the way car headlights can drown out fainter light from nearby objects. As for the non-parallel shadows cast by the astronauts, rocks and the lunar module, they are thought to be possibly due to the uneven lunar surface - as simple as that.

The famous lunar rock with the letter C on it, looking as if it was a stage prop, can be explained by the possibility that a small hair or piece of thread may have got caught in the machine while it was being copied from a much larger image.

Image I - In 1969, the display of a replica of the Apollo 11 Lunar Module in Victoria Square in the city of Adelaide, South Australia, was fascinating for me. You can see me in the foreground. Less than eight years later I enrolled in a Bachelor of Science degree at Adelaide University.

"Chariots of the Gods" - Unsolved Mysteries of the Past, 1969

Most of us are familiar with this very successful book, first released in 1969, about extra-terrestrial intervention in human history. I cannot remember how old I was when I bought this book, but if it was around 1969 then that would make me only eight years old. However, I am absolutely sure that I bought one or two subsequent books, including "Return to the Stars" which was released in 1970 by the same author.

I became so fascinated with the concept outlined in the books - the possibility that "God was an astronaut" - that for a while I retained the two parallel thoughts of religion and science that rang loud in both my world within my family when it came to church on Sundays, and my world when I was alone reading my books.

In the 1970s the release in the cinema circuit of a documentary focused on the material within the first book, "Chariots of the Gods", firmed up my entrance into the world of mysteries and the unexplained, as I sat there in the cinema. I did not openly discuss my thoughts on this subject with my family, but on occasion, I felt helpless with no one to talk to about it.

My First UFO Encounter, 1985

The very first time I saw a UFO was around 1985, when I was in my early twenties. My mother and two young nieces and I were returning from a family friend's party at Aldinga, a beachside suburb 45 minutes south of Adelaide. I remember it was a warm and clear night and I was driving on Main South Road, a lonely stretch of road that connects to the larger arterial, and which had limited street lighting at the time. High in the sky directly in front of me was a dark cigar-shaped object with a light in the front and rear.

I quickly pulled over and jumped out of the car. At this point, it was directly above my head, moving slowly and silently towards the coastline. I glanced over my shoulder and noticed that further down on the opposite side of the road a convertible had also pulled over some time before, and a man was standing beside his car observing the same object.

The object travelled towards the ocean, then made a sharp right-angled turn to the left following the coast. The surrounding area was sparsely populated farmland back then. When the object was above me, it seemed to eject a small bright object that made an arc towards the ground some distance away. Over the next several days I spoke with the acclaimed Adelaide UFO researcher Colin Norris ("Mr UFO", 1920-2009), who basically advised me that my sighting did not warrant any further investigation. As the object didn't land, and I could not provide any photographic evidence, he said it would not be of any interest to him or the public. I acknowledge the well deserved credit given to Colin Norris at the time for bringing the field of Ufology into the public forum while removing the stigma associated with it.

The Taos Hum, 5 January – 12 March, 2008

As I recall a strange encounter that consumed me in early 2008, I literally break out into a cold sweat. It is like a theatrical play in the mind's eye, with three key characters - my mother, my sister, and myself.

The name of the Taos Hum comes from a small town in New Mexico, Taos. It's a quiet little town except for one special feature: a mysterious humming sound was reported in the early 1990s. It seemed to commence as the sun goes down and would not cease until the sun came up, preventing a good night's sleep for those who heard it.

Hearing such a sound is not unique to Taos, New Mexico, as it occurs all around the world. Many theories have been put forward over the years about the Hum, including that it is the High Frequency Active Auroral Research Program (HAARP), or that it was part of a secret government mind-control program, right through to it being emitted by underground UFO bases. Investigators and researchers from the University of New Mexico conducted research into the Taos Hum, in which several pieces of sensitive equipment were set up in the homes of those that could hear it; but nothing out of the ordinary was ever recorded.

The other strange aspect to this phenomenon is that you can only hear it indoors and not outside. It is common for distressed sufferers to set up tents in their backyards in order to get a good night's sleep. And sadly, some people have harmed themselves to escape the clutches of the Hum.

I suffered from this very same thing for over nine weeks, from 5 January until 12 March 2008. It was an unrelenting hum that sounded like a diesel engine idling right outside my bedroom window. The internet has available several audio reproductions of the Hum which are eerily very close to what I heard, and some allege to have actual recordings of it. The Hum seemed to produce a three-dimensional effect comparable to the effect of virtual placement of sound sources such as speakers in three-dimensions of space, including behind, above or below the listener.

It was three years since I had moved into my house, and before I knew anything at all about the Hum. I began to hear the strange sound as I lay in my bed. I used to get up rather early in the morning to go to work so I was accustomed to going to bed early, and as it was Daylight Savings time in January the sun would go down between 8:30 and 9:00 pm. So I would only secure a couple of hours of sleep before the "fun" started.

As I peered through my bedroom window, my thoughts were immediately directed towards my next-door neighbours, contemplating whether they had recently bought an industrial refrigerator; and as my bedroom window faced the side entrance to their property, I thought that it was an odd place to install it. I did not realise how ridiculous my assumption was at the time. I just needed to find a solution to this living nightmare. Throughout this experience, from my perspective the sound was quite loud; so it was very frustrating when I would ask my mother (who was living with me), whether she could hear it, and her reply was always: "No, nothing". My sister tried her best to demonstrate that she could hear something as she placed her ears against the walls in every corner of the house, but she failed to convince me.

Night after night this would continue. While attempting everything in my power to suppress the Hum so that I could get some sleep, nothing worked. I tried various earplugs, music via headphones and white noise to no avail. I could still hear it close by, "calling me", with or without these external devices. It was as if the droning noise was bouncing around inside my head. Perhaps it is a manifestation of tinnitus, I thought. However, by definition, tinnitus means, "tinkling or ringing like a bell", and that certainly was not what I was hearing.

The only immediate solution that allowed me to function mentally and survive my daily onslaught of meetings, was to consume high volumes of coffee during the days. As I could not sleep, I would walk the neighbourhood streets trying to find the elusive electrical appliance that was in dire need of repair. I made moonlight of the situation as it illuminated my way in trying to find the culprit.

I remember complaining to two mechanics who worked in a workshop further down my street, but they denied that they had anything to do with it. I also directed complaints towards a high-rise apartment building situated even further from my house, on the assumption that the roof had a ventilation system that might be the cause. With the elimination of all possibilities in a radius of 40 or so metres from my house, in desperation I started investigating at many more times the distance, looking for that offending mechanism. It just had to be a faulty appliance, I thought to myself.

Each time, I returned home embarrassed and tired after virtually zero hours of sleep the night before. In the circumstances, the best I could offer humanity was to be the object of admiration since I was operating on an average of between two or three and zero hours of sleep per night. It was common for me to lament all the way to work, as I concluded that I must have been going insane. After about eight weeks, I remember scanning the web, typing all sorts of search criteria, when I came across the "Taos Hum". My excitement was overwhelming as I read article after article containing such similar stories to mine, and I learned that fundamentally this was a worldwide phenomenon. So, happily, I was not losing my mind. Some articles provided a glimmer of hope as to the cause; for example, that it could be unique to the structure of the roof of the house. I started to think that perhaps I should sell up and move to a house that did not have such a high arched roof.

Conversely, on 5 March 2008 I located a website in England dedicated to The Hum sufferers, which gave notice of an upcoming forum which would allow everyone to document and share their experiences, and provide advice on how to manage the problem. We wrote many emails to each other; and the two emails reproduced here in their original form (grammatical errors included) will demonstrate the thrill at discovering that this was not unique to my life alone. The second email records how, as suddenly as the phenomenon entered my life, it swiftly disappeared on 12 March 2008. Strangely enough, when the Hum stopped I felt a sense of loss, as if a close friend had died unexpectedly. I actually experienced a mild form of bereavement. I felt as if I had been a cancer sufferer cured of the deadly disease while discovering this for the first time.

I will say in conclusion, though, that in recent times The Hum is still noticeable to me, but only during absolute silence such as when I get up very early in the morning. And it is in no way as intense as it was back in 2008. I consider it to be just background noise, and in fear of it taking hold again I try to ignore it, and draw my attention away from it in small ways, such as focusing on the keyboard as I type. I never hear it in my bedroom because I always play soft background music on my trusty mp3 player all night, every single night, in fear that it may return.

I am not sure if my correspondent is still involved with the Hum, so I have blacked out key information for privacy reasons.

THE DISCOVERY THAT OTHERS ALSO SUFFER FROM THE HUM

From: ███████████████████.com.au]
Sent: Wednesday, 5 March 2008 6:35 PM
To: ████████████████
Subject: The HUM "My current experience"

Hi █████,
5 March 2008.

I wish to send you an e-mail regarding my horrific experience with the HUM.
But before I do, please ensure that what I wish to discuss with you will not be published in detail (for fear of ramification).

In summary:
• I am 46 years old and live in Melbourne, Australia. (Where are you?)
• I have suffered an absolute nightmare since around 05 Jan 2008.
• I have slept an average 2-3 hours a night (If any at all).
• I wish to make some comments to you as well.
Please return my e-mail as soon as possible.
P.S. When I discovered your site today (05 March) I was "relieved" that finally something is making sense.
Please email me on ████████████████████.com.au

Thanks
"█████"

Image II - As seen from this email I was very excited to have found that my problem was in fact worldwide.

13

AS QUICKLY AS IT CAME IT SUDDENLY STOPPED

-----Original Message-----
From: ██████████████████████.com.au]
Sent: Saturday, 5 April 2008 9:41 AM
To: ████████████████████
Subject: Re: The Hum

Hi ████,
Congratulations on getting your Forum up and running.
I have been reading everyone's comments and I still feel uncomfortable posting anything but I just wish to make a few comments to you.

It is conclusive that the hum affects people differently even though the sound certainly is similar. As I have explained previously my sister and I suddenly heard the hum at the same time in the first week of Jan 2008.

I wish to let you know that on Wed 12 March for some strange reason the Hum began to subside. It ceased for the next few days completely and then for a few days returned at a lower volume. Since then it is hardly noticeable.

It is now 3 weeks since it subsided and I can hardly hear it. Unfortunately, my sister can still hear it at my place when she visits on weekends. I have asked her to stay this weekend to see if it is so loud for her that it affects her sleep.

Everyone has their theories but I found that it is very difficult to come to any conclusions. I suppose I have been fortunate that my sister also heard it at virtually at the same time so I can draw some comparisons here:

████████████████████████████████████

████████████████████████████████████

████████████████████████

- We both heard the noise at virtually the same time.
- The physical effect can be felt throughout my body, heart beating faster.
My sister did not describe any physical affects.
- I now virtually do not hear it yet she still hears it at a similar intensity as before.
- We are currently investigating her complaint that she thinks she now also can hear it at her place (I cannot hear it there).
- There have been no obvious changes to my area or house.

It is only after 2 wonderful weeks of good sleep that the dark circles and bags under my eyes have gone.
I really hope that the HUM does not return because every now and then, my mind dwells onto what transpired over those 9 - 10 weeks and I get over come with fear.
Yet at the same time, I recall (amusingly) that on March 12, when it stopped for a few days, I remember sensing that I almost missed it as if someone I was close with for so many weeks suddenly left me.

If I am fortunate and it never returns I still will never ever for get the HUM! I am slowly weaning myself of the many cups of coffee I was drinking just to function at work.

Regards
" ████ "

Image III - Email testifying to the fact that "I have finally been cured" of the Hum, after 8 or 9 weeks of sleepless nights.

Working, Renting, and Finally Buying a Home in Melbourne - 2000

My life was a whirlwind when I first moved to Melbourne in 1994, as my utmost priority was to find a job and buy a property. Within six to eight months, I managed to find employment in a large company. However, although I was working full-time, my job was only a temporary position, making it impossible for me to get a bank loan. For six years I had been renting the dreariest one-bedroom apartments and small studio or bachelor pads in the worst part of town, comparable to a red-light district. My aim was to save enough money for a deposit towards the purchase of my own apartment.

My rented apartment building came complete with the strangest characters you can imagine, which made me feel as if I was living in a TV show. For instance, there was the drug-taking flute man next door to me who played the flute any time of the day or night he so desired, but without a recognised tune or melody. During the breaks in the composition, the virtuoso would take his drugs and throw the used syringes out of the third-floor window, letting them accumulate on the ground beside the building wall. When I was advised that the agents already were aware of his heroin use, I expressed my concern for children who also resided in this building.

Then there was the elderly woman who lived across the hall from me. I felt sorry for her because she did not seem to belong there. We would always say hello to each other in the hallway or at the entrance to our apartments, but it happened very rarely; she slowly and quietly unlocked the door to her room and disappeared inside until I saw her again after a week as she ventured out to the local supermarket.

When I finally received my full-time position at work, after six years of contracting, I had accumulated enough money for the mandatory deposit. In the year 2000 I successfully presented an application for a bank loan to buy a one-bedroom apartment on the better side of town. On the last day of packing to leave my rented apartment, as Christmas was approaching I placed two $50 notes inside a Christmas card and slipped it under her door.

About five years later, apartment properties had increased in value significantly, which allowed me to sell mine in 2005, increase my loan and buy a larger 2-bedroom house with a small front yard and backyard. Therefore, for the first time in many years I was once again able to stand in awe at the beautiful blue sky and the vastness of black velvet space.

There are two high-profile UFO incidents local to Melbourne, Victoria. One was just a 30-minute drive from my house, and the other two and a half hours' drive from where I was residing.

The Famous Westall, Melbourne, UFO Sighting - 1966

One day as I was surfing the web I came across an article about an amazing UFO sighting in the outer Melbourne suburb of Clayton South. At 11 am on 6 April 1966, for about 20 minutes, more than 200 students and a number of teachers witnessed a UFO flying at low altitude. With mixed emotions these young students followed each other and the object for a few hundred metres before it landed in a nearby clearing.

Because this event lasted nearly 20 minutes, and because it landed and some students even approached the landed craft and felt the warmth emanating off it, this proves to be one of the most mysterious and fascinating UFO witness accounts ever. In addition, Air Force personnel located nearby came in no time, and they confiscated the black and white photographs taken by a science teacher.

The first witnesses involved were a class of students and a teacher from Westall High School, who were on the main school oval at the time as they were completing a sports activity. They noticed above them a grey-silver disc-shaped object with a purple or green hue about it. The object descended then crossed the school grounds and headed towards a paddock surrounded by trees, called The Grange.

With witnesses, mainly students, now numbering over 200, it then climbed at high speed and departed towards the northwest. Adding to the mystery, as the object gained altitude, five unidentified aircraft circled it and pursued it from the scene.

Westall High School (now Westall Secondary College) was only 30 minutes from where I was living at the time, and I made numerous visits to the site. I stood at the southwest corner of the grounds of the Westall, looking at the high electrical transmission towers where the UFO climbed up before heading off in a southeasterly direction towards the Grange Reserve a few hundred metres away, where it finally landed, leaving a perfect circular impression on the ground.

There is an eerie feeling as you stand amongst the trees at The Grange, attempting to visualise the trauma and emotions the students felt as they were chasing this object, and observing it land and then ultimately take off at enormous speed. The dismissal early on of suggestions that it may have been aircraft was swift. A light aircraft airport (Moorabbin Airport) is close by, so the students and teachers were very familiar with all types and sizes of aircraft. Although the UFO was of similar size, everyone understood that it was not a plane or a weather balloon.

A television network that ran a story not long afterwards had the archived footage lost, missed, or stolen.

The Frederick Valentich Disappearance, Melbourne - 1978

Valentich was a 20-year-old pilot who went missing over Bass Strait on the night of 21 October 1978, leaving nothing behind except a mysterious radio transmission. Valentich disappeared while on a 125-mile (235 km) training flight in a Cessna 182 light aircraft over Bass Strait, south of Melbourne, Australia.

Valentich was a "flying saucer enthusiast", which makes his disappearance even stranger, and just like the Westall case. He took off from Moorabbin Airport. At 6:19 pm over Bass Strait, as he was heading southeast towards King Island, he saw what he thought was another aircraft pass over him. He radioed Melbourne Air Flight Service at Cape Otway Lighthouse, asking what aircraft was visible on radar near him. The response was that there was none. As he continued to describe the encounter, it seems the craft was playing with him, as it circled at enormous speed.

There are transcripts available of the actual conversation between the pilot and Melbourne Air Flight Service, informing that he was being accompanied by an aircraft about 1,000 feet (300 m) above him and that his engine had begun running roughly. Then towards the end, after the radio controller assures the pilot that there are no military planes - or any planes for that matter - in the vicinity, he asks him to describe the aircraft and its size. Valentich's final response was: "That strange aircraft is hovering on top of me again … it is hovering and it's not an aircraft." Then there were some metallic sounds and silence.

On the night of the disappearance there were unconfirmed or unsubstantiated reports of a UFO sighting and a photo of an alleged UFO sighting on the coast off Melbourne. A search was undertaken and there was no oil slick to indicate that the pilot had crashed his plane.

Valentich's family, especially his father, endured media frenzy following his disappearance, and they have held a vigil at the lighthouse at Cape Otway every year on the anniversary of his disappearance. Twenty years after the doomed pilot and his plane vanished, his family erected a memorial plaque at Cape Otway.

Millions wonder: "Do flying saucers exist, and is man alone in the universe? Is there life on other planets, and are we being visited by alien beings?" These are perplexing questions, and few subjects are as intriguing. I try to keep an open mind but at the same time respect my religion.

So how would different religions and faiths handle the revelation that we are not alone when disclosure finally comes forth? Some religions are more accepting of the idea of extra-terrestrials than others, and a poll has shown that a wide cross-section of the population believes in the existence of aliens.

The UNKNOWN

This Plaque commemorates the landmark of the Mysterious disappearance of FREDERICK VALENTICH On October 21 October 1978.

Frederick was flying a Cessna 1821, and at this point he changed direction to south from the lighthouse towards the sea.

Twelve minutes flying south from here at precisely 19:12:28 hrs radio transmission was cut off and in his last radio contact he explained "that strange aircraft is hovering on top of me again, and it is not an aircraft......"

After an extensive land and sea search, no trace was ever found of the Cessna VH-DSJ or of FREDERICK VALENTICH.

And so to this day, his disappearance remains a mystery.

Image IV – Text from the commemorative plaque placed near the site of the pilot's last known radio transmission on 21 October 1978, 227 km (141 mi) south of Melbourne, Victoria.

This book is set out in straightforward chronological order from my first photographed UFO of a classic disc. I photographed it with a 3.2-megapixel mobile phone camera on 19 February 2012 and then immediately grabbed my 10-megapixel digital camera to take a second shot of the UFO as it moved to a different position in the sky. We progress through to March 2018, when photographs and videos were taken with a 16-megapixel digital zoom camera.

You will notice a progression and slight change in some of the theories I put forward when explaining what these objects are and where they came from.

I hope that my sightings continue to mesmerise and impress my readers and myself enough to warrant me publishing a follow-up book. As you read these pages, please keep an open mind, as this will be the most difficult element to master. Allowing the mind to be receptive to different opinions and ideas, with admiration for what you seek with full interest, will bring newfound discoveries, knowledge, views, and opportunities. Come along with me as we discover new aerial phenomena and push the boundaries of our scientific and technical limits. For centuries the scientific and metaphysical minds have utilised curiosity and analysis to explore the heavens and beyond.

Please note that alongside these documented cases are many missed opportunities where either the object was travelling too fast, or I could not focus quickly enough or even grab the camera whilst driving. This happened with one of my closest and best sightings yet, when I was driving beside the Albert Park Lake, Melbourne (site of the Australian Grand Prix) in broad daylight (please refer to details later). In such instances, I have chastised myself for days or weeks, with something like a 50 mm film stock running through my mind as I try to piece together what went wrong. How did I miscalculate the focus or why was I not compelled to turn around to observe another section of sky at the exact right moment, thus missing the perfect opportunity? This stayed with me until the next good sighting and capture.

Now let us start this exciting journey together.

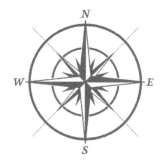

CHAPTER 1

**The Shape of Things to Come,
Super Highways and
Quantum Mechanics in the Macro**

Infinite Shapes

The following captures the essence what this book is about and what will be discussed. From what I can see there seem to be five categories of aerial phenomena:

Solid UFO – Metallic Disc (saucer shape), Cigar, Triangle,
H-shape, Boomerang shape etc. - VERY RARE
ORBS - "High Aerial Singularity Reactors", with
extreme morphing ability - RARE
ORBS - "Jelly Fish" - With other shapes - COMMON
ORBS - Yellow-Orange Orbs – moderately COMMON
BALLOON – With strange tethers and morphing ability - VERY COMMON

Solid UFO: UFOs come in many shapes, colours and sizes, mainly symmetrical in nature, most commonly the classic saucer shape with variations such as flat-bottomed, flat-topped, lens-shaped (top and bottom the same), hat, or helmet shape (this is the type that I first photographed in February 2012). The appearance is mainly bright metallic polished silver or chrome, but sometimes dull aluminium with a slight orange hue.

Most of the closer sightings documented by witnesses are smaller discs ranging from the size of a family car up to 16 feet (5 metres). Eyewitness accounts of triangle-shaped UFOs have been reported frequently since the 1970s, although the dark or black triangles and boomerangs were first reported as far back as the 1950s. They can be quite massive. For example, the Phoenix, Arizona, lights sighted on 13 March 1997 purported to be a dark V-shaped UFO the size of several football fields. Triangle-shaped UFOs usually have three lights beneath the object that shine down. I captured a morphing UFO that turned into a V-shape in Glyfada (Athens, Greece) while holidaying there in late 2016.

Cylindrical-shaped UFOs are usually bright metallic with a silvery finish and often seen with a luminous haze about them. These can be huge: some have been reported by jet airline pilots to be over 300 metres (984 feet) long, virtually as large as an aircraft carrier.

Spherical shaped orbs, or glowing balls of luminous light, are commonly orange-yellow in colour or plain white. These spheres range in size from 3 feet (1 metre) to the size of a small softball.

With all my sightings, I find it very strange that I would very rarely see the same UFO more than once. I would see a variation of it (refer to the "Golden Man" sightings), but not the exact same shape. Therefore, we all agree that there are numerous different shapes of UFOs. Besides the saucer-shaped UFO, I have seen balloon-like objects with glowing tethers below; boomerang-shaped UFOs; I have been mesmerised by glowing white balls of light (or orbs) moving at incredible speeds; I have seen constantly changing morphing UFOs (refer to "HAQSR - High Altitude Quantum Singularity Reactors"); and even the closest sighting yet of a pair of rectangle-shaped UFOs about 65 yards (60 metres) away, 50 feet (15 metres) above a lake, and probably 8 to 10 feet (3 metres) long.

This last sighting was extraordinary, since not only was it in daylight (at 9:00 am on a Sunday morning), but it was at the site of the Australian Grand Prix, used regularly by joggers around the perimeter of the lake.

I have noticed that people lose interest when you talk about UFOs with anything other than a disc shape. However, if you were to film several of these bright shining objects coming, for instance, from the west of Melbourne (where the ocean is), and if while you were taking photos one of them suddenly performed a sharp turn and came towards you as if aware that you were filming them, I am sure that your indifference would wane. You too would be overcome with excitement and amazement the moment it paused exactly overhead as if to communicate to you before moving off to join the others. How can such a sight not move anyone to astonishment about aerial anomalies? I find it truly remarkable that such an object would pause for a short time, seeming to observe me before it takes off again to join the other two white orbs that by now have moved some distance towards the southeast. It still gives me goose bumps to think about it.

There is a self-luminosity appearance to most UFOs, probably due to the ionisation of the air around them. It is usually described as an aura, or a fuzzy shimmering haze of orange and yellow, producing a heat-haze appearance in daylight. Daylight sightings result in reports of polished silver like chrome; and some have even been described as reflecting sunlight like a mirror, which is how I would describe some of my daylight sightings. I would say it is almost as if someone in the sky is shining a mirror at the perfect angle, punching the rays from the sun in my direction. The brilliant plasma surrounding a UFO might be adding to the reflection off its body. In contrast, there have also been sightings of UFOs that are matte black and/or charcoal grey in colour, or even glossy black where most of the boomerang, V-shaped, and triangle UFOs appear to be. From most reports the rotation of UFOs appears to be in a counter-clockwise direction, opposite to the movement of a clock. When hovering or moving slowly, a UFO seems to wobble like a gyroscope about to complete its spin and topple over.

Earth's Geomagnetic Field and Super Highways

The earth's magnetic field, also commonly known as the geomagnetic field, is the extension of the magnetic field from the interior of the earth's core out into space. This field is tilted 11 degrees from the earth's natural spin axis and has an effect similar to that of a bar magnet. It is believed that the magnetic field originates from within the earth's molten metal core is due to the circulating electric currents, which is the basic principle of electromagnetism in physics.

Electromagnetic force is a physical force between electrically charged particles, and produces one of the four fundamental interactions in nature (the other three are gravitation, the weak interaction, and the strong interaction). Over the years, the greatest minds in mathematics and physics have attempted to combine all forces into the one unified field theory, to describe all the fundamental forces of interaction and the relationships between the elementary particles within a single theoretical framework.

Just as Einstein, within the Special Theory of Relativity, described space and time as two aspects of the same thing called space-time (essentially three dimensions of space and one dimension of time), electricity and magnetism also are thought of as two sides of the same coin.

A changing electric field creates a magnetic field and a changing magnetic field creates an electric field, so we call this electromagnetism or electromagnetic forces. If you simply place a magnetic compass next to a wire in a circuit, the compass will deflect. This was exactly how Professor Hans Oersted discovered the magnetic field of a current in

1819, during a live physics lecture at the University of Copenhagen. We can also perform it in reverse by moving a magnet relative to a conductor, thereby producing a current called induction. If the magnet remains stationary, however, nothing happens until a movement, rotation or oscillation occurs. The same applies to moving charges or currents, which will produce magnetic fields. Non-moving charges, however, only produce electrostatic force, which is the attraction or repulsion of particles or objects because of their electric charge.

There are two types of charged particles: protons, which have a charge of +1 (positive charge) in atomic units; and electrons, which have a charge of -1 (negative charge). Hundreds of other charged particles have been identified in particle physics; new ones emerge during high-energy collisions at CERN, the Large Hadron Collider, but most are unstable and very short-lived.

As the magnetic field of the earth extends from the earth's interior out to space, it meets the solar wind, a stream of charged particles emanating from the sun. The Earth's magnetic field has a function and that is to deflect most of the solar wind and solar flares; otherwise, the charged particles would strip away the ozone layer that protects the earth from harmful ultraviolet radiation.

During the many sightings documented in this book and on my website, I have seen that the UFOs seem to be repeatedly following similar paths. In July 2012, NASA announced that they had discovered hidden portals in the earth's magnetic field. This was about the time that both CMS and ATLAS teams announced the discovery of the much-anticipated boson particle at CERN. The latter had occurred in the mass region of 125-126 GeV, which met the formal level requirement; hence the announcement of a new particle discovered soon after. When more precise measurements were undertaken, the observed properties were indeed consistent with the Higgs Boson.

One important point to note here is that CERN's first research run took place from March 2010 to early 2013 at energy of 3.5 to 4 teraelectronvolts (TeV) per beam (7 to 8 TeV total), which is about 4 times the previous world record for a collider. Thereafter, the accelerator began an upgrade period for the next two years in order to function at a higher power output. In early 2015 it was restarted for its second research run, reaching 6.5 TeV per beam (13 TeV total, the current world record).

I find it extremely interesting that in the period of experimentation when they discovered the boson, NASA announced the portals within the Earth's magnetic field in its interaction with the solar wind. In 2012 NASA explained that portals exist where the magnetic field of the earth connects to the magnetic field of the sun, leading to a continuous path from the earth to the sun's atmosphere over 93 million miles away. NASA has observed these magnetic portals open and close dozens of times each day where they are located tens of thousands of kilometres from Earth. The magnetic field is distorted, tangled, and twisted by the solar magnetic field where it is almost horizontal over the earth's equator and connects at higher altitude, creating magnetic portals.

Most portals are small and do not remain open for long. Others are huge and remain open for much longer periods of time, allowing tons of energetic particles to flow through, causing geomagnetic storms and igniting polar auroras.

I propose that the distances quoted by NASA for these portals - approximately 40,000 mi (65,000 km) to 56,000 mi (90,000 km) - might be correct, but that there are probably also natural portals occurring closer to earth, where UFOs may enter and leave our dimension. This may explain why I tend to see UFOs following the same path most of the time, while on the other hand during periods of inactivity the portals are probably closed, not including periods of cloudy skies.

Perhaps you will agree when you have seen some of the strange aerial phenomena I have captured on camera. Some of these objects, that almost look like living organisms, may be coming through portals in the fabric of space and time caused by CERN. Some of the very scientists who work there have warned of this.

Most scientists say that there is nothing sinister at CERN. It is described as the world's largest and most complex scientific instrument for the study of the basic constituents of matter – the fundamental particles within the atom itself. Particles are collided together near to the speed of light, allowing physicists to discover clues about how the particles interact, and providing insights into the fundamental laws of nature.

In late 2009, the Director for Research and Scientific Computing at CERN briefed reporters with an unexpected statement which sounded like a warning. He "warned" that the titanic machine may possibly create or discover previously unimagined scientific phenomena, or "unknown unknowns". For instance, he spoke of "an extra dimension", and said that "out of this door might come something, or we might send something through it". The expectation was that when we experiment with the very fabric of space-time itself in this way, a strange phenomenon may reveal itself.

One of warnings was that the result of these experiments might be a miniature black hole falling into the centre of the earth, which causes the earth to implode. These remarks seem to imply the creation of "space warp wormhole portals" into alternate universes.

You will see later that these objects may be manipulating the earth's magnetic fields closer to the upper atmosphere, resulting in portals that can be passed through. I possibly have video of an object's erratic transformation when in the process of developing or opening such a portal, but I do not have footage of it disappearing into it. This southwestern section of sky is always the same area, to which I have seen many objects move from the west, east and north. I have seen with own eyes a star-like object at about 2:30 am, similar in magnitude to the star Sirius, move from the north to that very southwestern section of sky then just "turn off" as if someone flicked a switch.

As mentioned before, my observations of these aerial anomalies conjure up the feeling that the objects are aware of being observed. On several occasions, at the exact moment my eye has caught the object - in the form of either a star or orb at night or reflective orb in the day - it has either slowly dimmed and disappeared or turned off immediately.

Further, it seems that there are pre-defined super highways leading to some form of interdimensional doorway, or at least a hyperspace portal transporting a UFO to another time and space as it disappears. I know of at least four:

Known Super Highways and Possible Portal Gates (With reference from my position)

- Running NORTHWEST to EAST, from the City of Melbourne direction to the suburb of East Hawthorn
- Running SOUTHEAST to EAST, from the suburb of Moorabbin direction to East Hawthorn
- Running SOUTHWEST to SOUTHEAST, from the suburb of St Kilda direction to the suburb of Moorabbin
- Running NORTHEAST to SOUTHWEST, from the suburb of Richmond to the suburb of St Kilda

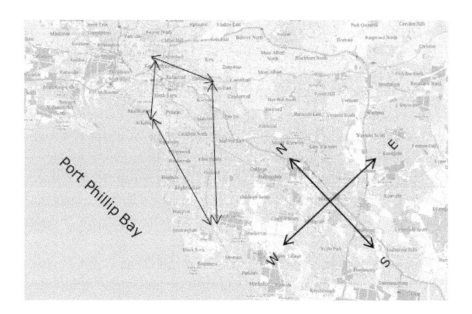

*Image V: Melbourne with some of the known
superhighways, from my perspective*

Quantum Physics at the Macro Level

I will be suggesting that some of these objects behave similarly to the way quantum particles would, but at the macroscopic scale. Quantum mechanics is the theory of the microscopic world describing atoms, particles, and molecules. Strangeness is of the essence before the theory slips through the axis across the world of the macro (perceived through our senses), to where the familiarity of classical physics begins.

Although we find it hard to see the quantum effects in the macro world, some scientists believe this effect routinely appears in the macro world and even probably in our cells. We need to see past the way the "quantumness" interacts with itself, and the way the macro world interacts with itself: somewhere in between is where we tackle this existence.

Some of the UFOs I have captured on video (such as the one in Glyfada, Greece) continually morph into peculiar shapes in a manner not unlike the wave functions of particles which are familiar to us in the field of physics.

These subjects interest me quite a bit. I have three consecutive photos showing the Glyfada UFO morphing from a V shape to a round blob, and then a well-defined saucer shape within. I have footage of the same object where it continues to change constantly. At reduced speed, the video footage appears to show that the object is propagating in a similar way to the quantum world that we have come to imagine through a multitude of experiments.

There seems to be a relationship between UFOs and light. Perhaps they have learned to use the properties of pure light rather than physically traversing the vastness of space. We all know that even travelling at the speed of light, it may take millions of earth years to arrive at a destination; but by utilising the "weirdness" of quantum mechanics, it may not be necessary.

Quantum weirdness might include, for example, "being in two places at the same time", or Einstein's favourite "spooky action at a distance". Such weirdness could allow them to leave our existence here on earth and project themselves into another part of the universe, reconfiguring as a solid object.

I will try to uncover whether UFOs follow supposedly distinct ley lines which follow grids of energy across the globe, connecting important and sacred sites such as Stonehenge and the Egyptian pyramid; or whether in fact there is something else at play here. I have witnessed many yellow-orange orbs that seem to follow similar paths in a predictable manner.

You will be amazed that for a short time the yellow-orange orbs I observed were predictable to such a degree that I would wait in advance with camera in hand, as they approached from the direction anticipated. I will conclude with an explanation of why so many UFOs documented in this book seemed to appear from or move to the southeast.

Most databases and investigations describe the observation of UFOs as random, which makes it extremely difficult to apply a scientific method in their study. They go on to explain that, by its very nature of unpredictability, it is very difficult to conduct experiments on this subject in a controlled manner. I will put forward patterns that I have seen and explain why I believe there are periods of minimal observations while at other times they are frequent.

When trying to live a normal life, hold down a job, and sift through large volumes of data, time constraints proved an enormous challenge. But I have done my best to ensure that only unnatural aerial anomalies are included in this book.

There are many ways to scientifically analyse UFOs. Ufologists usually use what is readily available, and take a logical and systematic approach - such as cataloguing and grouping sightings where possible, to reveal any pattern, or doing detailed studies case by case. I have tried to use both of these, but the prevalence of unprovable subjective analyses and hypotheses may be frustrating to some because we humans want definitive answers.

Ufologists have never really had any help or involvement from mainstream science, apart from some recent brief comments from prominent scientists, physicists and air force personnel. Mainstream science has never really come to openly discuss the possibility that UFOs may be extra-terrestrial in origin. It seems to be only mainstream media that ignites the flame for truth and disclosure, as articles are published with moderate frequency, as well as photos and videos of possible sightings. My hat goes off to them, as this may be just the beginning.

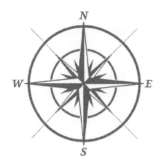

CHAPTER 2

A Brief History of UFOs

4,000 BC: The Vedas, Ancient Indian text, talked of UFO clashes.

April 570 BCE: The Prophet Ezekiel witnessed alien craft landing.

1940s, WWII: "Foo fighters" sightings by fighter pilots world-wide.

February 24 to 25, 1942: The Battle of Los Angeles.

July 16, 1945: First atomic weapons test - Alamogordo, New Mexico.

June 24, 1947: Pilot Kenneth Arnold sighted

9 UFOs, Mount Rainier, USA.

July 7, 1947: UFO Crash, Roswell, New Mexico – bodies recovered.

1950: Hollywood, USA – The Flying Saucer.

1951: Hollywood, USA – The Day the Earth Stood Still.

July 12-29, 1952: UFOs over Washington, DC, and the White House.

1952: Project Bluebook, USA Government-compiled reports.

4,000 BC - The Vedas in Sanskrit

In the centuries-old documents written in Sanskrit, the classical language of India and Hinduism, there is a wealth of information which is widely believed to be proof that aliens from outside earth visited India from 4,000 to 6,000 years ago. Modern translations reveal fascinating stories of flying machines, including captivating science-fiction types of weaponry.

These detailed descriptions of flying vehicles, written many thousands of years ago, conjure up images of nothing less than the classic UFOs we have come to know about: *Arrived shining, a wonderful divine car that sped through the air,* and *Bhīma flew with his Vimana on an enormous ray which was as brilliant as the sun and made a noise like the thunder of a storm.*

Amongst the texts, there are details of fighting and clashes with these vehicles, which used indescribably fearful weapons: *Gurkha flying in his swift and powerful Vimana hurled against the three cities of the Vrishis and Andhakas a single projectile charged with all the power of the Universe. An incandescent column of smoke and fire, as brilliant as ten thousand suns, rose in all its splendour. It was the unknown weapon, the Iron Thunderbolt, a gigantic messenger of death which reduced to ashes the entire race of the Vrishnis and Andhakas.*

Finally, there are passages detailing how to construct the Vimana flying vehicles: *Strong and durable must the body of the Vimana be made, like a great flying bird of light material. Inside one must put the mercury engine with its iron heating apparatus underneath. By means of the power latent in the mercury, which set the driving whirlwind in motion, a man sitting inside may travel a great distance in the sky. The movements of the Vimana are such that it can vertically ascend, vertically descend, and move slanting forwards and backwards. With the help of the machines human beings can fly in the air and heavenly beings can come down to earth.*

The text alludes to the fact that the knowledge of flight was a gift from "those from upon high" as a means of saving many lives.

April 570 BCE - The Prophet Ezekiel

The Old Testament book of **Ezekiel** in the King James Bible is one of my favourites. It is second to **Ecclesiastes**, which is about King Solomon's unsatisfied desire for wealth and his desperate search for the meaning and significance in life, while God remained present throughout. The ancient document of Ezekiel is supposedly a detailed description of extra-terrestrial contact. If this is true, and it is an eye witness account of an alien craft in the sky in the process of landing, and then four Interplanetary Beings stepping out of this UFO, then you can see within the writing the struggle to describe the object and to make sense of what is being seen.

There are countless books and web pages on this subject, including *The Spaceships of Ezekiel* written in 1974 by Josef F Blumrich. At that time, Blumrich was chief of NASA's systems branch of the program development office at the Marshall Space Flight Center. Erich von Däniken also touched on Ezekiel earlier in *Chariots of the Gods,* in 1969.

In the first chapter of Ezekiel, the prophet, who was in exile near Babylon at the time, recounts a vision (Ezek. 1:4–28):

As I looked, behold, a stormy wind came out of the north, and a great cloud, with brightness round about it, and fire flashing forth continually, and in the midst of the fire, as it were gleaming bronze. And from the midst of it came the likeness of four living creatures. And this was their appearance: they had the form of men, but each had four faces, and each had four wings. Their legs were straight, and the soles of their feet were like the sole of a calf's foot; and they sparkled like burnished bronze. Under the wings on their four sides they had human hands. And the four had their faces and their wings thus: their wings touched one another; they went straightforward, without turning as they went.........

Now as I looked at the living creatures, I saw a wheel upon the earth beside the living creatures, one for each of the four of them. As for the appearance of the wheels and their construction; their appearance was like the gleaming of chrysolite; and the four had the same likeness, their construction being as it were a wheel within a wheel. When they went, they went in any of their four directions without turning as they went. The four wheels' rims were so high that they were dreadful and their rims were full of eyes round about. And when the living creatures went, the wheels went beside them; and when the living creatures rose from the earth, the wheels rose. Wherever the spirit would go, they went, and the wheels rose along with them; for the spirit of the living creatures was in the wheels. When those went, these went; and when those stood, these stood; and when those rose from the earth, the wheels rose along with them; for the spirit of the living creatures was in the wheels.......

Like the appearance of the bow that is in the cloud on the day of rain, so was the appearance of the brightness round about.

Such was the appearance of the glory of the LORD. And when I saw it, I fell upon my face and I heard the voice of one speaking.

1940s, World War II - "Foo Fighters" Sightings

During and towards the end of World War II, beside the aerial dogfights between the allied forces and Germany there were unusual reports of inexplicable lights following the aircraft with as many as "8 to 10 bright orange lights off the left wing", for instance. They seemed to be balls of light hovering and following airplanes of all nationalities. There were many reports about the objects' high speed as they flew alongside the aircraft at 200 mph with colours of red, orange, or green and appeared as single objects or in clusters of 10.

These objects were often portrayed as out-manoeuvring the airplanes they were chasing, and radar operations nearby discovered that they never showed up on radar. The adopted descriptive term "Foo Fighters" was taken from a firefighter cartoon at the time. Military aviation enthusiasts, novice psychologists and conspiracy theorists offered explanations of hallucinations, fatigue and German secret weapons; but the pilots were quick to dismiss these. They stood their ground, explaining that actual physical entities had performed as no known aircraft at the time could perform, demonstrating extreme manoeuvrability, impossible instantaneous acceleration and deceleration in all directions of space, and hovering motionless. Sometimes they were glowing balls of light and at other times they were high illuminated disc-shaped objects. It is disappointing that with all the sightings and reports, and so many gun cameras able to take high altitude photographs, there has never surfaced a good quality photograph of Foo Fighters from the period.

24 February 1942 - The Battle of Los Angeles

I have always been intrigued by this event. It occurred during the early morning hours of 25 February 1942, midway through World War II. Fresh in everyone's mind was the Japanese bombing of the American fleet in Pearl Harbour, Hawaii, just over two months earlier on 7 December 1941, which resulted in the United States entering the war.

Thousands of rounds of anti-aircraft shells were exploded in an attempt to bring down a Zeppelin blimp (as it was thought to be) which was first sighted on military radar around 10:30 pm on 24 February. As it was a slow-moving object, they felt that it had to be a Zeppelin. Therefore every searchlight available from Santa Monica to Long Beach focused onto this single object.

The slow-moving object seemed immune to the constant barrage of explosive armament, which commenced shortly after 3:00 am on 25 February. With no visible effect whatsoever, it eventually disappeared out over the Pacific after following the coast south towards Long Beach and cutting inland for a short time. There was never a clear explanation for this huge object, and it was ignored by the authorities at the time.

Nothing fell to the ground and not a single bomb was dropped by it, even after 1,400 rounds of ammunition had been fired at it, so it could not be an enemy aircraft. It was not until 1983 that the military concluded that it was probably just a drifting weather balloon. Most witnesses described it as a large round object pale orange in colour and glowing.

16 July 1945 - First Atomic Weapons Test

The world's first atomic weapons test took place at the Trinity bombsite in central New Mexico. The development of the bomb began three years earlier as part of the Manhattan Project, in August 1942. Scientists from allied nations came together to see the probability of developing a nuclear weapon as proposed on paper by high profile scientists at the time. It was viewed by scientists such as Albert Einstein and Dr J. Robert Oppenheimer, Director of the project, who uttered the following words from an ancient Hindu text as he watched the first mushroom clouds in the New Mexico sky above: "Now I am become death, destroyer of worlds".

In fact, Albert Einstein, whose discoveries led to the bomb, played almost no role in the development of the atomic bomb because the US Government would not give him the necessary clearance. Einstein, amongst others, believed that the Germans were on the verge of developing the bomb themselves; so in a letter he had urged President Roosevelt to support research by American physicists into the feasibility of the chain reaction event critical to the development of a nuclear bomb. Einstein later deeply regretted the letter to Roosevelt, explaining that he would not have penned it had he known that the Germans would not be successful in the bomb's development.

NASA's former Apollo 14 (1971) astronaut, Edgar Mitchell, who is a firm believer in aliens visiting earth, once said during an interview that "aliens came to Earth to prevent a nuclear war between the US and the Soviet Union during the Cold War". Edgar Mitchell referenced the detonation of the world's first atomic bomb on 16 July 1945 at White Sands Missile Range facility in New Mexico.

Mitchell, the sixth man to walk on the moon, once said that high-ranking military officials witnessed alien ships during weapons tests throughout the 1940s. The UFOs, he says, were hovering over the world's first nuclear weapons test in the desolate White Sands deserts of New Mexico. He has also said that high-ranking officers had told him that alien spacecraft frequently shot down test missiles.

It may not be coincidental that the UFOs suddenly appeared during this period in the 1940s, when nuclear weapons were being tested and rocket technology was being developed. In early 2015 physicists suggested an ancient civilisation on Mars may have been destroyed by a nuclear attack from another alien race, and that there is evidence of the destruction today.

In 2011, a scientist theorised that the red colour on Mars was due the effects of thermonuclear explosions. The surface of Mars has a very thin layer of radioactive materials such as uranium, thorium and radioactive potassium, suggesting that the debris may have covered the whole planet after nuclear explosions. Finally, he concluded that – as is the case with Hydrogen bomb tests on earth - nuclear isotopes in the atmosphere of Mars are evidence of a nuclear attack from space.

24 June 1947 - Pilot Kenneth Arnold - 9 UFOs

The credit goes to Kenneth Arnold for coining the phrase "flying saucer" when on 24 June 1947he saw something in the skies that caused millions of people to wonder if we were not alone in the universe. He was flying over the Cascade Mountains, near Mt Rainier, helping with the search for a lost military transport plane, when he was startled by a bright flash of light, and sighted nine strange objects.

The strange looking aircraft were flying from north to south at about

3:00 pm, and Arnold watched the aircraft for two or three minutes. Soon after Kenneth Arnold told a friend about his experience, word got around and reporters wanted to interview him. He said each of the objects was roughly 50 feet across and looked to be circular in shape, except for one that seemed to be in the shape of a boomerang or crescent; but when he described how they moved in the sky "like saucers skipping on the surface of water", reporters adopted the term "flying saucers". He watched them for about two minutes until they disappeared over Oregon at speeds approaching 1,400 mph.

Capturing the public's imagination, the fascination with UFOs began.

7 July 1947 - Roswell, New Mexico - UFO Crash

Just two weeks later, farmer Mack Brazel found strange debris strewn across his farm about 60 km northwest of Roswell in New Mexico. Most of it was silver foil in nature, and when he crumpled it in his hand it quickly regained its shape. Brazel contacted the local Sheriff, who alerted the nearby Army base airfield, Walker Air Force Base at Roswell, that one of their aircraft appeared to have crashed on Brazel's ranch.

Major Jesse Marcel, an intelligence officer, went to investigate. After seeing the debris he was convinced that the rancher had found the world's first evidence of aliens and that they were looking at the remains of a "flying saucer". When he reported what he had seen back at the base, the press release officer put out an announcement on July 8 that a flying disc had been recovered from the ranch near Roswell.

The following day's edition of *The Roswell Daily Record* carried the headline: "RAAF Captures Flying Saucer on Ranch in Roswell Region". The article contained the following captivating words:

The intelligence office of the 509th Bombardment Group at Roswell Army Air Field announced at noon today, that the field has come into the possession of a Flying Saucer.

The RAF later retracted its original release with the following words: "What was found were nothing more but parts of a downed conventional weather balloon". However, as worldwide interest took hold no one wanted to believe that it was just a weather balloon, but a "flying disc". Eventually the story fell into obscurity until the 1970s, when it quickly gained interest amongst ufologists, and elaborate conspiracy theories began to evolve. The military then engaged in a cover-up of the recovery of one or more alien spacecraft that had crash-landed, as well as the extra-terrestrial occupants. Subsequently, in the 1990s, the US military published two reports disclosing that the crashed object was an experimental high altitude balloon. The codename was Project Mogul, which the US military hoped to use to monitor Soviet bomb tests. Nevertheless, the Roswell incident continues to be of interest in popular media, and conspiracy theories surrounding the event persist. Roswell is described as "the world's most famous, most exhaustively investigated, and most thoroughly debunked UFO claim". Understandably, the Roswell incident fired up the public imagination, and the number of reported sightings of strange aerial phenomena of unknown aircraft - UFOs - soared. The military found this a very useful means of gauging when their secret experimental aircraft became indiscreet, as the public reported any suspicious aircraft.

For years UFO theorists have speculated about the possibility of the retrieval and movement of dead and living aliens, along with the downed craft, from the Roswell crash site to Wright-Patterson Air Force Base for examination and back engineering.

1950 – Hollywood, USA – The Flying Saucer

The first time an alien ship was depicted as a flying disc was in 1950, when Hollywood released the film *The Flying Saucer*.

1951 - Hollywood – The Day the Earth Stood Still

In 1951, the film *The Day the Earth Stood Still* depicted a saucer landing to warn humanity about nuclear annihilation. The message delivered by this visitor from space was that if we earthlings extended our savage ways to other planets, we "would be handled harshly". Further:

> *It is no concern of ours how you run your own planet, but if you threaten to extend your violence, this Earth of yours will be reduced to a burned-out cinder. Your choice is simple, join us and live in peace, or pursue your present course and face obliteration. We shall be waiting for your answer. The decision rests with you.*

Obviously, in the early 1950s, the possibility of a worldwide nuclear annihilation had caught the public's attention and true to Hollywood's practice, most movies were born out of that fear.

12-29 July 1952 - UFOs Over Washington, DC

This incident, also known as the invasion of Washington, consisted of a series of reports of unidentified flying objects over Washington DC from 12 to 29 July 1952. Project Blue Book and the Air Force received more reports of UFO sightings in this July period than had ever been seen before.

To calm public anxiety over the wave of UFO reports, Air Force Major-Generals John Samford (USAF Director of Intelligence), and Roger Ramey (USAF Director of Operations) held a press conference at the Pentagon on 29 July 1952. The intention was to quell the numbers of UFO reports and sightings to Project Blue Book, while at the same time respond to the media's questions about the sightings.

This was the largest press conference since World War II, and the only answer they could provide to the USA was that the visual sightings over Washington were nothing more than misidentified aerial phenomena such as stars or meteors. The unknown radar targets were explained as temperature inversions, which were apparently present over Washington during the two nights on which witnesses reported the radar anomalies.

It became apparent that the true purpose of the news conference was to allay any fear the public may have about these objects of unknown origin. It was stated that the solid objects were not a threat to national security and did not cause the unknown radar contacts. The media responded by asking whether the same or similar radar targets were also on the Air Force radars. The response was that yes they were, and there were attempts to intercept them with fighter jets; the matter was summarised with the statement that it was pointless, as nothing real was there. No doubt the Air Force was happy with the outcome, as things did seem to settle down.

1952 - Project Bluebook

Ever since businessperson and civilian pilot Kenneth Arnold reported seeing nine objects moving at high speed through the skies over Washington's Mount Rainier, there had been an increase in the number of reported sightings not only by the public but also by personnel in the aviation industry. This led the US Airforce to begin their own investigation called "Project Blue Book". It became the longest running official government inquiry into UFO sightings, compiling reports on more than 12,000 sightings or related events from 1952 to 1969, when it stopped reporting. In the end, the dubious findings from the thousands of photographs were analysed and filed. According to "Project Blue Book", the public incorrectly identified most of the sightings, which were natural phenomena such as clouds, stars, and conventional aircraft.

The US Air Force had established "Project Sign" In 1948 (later renamed "Project Blue Book" in 1952) to investigate all sightings by the public. It was at this time that the USAF coined the term "Unidentified Flying Object", or UFO, to describe any aircraft of unknown origin squeezing through similar loopholes via the plethora of aerial phenomena witnessed through the years. "Project Blue Book" only referenced unidentified aircraft and was never meant to reference the overlap of mind-provoking concepts such as alien visitations.

President Harry S Truman was alarmed by the huge amount of UFO sightings in 1952 and feared public hysteria might take hold, so the Central Intelligence Agency (CIA) assembled an expert panel of scientists, military, and Project Blue Book officials to discuss the UFO issue for three days. At its conclusion to the review of potential UFOs from photos and film, the panel surmised that there was no proof for the extra-terrestrial hypothesis and that the so-called UFOs posed no threat to national security. The explanation provided was that 90 percent of the sightings were astrological or meteorological phenomena, or manufactured objects such as balloons and aircraft. The findings by the panel remained classified until 1979, and this had fuelled the government conspiracy theories.

In December 1969 Project Blue Book at Wright-Patterson Air Force Base in Ohio (where the head office resided) was ordered to be shut down. The following published results of the investigation are still used today:

1. No UFO reported, investigated, and evaluated by the Air Force was ever an indication of threat to our national security.

2. There was no evidence submitted to or discovered by the Air Force that sightings categorized as "unidentified" represented technological developments or principles beyond the range of modern scientific knowledge.

3. No evidence was available to indicate that sightings categorized as "unidentified" were extra-terrestrial vehicles.

Over the next 17 years, Project Blue Book had reports of 12,618 UFO sightings or related events, and it concluded that 700 incidents remained "unidentified". These included cases in which there was insufficient information to assign the event a known cause, and which were classified as unexplained, even after stringent analysis. The UFO reports were archived and are available under the Freedom of Information Act with the redaction of names and other personal information of all witnesses.

In 1966, the Air Force formed another committee, which released its "Scientific Study of Unidentified Flying Objects", better known as the Condon Report, in 1968. These findings arose from looking into the details of 59 sightings investigated by Project Blue Book. According to the Condon Report, the sightings they examined showed no evidence of any unusual activity and it was recommended that the Air Force stop investigating UFO-related incidents.

Ultimately, in 1969, directly because of the Condon Report and the comparatively declining number of UFO sightings, Project Blue Book officially ended. One of the project's main conclusions was that the "unidentified" sightings did not have enough evidence that they were the result of technology beyond the range of modern scientific knowledge or that they were extra-terrestrial vehicles.

As civilian investigations took over because of the dissatisfaction of the government findings, ufology was born. The adviser to Project Blue Book, Allen Hynek, also created the follow-up Centre for UFO Studies (CUFOS), which continues to investigate UFO sightings and to present arguments that they could be evidence of extra-terrestrial activity.

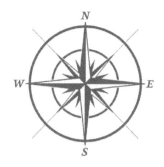

CHAPTER 3

The Classic Saucer

Date: 19 February 2012   Angle: E, 60°

Time: 5:55 pm   Direction: E to N

Height: 13,123 ft (4,374 yds, 4,000 m)   Photo: 2

Horizontal Distance: 6,561 ft (2,187 yds, 2,000 m)

Temperature: 81°F (27°C)   Video: N/A

Camera 1: Mobile Phone 3.2MP   Wind: S, 16 mph (26 km/h)

Camera 2: Digital Camera 10MP   Visibility: Passing clouds

Estimated Size of Object: 17.4 ft (5.3 m)

Well, this is when it all started, really. It was the modern era of ufology for me, and all year we had been debating what form the end of the world would take, especially with the approach of the now infamous date of 21 December 2012. Ten months prior to that "fateful" date, I had the shock of my life when I captured on camera what looked like the classic saucer UFO - and not on one digital optical device, but two, within 60 seconds of each other.

If you recall, a cataclysmic or New Age type of transformative event was to occur on or around 21 December 2012. This date was widely believed to be what the ancient Maya or Mesoamerican culture calendar had predicted. For the Maya, the end of the long count calendar represented the end of an old cycle and the beginning of a new one. However, we humans dwelled on the ultimate negative, and through the year we saw an infinite number of articles and YouTube videos predicting earthquakes, super volcanoes, asteroid impact, nuclear war, worldwide diseases to end humanity, and even economic collapses.

No, that day came and went and Mr Wonderer and the merriment of life went on. In the month of February my family took time out to celebrate my mother's birthday.

It was a beautiful day on Sunday 19 February 2012, with just a few scattered clouds and a temperature in the high 20s Celsius. Late in the afternoon my mother and I sat outside on the garden bench in our small backyard, facing towards the east and having a nice chat. I had bought a new mobile phone a week or two earlier and I was familiarising myself with some of its basic features, such as the camera, so I started to snap random pictures of the sky here and there. I only took a handful, and as I began to view the photographs I noticed what looked to be a tiny dark object clearly visible against the backdrop of the blue sky.

The garden bench we were sitting on has quite an angled back and it takes a bit of effort to get yourself out of it. I frantically raced to find the function that allows you to zoom into a photograph, and when I did, it suddenly became apparent that the shape took the form of a circular disc-like object with a dark bottom. Overcome with excitement, I jumped seemingly effortlessly from the bench, took a quick stare in the direction of the object, and ran inside to get my 10MP digital camera, which has 12x optical zoom. My poor mother was left behind confused over my actions, and made indiscernible comments as I ran inside.

Running back out, almost taking the sliding door shades with me, I started randomly taking pictures again with the superior camera. I aimed it all over the sky as I was not sure in which direction the object would be travelling, even though I knew where it was last. The bottom line is that we could not see the object, as it was either too far away to see or cloaking itself by blending into the background sky. But I do not think it was cloaking into the infrared spectrum, making itself invisible to me, as both of the non-infrared cameras produced photos.

I took some photos to the right then progressively more to the left, finishing over the roof of my house. As I was reviewing the photos, I broke out into a cold sweat because it dawned on me that just the day before I had been playing around with the macro settings to take pictures of bees landing on flowers, and had forgotten to return the settings to normal.

Image 3A: Single Photo taken with 3.2MP mobile phone, 19 February 2012.

Nevertheless, my efforts were successful. I caught the moving object within frame in virtually the last photograph, although I believe that it would have been clearer without the macro settings turned on.

My thoughts skirted around the idea that the object was cloaked after all - as is regularly discussed on the internet – which would mean that I could only not see it with my eyes, but only through the camera lens. Perhaps it just made itself visible to me at the exact same moment I pointed the camera? Highly unlikely. We can record events with a digital camera that happen too fast for the human eye to see; the camera can capture "the moment", while your eye cannot.

In a sense, though, our eyes are better at seeing faint light such as distant stars, than cameras would. Use a camera to take a quick single frame of those stars, and you are more than likely to capture the very brightest ones only. However, with the latest camera sensors and high ISO capabilities we are getting quite close to matching the sensitivity of the human eye. Having said that, of course, by using a long shutter speed, we can capture very faint stars that the human eye cannot even see.

Correspondingly, my photo of the disc UFO had been taken in daylight, so is there something else at play here? Was the UFO cloaking in the infrared after all, so I could not see it? It is difficult to say if this is the case, as in most cameras the sensor used to filter out the infrared is inside behind the lens. Infrared (IR) cameras interpret and convert the energy electronically to process a thermal image.

I am not sure if I will ever get an IR and thermal imaging camera, but the shifting prerequisite for me will be when the magnificent crystal in the form of a shiny orb wanes or the number of daylight UFO sightings declines. For this reason, if the UFO wants to remain camouflaged, then so be it. When it is ready, it will show itself.

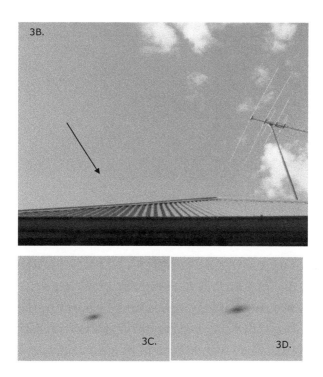

Image 3B-3D: Final random photo taken with a 10MP digital camera, with the disc clearly visible when magnified.

The object appeared to be travelling from east to north, finishing up directly over my house. I have often wondered whether this is why I heard the Hum at its peak a few years before: are these objects following certain highways in the sky, one of which happens to be over my house? Let us try some basic calculations to see if we can determine the size and speed of the object.

Estimated size of object:

Object size in image = object size * focal length/object distance from camera, or

Object size = (Object size in image * object distance from camera) / (focal length)

The Pythagorean Theorem to calculate distance from me is:

$a^2 + b^2 = c^2$ or (vertical distance)^2 + (horizontal distance)^2 = (distance from camera)

(4,000 m)^2 + (2,000 m)^2

(16,000,000) + (4,000,000) = $\sqrt{20,000,000}$ = 4,472 m (distance from camera)

10MP Digital Camera

Sensor size = 7.176 mm x 5.319 mm

Average = 6.25 mm (0.00625 m)

Size on image = 1 mm (0.001 m)

Vertical height of screen = 150 mm (0.15 m)

% of screen taken by object = 0.67

% of above compare with sensor size = 0.041 mm (0.000041 m)

35-420 mm (focal length used ~ 35 mm) = 0.035 m

To calculate size of disc (m) = ((0.000041 x 4,472) / (0.035))

= 5.32 m (17 ft)

The size of an average helicopter is 17-22 feet. I always compared the object to the size of a helicopter, except that I could not understand why I could not see it. Many helicopters perform frequent flyovers over my house, as I live near a major hospital accommodating a helipad alongside the main building for patient transport purposes. As in other built-up urban areas around the world, we have the occasional Police helicopter, television camera helicopters and Surf Rescue helicopters flying overhead.

As for the estimated speed, we can calculate this using the simple formula: speed = distance / time.

The feeling I have, and judging by the photos of the object, is that the height of the object remained constant; but I estimate the distance from where I first saw it in the east to the position in the final photo above my roof to be approximately 1 km (3,280 ft). Using this figure, the estimated duration between the first shot and when I snapped it over my roof would have been no longer than 60 seconds.

Speed = 1 km / (60 seconds / (60 x 60 hours))

= 1 / (60/3600)

= 60 km/h (37 mph)

Therefore, it was not really travelling fast at all.

Just to recap the facts, assumptions, and subjective analysis surrounding this sighting: I did not see the object at first and something made me take one shot in that direction, capturing the first image. Hoping to capture it for a second time, I took numerous photos in random directions with a different camera, one minute apart; this proved that it was not an anomaly within the mobile phone or MicroSD memory card.

What is the dark shade below the object? We can safely assume that it is of some significance to the disc and could be part of its propulsion system or its method of anti-gravitation. It is definitely part of the underside of the disc, as it appears in both photos, which were taken with two cameras. We assume that UFOs are capable of generating artificial gravity fields to manipulate the curvature of the fabric of space-time similar to the way we produce magnetism with electric currents. UFOs seem to defy our current accepted physics of conservation of momentum, as UFOs accelerate without throwing any material out the back. Another hurdle in understanding antigravity is that for it to be possible, it requires the existence of "negative mass" (or energy).

Looking back, what are the chances of capturing the object twice, and perfectly framed? Call it dumb luck if you will, call it deliberate intention on the object's part to materialise long enough for the camera to capture it. We can consider that chance and randomness are two sides of the same coin. What I saw happened randomly, as it occurred by chance. To scientists, chance and random outcomes develop when the physical causes may result in many different outcomes, and therefore we cannot predict what the outcome will be.

Risk, probability, chance, and coincidence play a significant role in the way we make decisions. Fair enough, the brain finds patterns and sometimes we go with our gut. For me, this all amounted to nothing over the next six to eight weeks as I took random, aimless photographs of the sky, amassing thousands of photos, analysing then deleting them. Most of the sightings in this book just happen by chance without me planning, predicting or looking for them. One thing I will add, though: as the years, months, weeks and days pass, the frequency of daylight sightings seems to increase.

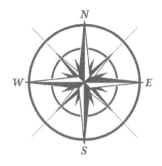

CHAPTER 4

Here Come the Glowing Orbs

Date: 26 February 2012	Angle: E, 60°
Time: 9:26 am, 10:37 am, and 3:24 pm	Direction: E to NE
Height: 15,000 ft (4,572 m)	Photo: 7
Horizontal Distance: 3,280 ft (1000 m)	
Temperature: 80°F (27°C)	Video: 0
Camera: Digital Camera 10MP	
Wind: N, 28 mph (46 km/h)	
Estimated Size of Object: 5.2 ft (1.6 m)	Visibility: Sunny

The next few chapters relate to my earlier sightings, where even though the photographs were taken with a 10 MP digital camera, the zoom capability was not sufficient to provide enough information. These few chapters only indicate that what I saw in the sky were strange flashing lights which I have never seen before, and which motivated me enough to record the events.

The number of objects that seem to fly directly over my house - whether just a normal looking balloon, bright orb or an object with strange long tethers - leads me to conclude that there seem to be specific paths that this phenomenon follows, high above. Occasionally I still hear the Hum (although very low) in the early hours of the morning. I look up to the ceiling and wonder if there is a link, and imagine how many objects fly over my house during the night.

It was frustrating when a week had passed since the classic disc sighting and taking random pictures of the sky proved to be a fruitless exercise. I was experiencing an unworkable apathy alongside a feeling of being disturbed. It was Sunday, just after 9:00 am, so the sun was well into its rise; and as I stepped outside and looked around the sky scattered with clouds, I saw a flash of light towards the west.

I wondered whether it could be a light plane, but the silence was deafening as I pointed the camera in that direction and took two consecutive photos in the wide-angle setting. It can't be a plane, I thought, and it certainly cannot be a sun dog (scientifically known as parhelion - plural parhelia). Relatively common, a sun dog is a halo usually seen around the sun, an atmospheric optical phenomenon associated with the refraction of sunlight by small ice crystals making up cirrus or cirrostratus clouds or by the sun shining through vapour or mist.

The shining orb I could see was something I had never seen before, almost like a small mirror in the sky reflecting off the sun when at the right position. I regret that (and am not sure why) for the next few years I never thought of taking a video recording with that camera, but only still photographs, thinking that the quality would be higher.

There seem to be three uses for the word "orb", in photography, metaphysics and ufology. In **photography**, an orb is normally a circular object or image, created when the flash illuminates dust or other particles. Orbs are especially common with modern compact and ultra-compact digital cameras. In the **metaphysical,** spiritual realm, they are thought to be spheres of energy. Many believe that orbs are spiritual beings such as angels or spirit guides. These are usually white, but can also have many different colours. In **ufology** orbs are usually seen hovering in metropolitan areas around the world, and they are recognised as having energy fields around them. They are also described as translucent, and their colours are very beautiful.

I have seen comments that these UFOs are usually seen over the summer months around the world, but quickly scanning the date stamps of the photo and video files that I have collected, I can see that I observe them any time of the year. There is an exception to this that I will describe later. The other exception, of course, is on winter days and nights when the clouds are abundantly present and there are minimal to zero sightings. I remember how a friend joked about my fascination overriding compromise as I watched the seven-day forecast waiting patiently for the next cloudless sky.

Looking back in detail again at the photos I took at 9:30 am on 26 February 2012, I can see that two were taken just seconds apart, and strangely the image in 4C is not in the second photo, although something similar appears at 3:26 pm (refer to Images 4D and 4E). There were at least five or six orbs in total, and the third photo (taken about 21 minutes later) shows that they have moved to the centre of that section of sky and one of them is larger than the others.

The orbs returned one hour later, then again five hours after that.

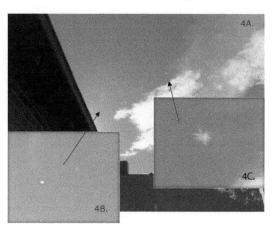

Image 4A-4C: Orbs appear in the east at 9:30 am on the left of frame. A very strange shape appeared to the right, although possibly just cloud.

Image 4D-4E: The orbs re-appeared in the same section of sky later the same day at 3:26 pm. When we magnify the orb, we see a shape similar to the object in 3C above, photographed earlier that day.

What I have tried to show here is that the captured evidence is only as good as the equipment you use. Please be patient, as the photographic evidence gets better after the next few chapters because after the Glyfada (Greece) UFO, I began experimenting with a telescope, attaching a small digital camera to the back of it with some good results. But still not happy, I decided to invest in a high resolution digital zoom camera with compelling potential. Still unsatisfied with the unsteadiness, I experimented with tripods and shoulder braces.

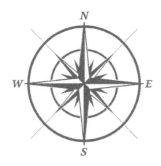

CHAPTER 5

Disc-Orb-Chemical Trail Cover-Up

Disc

Date: 19 June 2013

Time: 11:45 am

Height: 10,000 ft (3,048 m)

Horizontal Distance: 3,280 ft (1000 m)

Camera: Mobile phone 2MP

Estimated Size of Object: N/A

Angle: East, 75°

Photo: 0

Video: N/A

Temp: 11°C (52°F)

Wind: SSE, 9 km/h (6 m/h)

Orb

Date: 19 June 2013

Time: 11:53 am

Height: 1,312 ft (400 m)

Horizontal Distance: 2,460 ft (750 m)

Camera: Mobile phone 2MP

Estimated Size of Object: 4.2 ft (1.29 m)

Angle: East, 45°

Photo: 1

Video: N/A

Temp: 11 °C (52 °F)

Wind: SSE, 9 km/h (6 m/h)

Chemical Trail Cover-Up

Date: 20 June 2013

Time: 11:57 am

Height: N/A

Horizontal Distance: N/A

Camera: Mobile Phone 2MP

Angle: East, 75°

Photo: 54

Video: N/A

Temp: 13°C (55°F)

Wind: N, 17 km/h (11 m/h)

There are three sections to this sighting, which occurred over two days and at the same time each day, 12:00 pm - no coincidence, just my daily walk at lunchtime. I witnessed the most incredible whitish disc sitting motionless in the sky, and then I saw an orb low in the sky on the way back to work. The strangest of all was that the next day at the same time and at the exact same location, there was the oddest chemical trail in the sky.

We are all working so hard to get somewhere that we forget to remain in the present. Walking for me is a meditative moment that I can fully exercise, engaging my full senses with the surroundings. I take the time to see what is around me and listen to all the sounds. I can still utilise my senses of smell and touch, so for an hour the worries of my day do not enter the equation at all. No need to worry about work, the boss, the emails, the promised retirement fund and whether it will be enough.

I was on my way back to work from the 45-minute walk, waiting for the pedestrian lights to turn green, when high in the sky I saw this whitish disc. What caught my eye was the fact that the object remained stationary amongst the small amount of scattered, passing clouds. I took out my mobile phone and snapped several photos and a short video, but I was not successful in framing it against the bright sky.

As I continued walking I played back the video to check what I had captured, but could not see anything. Disappointed, I looked around to see if the object was still there but could not locate it amongst the scattered clouds. Still glancing behind me hoping to see the disc again, I resigned myself to the fact that I had missed a good opportunity, so in desperation I commenced to randomly take photos of the sky around me. Thinking that it would be an ineffective exercise, I didn't even bother looking at the shots until I got home and uploaded them onto the computer - and saw a glowing saucer-shaped object. It had a dark trail above it which eventually became part of the object as it glowed (Images 5A-5B).

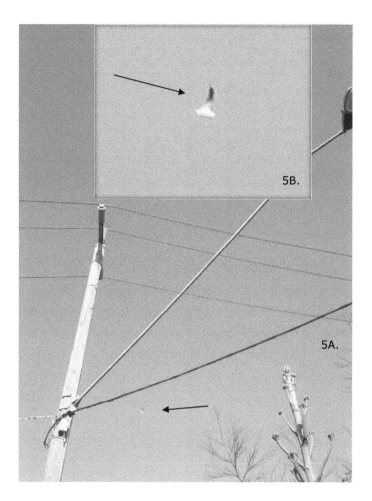

Image 5A-5B: *This is what was captured after random photos were taken across the eastern sky.*

Estimated Size of Object:

*Object size in image = object size * focal length / object distance from camera, or*

*Object size = (Object size in image * object distance from camera) / (focal length)*

The Pythagorean Theorem to calculate distance from me is:

$a^2 + b^2 = c^2$ or (vertical distance)^2 + (horizontal distance)^2 = (distance from camera)

(400 m)^2 + (750 m)^2

(160,000) + (562,500) = $\sqrt{722,500}$ = 850 m (distance from camera)

Mobile Phone 2MP

Sensor size = 4 mm x 4 mm

Average = 4 mm (0.004 m)

Size on image = 2 mm (0.002 m)

Vertical height of screen = 150 mm (0.15 m)

% of screen taken by object = 1.3

% of above compare with sensor size = 0.053 mm (0.000053 m)

(focal length used ~ 35 mm) = 0.035 m

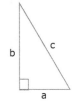

To calculate size of object (m) = ((0.000053 x 850) / (0.035))

= 1.29 m (4.2 ft)

The next day I followed the same lunchtime routine, my patience rattled as I stared at the sky. I couldn't believe my eyes as I turned around the corner to where I had seen the white disc in the sky the day before. There in front of me taking up half of the sky was a massive chemical trail in the shape of an "X". The centre of the X was about where I had seen the first disc the previous day, and not the glowing saucer-shaped object that was lower in the sky. After a couple of decades of observing these chemical trails, in Adelaide then in Melbourne, such a cross pattern was a first for me. I believe I had noticed two chemtrails intersecting once or twice before, but certainly not as an X shape.

The internet has literally thousands of web pages about chemical trails and the inherent conspiracy behind them. When a jet engine emits hot, humid air into the atmosphere, which is cold and has low vapour pressure, the result is "contrails" (short for condensation trails); but this is short-lived as the trails quickly dissipate behind the jet. One explanation the "experts" have offered is that when the atmosphere is more humid, the contrails linger around, but when the atmosphere is dry, the contrails disappear more quickly.

This may be correct, but the cover-up and fake data surrounding first global warming then climate change leave much to be desired (remember the hockey stick graph for man-made carbon dioxide emissions?).

Worldwide, many believe that the population is experimented on, not unlike lab rats, when they are sprayed illegally with highly toxic chemtrails. It's a massive project instigated by the elite, the military and government officials, where they spray every night and every day in most countries from recognised commercial, private jets and unmarked military jets.

Despite many groups' activities protesting against this atrocity, officials refuse to respond and acknowledge that it is happening. In fact, I felt I had to make a complaint several years ago as the chemtrails were deposited in the same part of the sky for two days in a row. After a couple of calls, I believe I was passed on to Melbourne Airport, and the person at the other end of the line explained that they are just condensation trails. I gave him a lengthy explanation showing that they cannot be contrails since they spread out like clouds and stayed visible for hours later, but it all seemed to fall on deaf ears.

The suspicion does count for the chemtrails across the world as the general belief warps chemtrails to a degree. But the evidence mounts up: there is a growing epidemic of thyroid disease worldwide, and an increase in Morgellons disease (a controversial condition involving skin lesions where contrail fibres and Morgellons disease fibres on the skin look identical).

The four ailments commonly associated with chemtrails are:
- Aneurysms: Chemicals associated with chemtrails are believed to block arteries and weaken arterial walls, leading to aneurysms and eventually deadly strokes.
- Strokes: Nano-particle aluminium builds up in capillaries, causing blockages and eventually leading to aneurysms and strokes.
- Heart Attacks: Barium dramatically lowers potassium in mammals, leading to heart fibrillations and heart attacks. In

fact, barium is used in animal testing to artificially induce heart attacks.

- Cancer: Most of the components of chemtrails suppress the immune system. When the immune system is suppressed for extended periods, cancer grows and thrives.

Of course, there are also the lesser ailments such as fatigue, headaches, joint pains and so on. On the other side of the coin, maybe in my case the chemtrails were drawn as an X to conceal potential UFO activity as per the day before. Perhaps the massive X drawn in the sky was almost an inside joke.

Image 5C-5D: Images showing the highly unusual criss-cross effect of chemtrails the day after a white disc was sighted virtually where the trails cross.

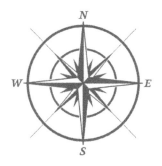

CHAPTER 6

2015-Mirrors in the Sky

Date: 21 March 2015	Photo: 4 Video: 4min 57 sec	Time: 3:34 pm
Date: 21 March 2015	Photo: 45 Video: N/A	Time: 4:22 pm
Date: 21 June 2015	Photo: 6 Video: N/A	Time: 8:09 pm
Date: 22 June 2015	Photo: 7 Video: N/A	Time: 2:34 pm
Date: 18 July 2015	Photo: 15 Video: N/A	Time: 1:53 pm
Date: 4 October 2015	Photo: 7 Video: N/A	Time: 11:23 am
Date: 7 February 2016	Photo: 16 Video: N/A	Time: 2:54 pm
Camera: Digital Camera 10MP		

Most of the sightings in 2015 were daylight orbs, unassuming except for the fact that they caught my attention simply by the sun reflecting off them, or they may have been self-luminous and/or pulsing. It is difficult to say as the camera I had at the time would only zoom 12x, which was nowhere near enough to determine shape with the distances involved, as I was able to with subsequent cameras. Another disappointing aspect is that I am still unsure why I never attempted to take video footage with the digital camera rather than just photographs. I recall an assumption that it would not be clear enough.

I did, however, have an old JVC camera with which I took some video of these orbs. But again, the actual shapes are indiscernible and will not be published. I do not have a keen interest in using infrared cameras to chase and photograph anything outside the visible spectrum. All the UFOs in this book, including the flashing, plasma-type orbs, can be seen with the naked eye in daylight. And less than 18 months later I was able to get a closer look at what these objects really are, with incredible detail.

From my perspective these phenomena appear to have only been witnessed around the world in recent years, and I for one have certainly never seen them before.

As a teenager in Adelaide, South Australia, when I bought my first telescope, I used to spend hours every single night using star charts and star catalogues to gaze at heavenly wonders. I saw Jupiter and four of its larger moons as they orbited the giant plant with the beautiful great red spot across its face.

When I first saw Saturn through the telescope it was breathtaking, and I remember the excitement as my mother also could not believe what she was seeing. The horse head nebula in the constellation of Orion and the Seven Sisters, or the Pleiades star clusters, were also amazing sights for my young eyes.

Even without a telescope, there were times that I would gaze at the sky during periods of solar and lunar eclipses and sun spot observation using filters and pin holes through white cardboard where the image was safely projected. During this period, even chemtrails were in their infancy, but I never recall observing anything unusual such as glowing or flashing orbs.

We are told that we live in an infinite ever-expanding universe, so that everything that is possible, is possible. The further away our telescopes and instruments observe, the closer to the speed of the light the space (and therefore the stars and galaxies) is moving away from us here on earth. Not only that, we have physics and mathematical equations that produce results indicating that there is more than one universe - that in fact an infinite number of universes exist as probabilities and collapse into one at the point we observe it.

This was the case with quantum mechanics calculations as far back as 1926, when Schrödinger's mathematical equation described the changes over time of a physical system for quantum effects, such as the wave–particle duality. The equation allows physicists to find the allowed energy levels of quantum mechanical systems such as atoms or particles, and the associated wave function gives the probability of finding the particle at a certain position.

Alternate realities and parallel universes do not have to be light years away across the universe. They can be here on earth, where a multitude of versions of you yourself exist until the wave function collapses at the point of observation as described mathematically. With every possibility existing at any one time, the act of observation from our perspective removes all the other possibilities, leaving only the one.

The other realities do not cease to exist during the wave function collapse; they all exist as well. Experiments have been devised to prove that the strange laws of quantum mechanics apply not only to the very small but also to the very large; so any object can be in many places at once.

There is a parallel universe containing antimatter which is in the equal amount of matter as seen in the physical universe, although if a tiny fragment of this antimatter was ever to meet matter it would result in an explosive force that would dwarf our nuclear weapons. Associated with every particle is an antimatter particle which has the same mass but opposite properties. For instance, the electron, which has negative charge, has the positron of positive charge as its antimatter.

Particle accelerators, such as the one at CERN, are used to experimentally produce particles called B Mesons and anti-B Mesons, comparing each one-trillionth of a second longevity, that may provide proof of where in the universe these antimatters are. The conclusion is that due to the very small differences in decay times, we have been left with the visible matter in the universe we see today - leaving the unanswered question that this does not account for all the missing antimatter in the universe. And so the search continues.

We may well live in three dimensions surrounded by a membrane within space, but it also has an extra fourth spatial dimension containing a parallel universe only a fraction of an inch away. Even though these two universes should not interact with one another, it is understood that occasionally they move towards each other and collide, producing matter and radiation and then separating again. Theoretical physicists and cosmologists have suggested that the Big Bang was not the commencement of time and space, but the result of two dimensions colliding. It is suggested it would be more aptly described as the bounce, corresponding to a collision and recoil of branes (a basic object in string theory).

The laws of physics are completely different in each of these two worlds that are so close to each other, less than an atom's width apart. We are already seeing evidence of this other universe in the effect of gravity on galaxies produced by what has been called "dark matter" in that parallel world.

Black holes in space may be the ultimate link between the third dimension and fourth spatial dimension of space. Some scientists think that our universe resides at the bottom of a black hole because of an enormous star collapsing. If this is so, would sending a message though a black hole result in the message being received in the parallel universe? If this is the case, then beings from this parallel universe should already be trying to communicate with us.

Besides my photos of orbs and shiny objects taken in 2015, you will see photos and videos from towards the end of 2016, that would blow your mind and make you wonder whether these are interdimensional beings. I have seen the objects materialise and dematerialise as if moving between dimensions, either due to a natural phenomenon (as they seem to always occur at the same points in the sky) or as a direct result of the objects themselves creating a portal.

Images 6A-6B: Images taken on 21 March 2015, 3:34 pm. Single orb facing east, hovering, and drifting south. The two dark objects below it only appeared in one photo.

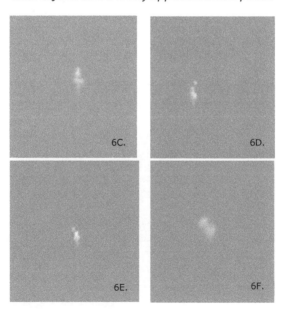

Images 6C-6F: Images taken on 21 March 2015, 4:22 pm. Single orb towards the south. It is difficult to say if it was the same object that was seen one hour earlier.

 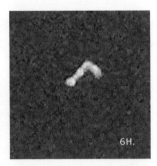

Images 6G-6H: Images taken on 21 June 2015, 8:09 pm, Single orb towards the south. I am not sure whether this was the actual shape, or whether it morphed very quickly between consecutive shots, or moved extremely quickly within the shot creating a trail, or is a result of camera shake.

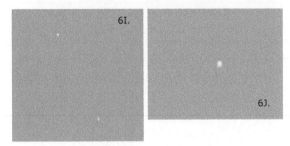

Images 6I-6J: Images taken on 22 June 2015, 2:34 pm. First two orbs were observed towards the south, then only the one remained.

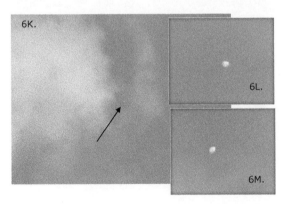

Images 6K-6M: Images taken on 18 July 2015, 1:53 pm. The orb was high in sky towards the south.

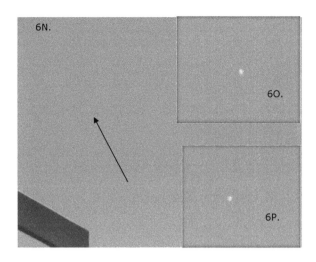

Images 6N-6P: Images taken on 4 October 2015, 11:23 am. Three orbs from the west moving east. Two continued on. while the third came in my direction for a short period then returned to the others.

If I am accurately recalling the above sighting at 1:53 pm on 18 July 2015, it was the time I saw three orbs come from the ocean side in the west, and as I was filming and zooming in, two continued along an easterly direction while the third one momentarily paused then did a sharp turn in my direction. It literally stopped right above me and I remember the strain I was under in order to take the photos.

It then turned around to join the others travelling in the easterly direction. This was one of those times that I will never ever forget, as my perception was that the object knew I was focusing and zooming in on it, so it moved towards me in acknowledgment, as if under intelligent control. As it came in my direction, it never made any alteration to its height of approximately 9,842 ft (1.86 mi, 3 km).

Images 6Q-6R: Images taken on 7 February 2016, 2:54 pm. One orb in the west

I have included this unassuming orb from February 2016 because it was nearly six months before the commencement of first of the major sightings beginning with Glyfada, Athens (Greece).

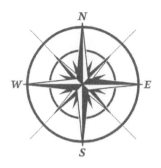

CHAPTER 7

The Glyfada, Athens (Greece) Red Orb

Date: 18 September 2016	Angle: S, 50°
Time: 8:15 pm	Direction: S to W
Height: 984 ft (300 m)	Photo: 46
Horizontal Distance: 3,280 ft (0.62 mi, 1 km)	
Temp: 79°F (26°C)	Video: 1 min 43 sec
Camera: Mobile Phone 16MP	Wind: S, 17 km/h (10 mph)
Estimated Size of Object: 2.6 ft (0.8 m)	Visibility: Clear

The week leading up to August 2016 was a very exciting period for me indeed. After a 25-year of period inactivity, holding off and never taking a decent holiday, with the help of my mother and sister I finally made meticulous plans to visit three key destinations.

The first would be Turkey, because my sister had visited Istanbul twice before and it was highly recommended; then Italy's colosseum; and Greece, which is only one and a half hour's flight from Turkey. We looked forward to being able to experience the different cultures and diversity these places offer: the romance of Venice, the Greek islands, shopping in Istanbul and various modes of transportation such as the massive ferries from the island of Chios to the Turkish coastal town of Cesme. We boarded the plane after the usual wait at the airport. Flying with Qatar Airways made it all worthwhile, as in our view it would function as the gemstone amongst the uncertainty ahead.

Qatar Airways has one of the world's youngest airline fleets, with an average aircraft age of approximately five years. There is nothing pretentious about the strength of its fantastic service. The state of the art entertainment technology is the best way to keep weary travellers occupied. I nevertheless chose the window seat with camera ready hoping to catch something unusual outside, but I did not see anything else unusual other than a terrifying storm with lightning in the distance that stretched for many kilometres.

At Doha International Airport I was shocked to hear that the temperature outside was 111 °F (44 °C). We waited a couple of hours before boarding another Qatar flight to Istanbul. When we landed, our private taxi was waiting to take us to our hotel, where we literally dumped our bags and took off so that I could experience Istanbul for the very first time.

Our taxi crossed over the Bosphorus Strait, which acts as a border between Europe and Asia, and we did a river tour which gave us a stunning view of Istanbul. Istanbul's historical buildings are difficult to take in unless you are at a distance, such as on a boat cruising along the Bosphorus. Highlights include views of several Ottoman palaces and fortresses along the riverfront. The Bosphorus leads into the Sea of Marmara and the Black Sea.

In June 2007 the Sea of Marmara played host to a very interesting and important UFO when a night guard saw and recorded a strange object hovering over the sea. The same UFO had been spotted previously around the same time, and it was observed and recorded by various other Turkish citizens in 2008 and 2009.

Several residents described observing a disc and oval-shaped object with a metallic appearance flying or hovering. When moving it was silent, and sometimes accompanied by strange red and orange lights. When it hovered, it was under a bright moon showing a lot more detail than would otherwise have been seen. The footage is purported to show in some detail not only the craft, but also what appears to be a cockpit with the actual alien "pilots".

To prove that all the recorded footage of the UFO was nothing more than another hoax, Turkey's National Council for the Study of Science and Technology analysed it, thinking that it was nothing more than a model, toy, or CGI to pull off the impressive hoax. What they proved, however, was the exact opposite of what was expected. After extensive analysis, they found absolutely no evidence that any part of the footage was a hoax at all.

The Council stated that the objects observed on the images have a structure made of a specific material and that they were not any kind of CGI animation, and by no means any type of special effect used for simulation in a studio or for video effects. They concluded that the observed objects were neither models, marquettes or fraud. Further, after analysing the footage, professors, special effects companies, and video specialists all agreed that the images were indeed authentic. Nobody has yet been able to disprove the footage.

After the Bosphorus tour we returned to Istanbul and familiarised ourselves with the immediate area around our hotel, including the Grand Bazaar and the various eateries. There is no doubt about it, Istanbul is a beautiful city architecturally, with reportedly almost 3,000 active mosques. One of the tours we had organised included the Blue Mosque. This impressive mosque was constructed between 1609 and 1616 and is famous for the hand-painted blue tiles which adorn the interior walls. At night the mosque is bathed in blue as lights frame the five main domes, six minarets and eight secondary domes.

The Blue Mosque is situated next to the Hagia Sophia, another popular tourist site that was also included in our itinerary. The 1,500-year-old Hagia Sophia is a very important World Heritage church of great architectural beauty, and it has been the inspiration behind many books and films. Hagia Sophia was once a Greek Orthodox Church, later turned into a mosque with the additional minarets, and now is a museum. Relics such as nails from Jesus Christ's crucifixion and the shroud of Mary were some of the very important treasures of the church until they were stolen during the attack of the Crusaders. It is widely believed that this magnificent building led Russia, in a way, to choose Orthodox Christianity rather than Catholicism.

We decided to do some shopping at the Grand Bazaar in Istanbul. It is one of the largest and oldest covered markets in the world, with 61 covered streets and over 4,000 shops which attract between 250,000 and 400,000 visitors daily. In one of the smaller shops outside the market I bought two mobile phones, one for my mother and one for myself.

It is difficult to resist the attractiveness of Istanbul with the many historical ruins dating back to 6,500 BC. The 100,000-capacity hippodrome of Constantinople (Sultanahmet square, Istanbul) was originally the sporting and social centre of Constantinople. The ancient Greek city of Ephesus (cited in the Bible's Book of Revelations; it is widely believed that the Gospel of St John may have been written there) which is a one-hour flight from Istanbul, was built in the 10th century BC, and has had a diverse history including visitors such as Alexander the Great, Mark Antony and Cleopatra. The Virgin Mary is believed to have spent her last years not far from Ephesus. The House of the Virgin Mary is considered to have been the last home of St Mary. The Temple of Artemis, also close to Ephesus, was completed in 550 BC and is one of the Seven Wonders of the Ancient World, although not much remains. Close to the Temple of Artemis is the St Johns Basilica site. There are just too many to name.

I was so glad I purchased the mobile phone in Istanbul, because in Greece I later captured on camera the most amazing object. After eight days we flew out of Istanbul, stayed in Macedonia in Northern

Greece for two days, the Greek islands of Chios and Mytilene for ten days, then finally stayed at the beachside tourist area of Glyfada in Athens.

Glyfada is situated in the southern part of the Athens suburban area and was the site of an American airbase until the early 1990s. It still has a heavy American influence in atmosphere and cuisine, while continuing to also offer distinctly Greek cuisine, entertainment and nightlife. The hotel we stayed at offered a wonderful breakfast buffet and on the second night we decided to have dinner at the rooftop open air restaurant.

For some strange reason, even though we always take along our 20.1 MP digital camera everywhere we go, on this occasion - you guessed it - we left it behind in our room. Fortunately, I had brought along my newly purchased mobile phone.

We were shown to our table and sat down. It was a beautiful evening as the sun was preparing to set over Glyfada Beach, an open ocean directly in front of us providing the best view I have ever seen. It was a comparatively small dining area with about five or so other couples in various stages of their meal. Some had just sat down while others had finished eating and continued having drinks.

After we ordered I walked around to take in the views in all directions. Towards the south I could see a typical metropolitan area and further beyond were the Glyfada Hills; towards the west was the magnificent Glyfada Beach of the Saronic Gulf; and to the north was the main highway leading to the main port of Piraeus and Athens. I stood there watching as a lady of the night, impervious to the fast-moving traffic, was performing her routine as if on a catwalk for 20 metres, returning briskly to her starting point then parading again for 20 metres. This went on several times until a car pulled over and she jumped in. Towards the east was the continuation of buildings and homes, and further in the distance the hilly area stretched from south to north.

Just before 8:00 pm we started eating our meal. All the lights of Glyfada looked pretty against the dark and star-filled sky. I remember clearly that we were saying it was a great idea to have included Glyfada as the destination after the hectic time in Turkey, Italy and Greece, full of tours and sightseeing. If relaxing and walking on the beach or having a coffee watching the sunsets over the ocean proved too leisurely, you could take the train along the coast to Athens for the day or night.

Suddenly a bright red light appeared out of the darkness to the left of me (south) and attracted my attention. My exact words were "that looks weird" as I jumped up, grabbing my mobile phone. I walked to the southern edge of the building to take some photos and I could hear my sister exclaiming not to worry about it and that the airport is in that direction, implying that it was just a plane. I kept taking photos, a total of six, because I knew instantly that it was not an aircraft, as it was one large red light, not flickering, and there were no other visible lights at all. I learned later that the international airport was some distance away, about 25 km to the east, not south.

From where I stood I could see that no other customers had noticed the light. They had their backs towards the object as many of the tables were on the ocean side of the building to take full advantage of the impressive views. From my perspective, the bright red light was at a low angle and probably about 1 km away, hovering for a moment before it began to move very slowly in a downward direction. I remember that no other discerning detail was noticed throughout the 50 seconds or so that this object was visible, perhaps due to the intensity of the red light. The camera, on the other hand, revealed a wealth of detail behind the blinding light, including the video I recorded.

Then just as suddenly as it had appeared, the light turned off as if someone had flicked a switch. I sat down again and tapped through the photos, knowing that it would be something extraordinary. Out of the six photos I managed to take, to my amazement, the very first photo clearly showed a V-shaped object, reddish in colour. When magnified, you could see it had three visible whitish nodules on the outside. The second photo showed that it had transformed into a circular kind of shape with no detail; but in the third photo it clearly looked like a reddish saucer with a dome on top, now displaying four visible nodules around the circumference of the object. The final three photos showed nothing but black sky, having probably been taken as the object disappeared. Later when I was back in Melbourne I uploaded the photos onto my computer; zooming in, I noticed some other incredible details.

Thinking that was the end of it and that I was fortunate to capture a night-time UFO overseas, about 15 minutes had passed when I whispered loudly to my mother and sister that it had returned, but this time directly above the ocean and peculiarly directly in front of us. It was the same size red light, and again no other shape was visible through the intense red light.

I recalled that as I was playing around with the phone earlier, I had found it could take 40 continuous photos when required. When I pressed the relevant button now, I could see nothing less than a unique shape in every single shot as if it was continually morphing, so I could not wait to go back to Melbourne to upload them to my computer. With the object still hovering, I quickly flicked the mobile phone to video again and started recording, but again after about a minute it disappeared.

Playing back the videos on the mobile phone did not reveal much except for a small light in the centre of the screen, and unable to zoom in I left it at that, happy that I had captured it on video. I found it truly fascinating that this object just vanished not far from me and then re-appeared over the ocean some 15 minutes later.

Once back in Melbourne, I uploaded all the photos and video onto my computer and started to analyse them. To my astonishment, the very first photo showed a V-shaped object. I could clearly see that there were three nodes, one at each end of the V shape, but also the street lights below for some strange reason also adopted the same V shape and were pointing in the same direction as the object.

The object was changing shape at an enormous speed and the incredible thing about it is that the first three photos show the exact time the object transformed from V shape to saucer shape.

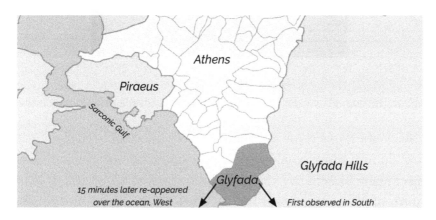

Image 7A: Red orb first seen to the left of us (south); disappeared and 15 minutes later re-appeared over the ocean directly in front of us (west).

Images 7B – 7D: The very first photo shows a V-shaped object with 3 nodules at each extremity; and peculiarly the street lights below the object also have the same V shape.

Image 7E–7G: The second photo shows the object morphed to a more circular object. The nodules are not visible and the street lights are no longer V-shaped.

Many questions come to mind. Why was the colour red significant? How did it disappear, only to re-appear in a different location? Is the object made invisible by changing to the infared spectrum, or is this a form of interdimensional travel? What did it achieve in the short time it appeared? How did the object's presence influence the shape of the traffic lights? Is this evidence of quantum mechanics in the macro? Is the object performing a wave-particle duality as a method of propagation? Is that what the rapid morphing of the object is revealing?

Images 7H–7J: The third photo shows the object morphed in a fraction of a second to a saucer shape with 4 visible nodules and red dome above it; assume another two nodules are on the other side. As before, the street lights are no longer V-shaped.

We will seek some answers in the next chapter by learning about the properties of light, which can be explained in terms of waves via the double slit experiment: when light was directed at the two slits an interference pattern resulted on the screen at the back, leading to a definitive conclusion that light behaves as a wave. Additionally, we cannot escape the fact that according to wave-particle duality, light behaves as both a wave and a particle at the same time.

Wave motion is represented by the three measurable properties of wavelength, amplitude and frequency. The propagation of waves, or wave motion, is the disturbance of electric and magnetic fields in space - the electromagnetic radiation.

UFO over

Glyfada—Athens

19 Sept 2016

Time, 8:15 PM

A. Bright Red light appears **South**
~ 1 kilometre distance
~ visible for 60 seconds

over **Glyfada—Athens** Residence

6 consecutive photos over **15 seconds**

UFO changes shape

1. V shape (red V with 3 white nodules)

2. Becoming sphere/saucer

3. Saucer (red dome with 4 white nodules)

4. 5. 6. Red light dims and disappears

B. **13 minutes** later, same Bright Red light appears **West** Over the Ocean
~ 1 kilometre distance

40 consecutive photos over **15 seconds**

UFO changes shape in every shot.

Red light dims and again disappears

Notes:

Bright red light appeared to be size of 60% of full moon.

4 videos also obtained

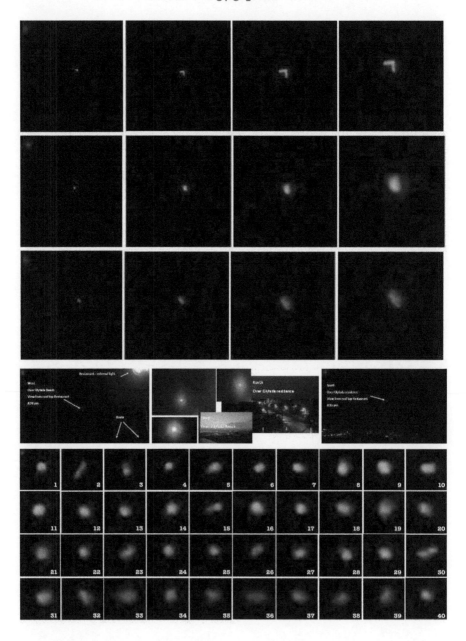

Image 7K: This collage of the Glyfada UFO adorns my lounge room wall. The bottom half shows the 40 consecutive photos, while the top half shows the initial changing of shape, from V shape to saucer shape. On the last row, second from the left, is the only other clearly defined saucer shape during the morphing.

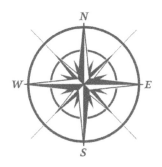

CHAPTER 8

Red Light Waves, Wave-Particle Duality

When we remove the intricacies of interacting electric and magnetic fields and quantum mechanics, light is basically energy in space. A wave is really a mechanism by which energy is transported from one location to another. In a vacuum, the speed of light is 186,282 miles per second (or nearly 300,000 kilometres per second). Due to this finite nature of light, it takes 2.5 seconds for a signal or light to travel to the moon and back, while it takes about eight minutes for a signal or light to reach earth from the sun.

Light, also called electromagnetic radiation, consists of a continuous range of energies of gamma-rays, X-rays, ultraviolet, optical, infrared, and radio waves. Visible light has wavelengths in the range of 400–700 nanometres (nm), or 4.00×10-7 to 7.00×10-7 m. On either side of visible light is the infrared (longer wavelengths) and ultraviolet light (shorter wavelengths). Higher frequencies have shorter wavelengths, and lower frequencies have longer wavelengths.

When electric and magnetic fields are disturbed - as when a pebble is thrown in a pond - the stationary charged particles vibrate and accelerate, disturbing the electric field around the particle and creating magnetic fields. The resulting outward moving disturbance in the electromagnetic field is the electromagnetic wave, or what we call light. White light can be separated into red, orange, yellow, green, blue and violet, each with their own unique wavelengths; but the speed is constant (speed of light).

The formula for light is $c = \lambda f$. This important formula shows the relationship between the speed of light, its wavelength, and its frequency.

c = the speed of light = 300,000 km/s or 3.0×10^8 m/s

λ = the wavelength of light, usually measured in metres or Angstroms ($1 \text{ Å} = 10\text{-}10$ m)

f = the frequency at which light waves pass by, measured in units per second ($1/s$).

Color	λ (Wavelength)	v (Frequency)
	(nm)	(THz)
Infrared	>1000	<300
Red	700	428
Orange	620	484
Yellow	580	517
Green	530	566
Blue	470	638
Violet	420	714
Near ultraviolet	300	1000
Far ultraviolet	<200	>1500

The longest wavelengths are **radio** waves, while the shortest wavelengths are **gamma** rays. When combined with the colours of light, these become the **electromagnetic spectrum**.

It is a well-known fact amongst the UFO community that UFOs seem to hide outside the visible spectrum of light, within the infrared. There is footage on the internet which has been captured by civilians using the many infrared cameras and lenses available. Air Force personnel around the world using highly sophisticated hardware have also released declassified footage using infrared cameras.

The double slit experiment, where a beam of light or particles is directed at two slits with a screen at the rear, results in a diffraction pattern due to interference effects. Due to the waves from the two slits, bands of light and dark constructively or destructively interfere. The exact same pattern is observed when individual particles are also fired at a double slit, leading to the conclusion that light can behave as both a particle and a wave, and this is described as wave-particle duality. A particle of light is called a photon of light; wavelength and frequency can still be applied and, as discussed earlier, the waves transport energy; so each photon of light carries energy, and the amount of energy depends on the wavelength or frequency of that photon.

The formula for light is $E = h\,c\,/\,\lambda$. This simple equation ties together the particle and wave nature of light by permitting us to convert back and forth from wavelengths to photons, and from photons to their corresponding wavelengths. Straight away this formula reveals that an X-ray photon has a large energy (and a small wavelength) compared with a photon of optical light.

E = energy
h = Planck's constant = 6.62607004 × 10-34 m2 kg / s
c = the speed of light
λ = the wavelength of light

So far, we have seen that there is a possibility that the Glyfada UFO may have mysteriously disappeared and re-appeared in a different position by cloaking itself in the infrared red spectrum that exists beyond red visible light, then returning to the visible spectrum over the ocean. The other possibility is that the object may be converting itself from an object (perhaps solid) into pure light for its method of propagation, at the same time moving into the infrared; hence the strange orbs captured on video around the world.

If you refer to image 7K, you will notice that of the 40 consecutive photos, even though they are dim due to the quality of the mobile phone, photos 31 to 40 in the last row are even darker compared to the earlier ones, which may mean the object was preparing to move into the infrared. Can the high rate of speeds of some of these objects be attributed to their somehow rearranging themselves at the quantum level to become pure light, enabling them to travel at the speed of light? The vast distances we know of in space can be overcome by coupling this with the ability for interdimensional travel through portals, natural or created (to be discussed later).

The only way of breaking the light barrier may be through general relativity and the warping of space time. This warping is what we sometimes call a wormhole, which theoretically would allow something to travel vast distances instantaneously, essentially enabling us to break the speed of light by travelling great distances in a very short amount of time.

Regardless, I remember that there was some movement when I first saw the object in the south above the streets of Glyfada. It was moving slowly in a downward direction. Further, there appeared to be an object behind the intense red light; and it morphed into different shapes continually at a very high rate of speed, impacting on the shape of the street lights below as captured by the camera.

Most street lighting around the world commonly uses high-intensity discharge lamps, often HPS or high-pressure sodium lamps. Such lamps provide the greatest amount of illumination for the least consumption of electricity. A sodium-vapour lamp is a gas-discharge lamp that uses sodium in an excited state to produce light at a characteristic wavelength near 589 nm.

A more accurate explanation for how High-Pressure Sodium Lamps (HPS Lamps) operate is that current first passes through Xenon gas (a noble gas with very low chemical reactivity); and the lamp also contains mercury (blueish), and sodium (orange) that vaporises, producing more of a full-spectrum light rather than an intense orange.

I believe that even though the object appeared to be neon red in appearance and self-luminous, its inherent characteristics tended to the orange due its effect on the sodium vapour street lamps below it. How? It could be due to absorption and emission of light or the interaction of light and matter, light from the UFO and matter from the sodium and mercury.

Atoms or molecules can absorb light (or energy). Atoms are made up of protons, neutrons and electrons, and each chemical element has a specific number of these, making them unique in the periodic table. Electrons are only found at specific, discrete distances from the larger and heavier nucleus, and that distance corresponds to different energy levels for electrons. The electrons bound to any atom can only be found in certain, specific energy levels with respect to the atom's nucleus.

As a simple example, the hydrogen atom only contains one proton and one electron. Left undisturbed, the electron occupies the lowest energy level, which is called the "ground state". However, things become interesting when a beam of light shines on the hydrogen atom, for example a distant star. Once the atom encounters a photon with just the right amount of energy to jump the electron up to the next higher energy level, the photon gets absorbed with that specific energy, and therefore specific wavelength, in the spectrum of light.

At this point the hydrogen atom is in an "excited" state and if no other photons are absorbed by the atom, the electron will eventually drop back down to the lower energy ground state, its natural state. Thereafter the process of emission occurs where a photon of the same energy it had absorbed is released. Other more complex variations can occur. For example, a sufficiently large photon can be absorbed, knocking the electron completely out of the atom (this is called "ionisation"). The atom will then no longer be able to absorb or emit light until it catches a free electron back into its energy level.

This pattern of absorptions (or emissions) is unique to hydrogen, and no other element can have this pattern, which produces a recognizable pattern of absorption (or emission) lines in a spectrum using a spectroscope. I suppose if I had directed a spectroscope at the Glyfada UFO, the absorption and emission lines would have been unique to both the orange and red component of the light spectrum. The morphing object appears to be both light and particle at the same time, so as the light emanates from the object and/or the object emanates from the light, it seems to be doing the same to all light in the immediate vicinity, such as the light from street lamps.

But why the morphing? What was it doing there at the time? What is the true shape of the object? Was it a V shape or saucer shape?

If quantum physics has anything to say on the subject and the mysterious wave-particle duality (where the object is behaving as both light wave and particle at the same time), it would explain the morphing from our perspective, as seen through the camera.

The object changes shape at such a rapid continuous rate, but as Einstein's special theory of relativity permanently ties mass and energy together in the simple yet fundamental equation $E = mc2$, it predicts that nothing with mass can move as fast as light, or faster. The closest humankind has ever come to reaching the speed of light is inside powerful particle accelerators like the Large Hadron Collider.

This colossal machine can accelerate subatomic particles to more than 99.99 percent the speed of light, but the particles will never reach the cosmic speed limit.

To reach the speed of light would require an infinite amount of energy, and in the process the object's mass would become infinite, which is impossible. For this reason, particles of light, or photons, can travel at light speeds because they have no mass. Physicists have found that certain entities can reach faster-than-light speeds and still follow the cosmic rules required by special relativity. While these do not disprove Einstein's theory, they give us insight into the peculiar behaviour of light and the quantum world. Examples are the Cherenkov radiation glows within nuclear reactor water tanks, and quantum entanglement or Einstein's "spooky action at a distance".

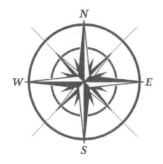

CHAPTER 9

Ring Shape and Morphing S Shape

Date: 19 October 2016	Angle: E, 75°
Time: 4:15 pm	Direction: E to E
Height: 13,123 ft (2.5 mi, 4 km)	Photo: N/A
Horizontal Distance: 3,280 ft (0.62 mi, 1 km)	
Temperature: 59°F (15°C)	Video: 3 min 09 sec
Camera 1: Digital Camera 20MP +	Wind: NNE, 4 mph (7 km/h)
Skywatcher Telescope x 66	Visibility: Sunny
Estimated size of Object: 3.87 ft (1.18 m)	

As usual, outrage manifests itself in the first section to this sighting in mid-October 2016, as I place it in the missed opportunity category of detailed observation only, with no video or photographic evidence. It was 25 days since our Turkey-Europe vacation, and eight months since a sighting of significance in Melbourne. It was a sunny cool Wednesday with hardly any breeze. Over one hour after coming home from work, I was thinking I would probably never see anything today as extraordinary as the Glyfada UFO. Nevertheless, still hopeful, every 10 or 15 minutes I religiously walked out the rear sliding door and gazed up at the blue sky.

For all these sightings I have indicated the wind direction and speed in comparison with the direction the object travelled in and the angle of sight, in the hope that anyone trying to disprove what I saw as nothing more than a balloon or Chinese lantern or even daylight sighting of Venus (which is known to happen) can be renounced. I do realise this may go against me, as the object may well be moving in the same direction as the prevailing winds.

Venus can never stray too far from the sun, so if Venus is to the east of the sun it will still be above the horizon during sunset, and it will be an evening star in the western sky. If it happens to be west of the sun, then it will be visible in the mornings before sunrise and so it will be a morning star in the eastern sky. I can say with 100% certainty that none of the sightings were in the east or west, at or near sunrise or sunset time.

The wind speeds indicated are average wind speeds at the standard height of 10 metres above sea level. Wind speed usually increases with height above the ground or sea surface. This is because the heating of the earth's surface disturbs the atmosphere's equilibrium as the sun creates the force that creates wind.

The vertical gradient of the mean horizontal wind speed in the lower atmosphere is the wind gradient. It measures the rate of increase of wind strength with unit increase in height above ground level, in units of metres per second of speed, per kilometre of height (m/s/km).

The wind is characterised by the direction in which it moves and by its speed. Normally, wind direction means the direction the wind comes from, so westerly winds, for example, are winds that blow from the west to the east. There are two types of winds: ground level winds that blow from the lower troposphere, and high-altitude winds. The troposphere is the lower layer of the earth's atmosphere, where nearly all the weather conditions occur. The average depths of the troposphere are 20 km (12 mi) to 17 km (11 mi).

The lowest part of the troposphere is where friction with the earth's surface influences air flow and it is the planetary boundary layer. It is also where unequal heating caused by unequal solar radiation causes breezes. This layer is a few hundred metres to 1.2 mi (2 km) deep, depending on the landform and time of day.

As some of my sightings have been higher than 3 km (1.8 mi), the wind direction may not be exactly as described at that height for that day compared to lower altitudes.

I stood there in a meditative state, transfixed, staring almost blankly and contemplating that my focus should remain in the east where the major Melbourne sightings were, in the region where I saw the disc-shaped object some years before.

As happened many times before, only ignorance handicaps my consideration of the reflective, mirror-like object I saw in the sky that afternoon as I pondered what complex intelligence was behind this wonderful display. Each of the objects I have seen seems to be unique. Whenever they present themselves, I have the feeling that I have seen something special for the very first time, just like seeing Saturn or Jupiter through a telescope. How does beauty in nature publicise its rainbow? Simply by somebody looking up and smiling at the dazzling display of colours as they take the dog for a walk as the rain subsides; or the taxi driver on the way to pick up the next fare, who turns the corner and between the skyscrapers catches a glimpse of the rainbow like a gift from nature.

I ran inside and grabbed my telescope, and not wanting to waste time attaching cameras, I pointed the telescope towards the object and took in the full unobstructed view of this heavenly body. It was circular in nature, ring-like, but it had a fluid motion. It was almost as if I was watching an oscilloscope, to observe the change of an electrical signal over time. The shape of a wave on the oscilloscope screen indicates voltage and time, and is continuously graphed against a calibrated scale. The observed waveform can be analysed for such properties as amplitude, frequency, rise time, time interval, distortion and so on. Well before the computer era, the oscilloscope was the popular choice in many old science fiction movies, and it was frequently displayed on consoles in spacecraft and laboratories.

The object was high in the eastern sky and moving towards the east, constantly changing shape as it went, yet retaining the circular doughnut shape, and presenting the underside and top side in my direction. It seemed to be darker and flatter on the bottom, compared with the more rounded sides and top. Its colour seemed to blend in with the sky; and the incredible feature of this object, which stood out the most, was that it had two intensely bright yet small lights at either end and on top of the ring.

2 intense bright lights at either
end of the object

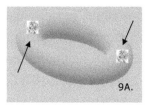
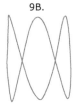

Image 9A and 9B: The circular object rotated with fluidity and had two strong lights above the object at both ends. It displayed wave motion like the image on an oscilloscope, and can be described as alternating from a doughnut shape to a figure of eight.

This object displayed the properties of a toroid. In geometry, a torus is a surface of revolution generated by revolving a circle in three-dimensional space about an axis in the same plane with the circle. If the axis of revolution does not touch the circle, the surface has a ring shape and is called a torus of revolution. A theorem exists which details how any closed surface is homeomorphic to a sphere, and such mappings preserve all the topological properties of a given space.

One example is a continuous deformation between a coffee mug and a doughnut (torus), which can be illustrated in 3D on a computer demonstrating that they are homeomorphic - one can be interchanged with the other. Another example is where one can bend a rectangle into a torus by folding the sheet into a tube and connecting the ends into a tube. "Toroidal space" is the name used to describe the area and volume of a torus or so-called doughnut, ring shape. This special form has been used to describe and represent several objects in the actual material world, as well as in a potential, abstract or imaginary world.

A major study in geometry involves a manifold, which is a curved space with some dimension like the surface of a sphere. The torus, surface of a ring or doughnut, are both two-dimensional manifolds. The mathematical object is defined on the background torus that is the manifold, comparable to the canvas for an oil painting. Einstein's Theory of General Relativity describes and calculates the universe, consisting of space and time, as a four-dimensional manifold.

The curvature of space that is responsible for gravity - especially near a black hole, where space and time are so curved they twist and turn upon themselves - can be described as a geometrical structure on the 4-dimensional space-time manifold, including light and subatomic particles. In mathematical physics, manifolds are used to understand the structure of the universe in cosmology, suggesting that the entire universe may be shaped like a torus, as well as the Theory of Relativity which introduced the idea of matter-energy interchangeability leading to nuclear power and the atomic bomb. The universe is now calculated to more closely resemble a 12-dimensional nested manifold.

The object I saw through the telescope was the exact representation of a torus as described above. Even if my calculations are incorrect and it could be significantly larger, the doughnut shape, fluid motion, and the way it was stretching in and out of shape, make it difficult to believe that this was a craft with occupants. I believe that these are particular components of intelligently controlled objects, which are only visible in our 3-dimensional world; and that the rest of each object sits outside our realm as an interdimensional entity.

We all remember the fictional masterpiece *Flatland: A Romance of Many Dimensions* by Edwin A. Abbott, which is a fictional introduction to the concept of the multiple dimensions of space, written over 100 years ago. It describes the journeys of a Square, a mathematician and resident of the two-dimensional Flatland, where women are thin straight lines and therefore are at the lower end of society due to their basic shape or lack of shape. Men on the other hand have any number of sides, depending on their social status. The story revolves around the interaction between many geometric forms, including Square who has adventures in Spaceland (three dimensions), Lineland (one dimension) and Pointland (no dimensions), and it culminates in a visit to a land of four dimensions.

We often wonder what the different dimensions above our third dimension look like. Our three-dimensional nervous system restricts us to the third dimension, making it virtually impossible for us to visualise the higher dimensions. The same applies to the Flatlanders living in the two-dimensional world, who are unable to visualise in the third dimension; and of course Lineland residents in the one dimension, who are unable to see anything beyond that. The magic happens when, in humour, the superbeing in the fourth dimension suddenly pokes his finger into our third dimension.

What we may be seeing is the sudden appearance of a light in the sky, perhaps a shiny orb or in any case a component, a fundamental aspect of the whole picture which is hidden from our prying eyes within a higher dimension. I believe that most of the self-luminous objects or orbs of peculiar shapes that I have seen would fall into this category – that is, they are partly in our third dimension but reside in a higher dimension.

The second part to the sighting in this chapter was an object I successfully filmed five or so minutes later in the same general area of the sky, but I cannot determine whether it was the same object taking on a different shape, or another object. At the time I only had a makeshift camera holder for a compact digital camera to screw the camera to the telescope, rather than a professional camera adapter or camera with a removable lens such as SLR. I pointed the laser scope towards the mirror-like object in the sky, and centring it on the camera display, I pressed record. What I saw was an object that continually changed shape from three connected nodules (9C), to many clumps together (9D & 9E), to which looked like a spacecraft (9F), to clumps and light formation (9G & 9H), three long cylinders with three bright lights (9J & 9K), to an S shape.

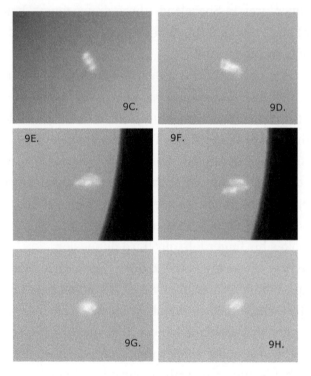

Images 9C to 9H - *It is difficult to say whether this morphing object is the same doughnut shape object I saw earlier through the telescope.*

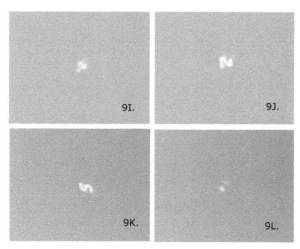

Image 9I to 9L: *The three-dimensional cylindrical and S-shaped morphing object is clearly seen here. All the while the changing of shapes occurred at high speed.*

You will see some similarities between this and the HAQSR in Chapter 18, taken on the same day. The object in that sighting changed from a boomerang, "L" or "J" shape with two bright lights at either end, exactly as this one did. It then continued to morph to such a high degree, with the release of light so intense, that it can only be described as high energy.

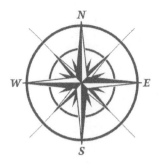

CHAPTER 10

Bright Yellow-Orange Orb 1

Date: 4 June 2017   Angle: S, 30°

Time: 5:59 pm   Direction: S to SW

Height: 9,842 ft (1.86 mi, 3 km)   Photo: N/A

Horizontal Distance: 6,561 ft (1.24 mi, 2 km)

Temperature: 48°F (9°C)   Video: 0 min 12 sec

Camera: Digital Camera 16MP   Wind: No wind

Estimated Size of Object: 3.3 ft (1.0 m)   Visibility: Clear

The strange thing about this early evening sighting is that the object completely disappeared from the small amount of footage I took. We can speculate that it may have known I was recording it and cloaked itself in invisibility or transported itself inter-dimensionally. Many would consider this speculation far-fetched considering the estimated height and distance involved, but as mentioned before I am 100% certain that on one occasion as I was photographing three distant orbs high in the sky, one of them stopped only to move in my direction, stopping again directly overhead for a few moments, and then joined the other two again.

This sighting was towards the south and the point in the sky where it had disappeared was very close to where most of my sightings have taken place. What this may indicate to me is that the portal through which they transport themselves to interspace or another dimension is not as narrow a window as I first thought. I would say this one disappeared about 10° or 15° further towards the south than the southwest.

Elsewhere in this book I talk about portals in the earth's magnetic field, and rather than the magical or extraordinary opening in space or time that connects this world to distant realms, they are called X-points or electron diffusion regions. These are basically places where the magnetic field of the earth connects to the magnetic field of the sun, creating a connected path from earth to the sun 93 million miles (149 million km) away.

NASA has observed that these magnetic portals open and close dozens of times each day. The explanation we have from scientists is that this occurs some tens of thousands of kilometres from the earth, where the geomagnetic field meets the speeding solar wind from the sun. But what if these portals also occur closer to earth - between 15 and 20,000 feet (2.84 mi or 4.57 km)? NASA has found that most of the portals are small and don't remain open for long at all, while others are gigantic and remain open for longer.

The outcome of all of this is the appearance of polar auroras as energetic particles flow through the openings, heating the earth's upper atmosphere, and creating geomagnetic storms.

This sighting of the yellow-orange orb included some moderate morphing, where occasionally it took on the shape of what looks like a saucer or disc (refer Image **12A**). The whole object looks yellow and is self-luminous, or the luminosity may be the result of the ionization of the air around the object. The strong energy field emanating from the object causes the air around it to break down, in such a way that allows energy to flow outside to neutralize the charge separation. What may happen is that the air breakdown creates a path that short-circuits the air around the object.

The energy field separates the surrounding air into positive ions and electrons, meaning that the air becomes ionized. What happens during this ionization is not actually a case of more negative charge (or electrons), more positive charge (or positive ions), than before; it only means that the electrons and positive ions are farther apart than they were originally in their atomic structure. Therefore, the electrons have been removed from the molecules of the non-ionized air.

So, the ionized air - or plasma, as it is called - is the stripping of the now freely moving electrons, allowing electrical energy to flow. The conductive property of this plasma, or the ionization of the air, is similar to that of metals. Similarities can be drawn with the oxidation of molecules where there is a loss of electrons when combined with oxygen. Plasma gases that we know of glow different colours: neon has a bright orange glow, argon is a deep purple, and nitrogen is a reddish purple.

Plasma is the fourth state of matter besides solid, liquid or gas. It can only be artificially generated by heating neutral gases or by subjecting such a gas to a strong electromagnetic field. We have talked about energy fields around the UFOs causing the plasma to be formed. But what about the speed of the object - is that likely to also create plasma from within the atmosphere?

When a hypersonic spacecraft (nearly 17,500 mph / 28,163 km/h), re-enters the earth's atmosphere, it is travelling very much faster than the speed of sound. The atmospheric gases in front of the aircraft compress, very quickly causing its temperature to rise. As the air temperature heats up, the bonds between the molecules of the air break up, producing an electrically charged plasma around the spacecraft.

Most witnesses report this luminous ionization of air around the UFO as generally only visible at night or at twilight, and it is described as an aura or fuzzy haze of orange-yellow colour. During daylight sightings this would cause the mirage or heat haze effect in the appearance of UFOs.

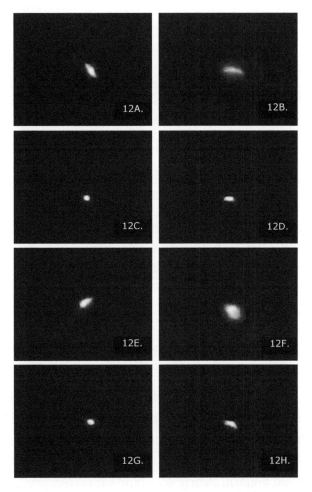

Images 12A–12H: Screen grabs showing the yellow-orange orb exhibiting a moderate amount of morphing. Interesting to note that the object was moving left to right and you will see the angle and tilt in 12A is repeated a few times in sightings of this type.

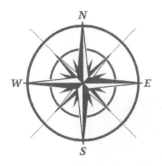

CHAPTER 11

Bright Yellow-Orange (White) Orb 2

Date: 2 July 2017   Angle: E, 60°

Time: 5:36 pm   Direction: E to SE

Height: 9,842 ft (1.86 mi, 3 km)   Photo: 3

Horizontal Distance: 3,280 ft. (0.62 mi, 1 km)

Temperature: 48°F (9°C)   Video: 1 min 49 sec

Camera: Digital Camera 16MP   Wind: N, 16 mi/h (26 km/h)

Estimated Size of Object: 2.9 ft (0.9 m) Visibility: Clear

This similar object was seen nearly one month later to the day, and at about the same time, in the east. There is also some morphing displayed by this object with the predominate shape being an upside-down saucer. If you refer to the slowed down video online or Images 13A–13H below, you will clearly see some aura effect around the object.

In December 2017 it was revealed by the US Defence Department that a program to study unidentified flying objects has been in existence, but the Department has never acknowledged its existence. The program collected video and audio recordings of reported UFO incidents, including footage from a Navy Super Hornet which was purported to show an aircraft surrounded by a glowing aura travelling at very high speed and rotating as it moved. The Navy pilots can be heard trying to understand what they are seeing, explaining on radio that there were many objects at the time. The Defence officials have not released the location and date of the incident. The images in that release are very similar to the images in the chapters of this book titled Bright Yellow-Orange Orb 1, 2 and 3.

Throughout these chapters, and from my observations as recorded on video and photos, the most prevalent and consistent UFO is the yellow-orange orb that appears in at least two separate undisclosed locations at about 1.8 mi (3 km) apart. For some strange reason these objects appear virtually at the same time and the objects are mostly in different shapes, from saucer, rectangle or spherical, to an abstract shape.

It's difficult to gauge height at night, but I can hazard a guess that most of the time these yellow-orange orbs appear to be at the same height of between 5,000 and 10,000 feet (0.94 – 1.89 mi or 1.5 - 3 km), and move at the same speed of approximately 9 mph, (14 km/h). On some occasions I note that they move silently at twice the speed, which is a challenge when trying to focus and video. A simple mathematical calculation reveals the objects to be approximately 3 feet (1.0 m) in size.

I would say that as this object is estimated to travel at 17 km/h, it would take about 10 minutes for it to reach the second destination; and as the observation times are very similar at both locations, I have concluded that they are not the same object. The only similarity is the times that they are visible overhead.

At the end of this book I will try and present examples to show how easily you can be fooled into thinking you have captured a UFO on video, not only by the normal run-of-the-mill balloons but also by planets such as Jupiter rising in the east, and some very interesting balloons easily mistaken for UFOs. Why do these yellow orbs appear with such frequency and regularity, always following similar flight paths? What is their objective, if all they do is fly in one direction without (as far as I can see) any of them diverting in any way from that?

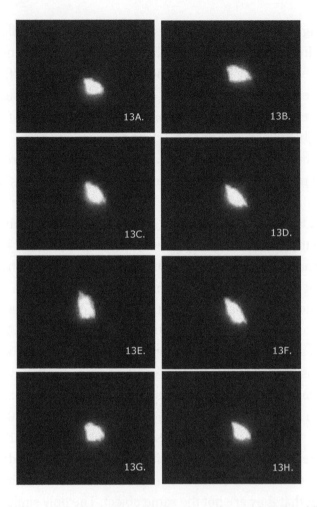

Images 13A – 13H: Screen grabs showing the yellow-white orb exhibiting a moderate amount of morphing but predominantly an upside-down saucer. Note the similar but inverse tilt as it moves from right to left this time.

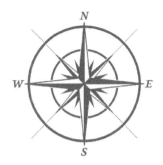

CHAPTER 12

Bright Yellow-Orange Orb 3

Date: 3 July 2017   Angle: W, 60°

Time: 6:19 pm   Direction: W to E

Height: 9,842 ft (1.86 mi, 3 km)   Photo: 3

Horizontal Distance: 3,280 ft (0.62 mi, 1 km)

Temperature: 46°F (8°C)   Video: 1 min 49 sec

Camera: Digital Camera 16MP   Wind: N, 10 mi/h (17 km/h)

Estimated Size of Object: 3.6 ft (1.1 m) Visibility: Passing clouds

This was an amazing sight not only because it was the very next day, but it was coming from the west and passed directly over my head before continuing off to the east. As on the past two occasions, the object has a yellow colour overall, and full body luminosity, but soft as a neon light. These bright yellow orbs exhibit a soft glow which engulfs the UFO in a sphere of light like an aura. On occasion I have seen an increase or decrease in brightness, but not pulsation or flickering.

Even though these orbs are described as full body self-luminous, the fact that there are no obvious lights on the objects indicates the luminosity is due to breakdown of the air around it, evident with the halo or aura effect displayed in the video and stills.

As usual, the disbelievers will say that they are not UFOs. How can I be seeing these orbs with such high frequency? I must be lying, or perhaps it's just a drone. I have seen these objects before dawn when it's deathly silent, so drones can be counted out because these magnificent objects fly silently overhead or in the distance. However, I must admit that there is a fine line between something with an earthly logical explanation and something out of this world and unexplainable. Most UFO reports have turned out to be fully explainable due to normal natural or manmade phenomena; others are of course blatant hoaxes (refer to the end of this book for examples of this).

I don't really blame the disbelievers, as many of the so-called sightings are certainly easily explained; but in recent years the increase of sightings with validating video and photographic evidence has fired up the disclosure argument. Nevertheless, when people observe strange aerial phenomena, whether it's a moving object in the sky, strange lights or objects morphing, the immediate conclusion reached is that "they must be aliens" or "undisclosed secret Government technologies", thereby fuelling the conspiracy theories.

Even though I have put forward an explanation about the plasma around the fast as well as the slow-moving objects, it's the plasma effect present in the lower atmosphere that they say must be given serious consideration as a possible driver of these sightings. The interest in plasma phenomena as a possible explanation for the mass UFO sightings started in 1967, at a conference in Colorado attended by experts from various university, military and government departments around the US.

Two summarised quotes from the proceedings mention that the plasma could only last for a short period of time in the lower atmosphere:

Participants with a background in theoretical or experimental plasma physics felt that containment of plasma by magnetic fields is not likely under atmospheric conditions for more than a second or so.

All participants agreed that the UFO cases presented contained insufficient data for a definitive scientific conclusion.

Surely the experts in the field of plasma physics would have known how short–lived the natural phenomenon is compared to the actual observed UFO phenomena. It is strange that the conference would go ahead when from the very outset the most important factor about plasma in the lower atmosphere was ignored; or perhaps the powers that be hoped something else would come out of the conference to silence or mislead the public. Note that some of my orb videos last well over four minutes, thus disproving the natural plasma theory.

Then in the 1990s a series of scientific studies was conducted in England, attempting to prove that UFOs were a natural phenomenon in the atmosphere. The associated declassified documents were released to the public by the Ministry of Defence in 2006. As always, the main conclusion was that UFOs are possibly some sort of electrical plasma occurring naturally in the lower atmosphere.

The report goes on to say that "the events are almost certainly attributable to physical, electrical and magnetic phenomena in the atmosphere, mesosphere and ionosphere". It says that the required conditions (that need to be just right) result in infrequent observations of these phenomena, and in some cases re-entry of meteorites may be the cause of "buoyant" plasma. At the end of the paper there seems to be an argument that the sustained plasma witnessed by some could be incomplete, or that scientific theories are not fully understood.

With regard to meteorites, it is assumed that the enormous velocity and the attainment of very high ionisation temperature forms a gaseous plasma which is viewed as a visible luminous stream, forming a single or several plasma bodies, and resembling UFOs.

I have contradicted virtually everything in these reports, not only with the length of time these objects were sighted and recorded, but with their relatively low height and the frequency of my sightings. What about the predictable manner and horizontal paths which I have noted in a few undisclosed locations around Melbourne, not to mention the red orb in Glyfada, Athens, in 2016?

Suggesting meteors as a likely explanation for the glowing orb-like UFOs is laughable, as there is no mention of any of the UFOs burning up in the atmosphere, and they never produce long-surviving plasma.

There was still a determination to find out what was causing the plasma to last so long in the lower atmosphere - and not only in the upper ionized atmosphere - where the UFO phenomena were prevalent. Papers have been written to prove, or at least suggest, that the lower atmosphere can behave like quasi-neutral plasma, where it exhibits the same number of positive protons or positive ions in a given volume, as it has unattached negative electrons in the same volume of space. They believe that this occurs between two layers of atmosphere of opposing charge, the region of highly charged electric fields, and where plasma is buoyant, giving the appearance of self-luminous UFOs.

Plasma is highly conductive but has very low voltage differences over small distances, while over large distances the opposite occurs, producing very powerful electric fields. As electric currents and magnetic fields (electromagnetism) dominate the plasma medium, some physicists believe that its interaction with these forces produces complex structures, for example cellular and filamentary. In other words, they give the appearance of UFOs.

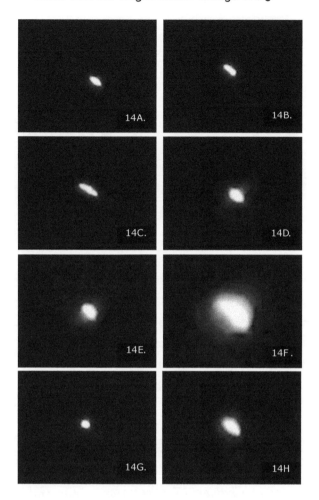

Images 14A–14H: Screen grabs showing the yellow-white orb exhibiting a moderate amount of morphing plasma/ aura which obscures the true shape of the object.

CHAPTER 13

Precursor - "The Golden Man" 1

Date: 3 October 2017   Angle: E, 60°

Time: 6:12 pm   Direction: E to NE

Height: 9,842 ft (1.8 mi, 3 km) Photo: 0

Horizontal Distance: 3,200 ft (0.62 mi, 1 km)

Temperature: 68°F (20°C)   Video: 1 min 58 sec

Camera: Digital Camera 16MP   Wind: N, 12 mi/h (19 km/h)

Estimated Size of Object: 6.2 ft (1.9 m) Visibility: Partly sunny

Please also refer to Chapter 17 (Precursor - "The Golden Man" 2), Chapter 19 (Precursor - "The Golden Man" 3), Chapter 21 (The Golden Man) and Chapter 28 (Return of the Golden Man).

This object was spotted in the east moving towards the northeast.

As I was going through my videos and photos in preparation for this book, I realised I had initially ignored this one (judging by how I had named the folder that contained this short, somewhat shaky, and unsteady video). Whenever I used to see UFO footage and photos taken by the public on YouTube, believe me, I was the first to complain about the poor quality of UFO images. They seem to be always out of focus or shaky.

When you are holding a good quality camera it won't be one of the lightest, so it is no easy feat to hold it at an awkward angle while trying to keep a moving object in frame and in focus. Even after one minute it sometimes proves to be difficult. I have tried using a tripod but this is virtually impossible at times, especially when using the viewfinder to look at the object high in the sky when it is almost directly overhead, rather than comfortably with the LCD camera display.

The main reason why I never use the LCD display when filming is that shooting in bright daylight makes it difficult to see the LCD display, as it usually looks washed out. The other reason is that these objects are so far away that they only are the size of a few millimetres in relation to an outstretched arm and fingers, so pointing the camera in the general direction first then looking through the viewfinder to locate it and focus on it usually does the trick. The problems commence as soon as you start zooming in while trying to keep the camera steady. I am currently trying to perfect the use of a shoulder mount support pad, hoping that it will alleviate these issues.

The reason I have titled this chapter **Precursor - "The Golden Man" 1** will soon become apparent. I believe that what I have captured in this short video is very important. As I was going through the directory files on my laptop I was aided by how I usually categorise sightings by date and then a short description. My naming conventions and rules for naming are not the best, and at times, not consistent and not logical, especially when I am pressed for time as I am working a day job and trying to live a normal life.

Even though I have learned to never delete anything, I had given this folder a name that would never warrant a second viewing: **2017-10-03_goldobject-Day_Video_*Damn* balloon.** Please use your imagination to replace the word *damn* with something more colourful. Thinking that it was just an image of a clump of gold coloured balloons let loose after some child's birthday party, I took no further notice. Having already written the chapter titled **"The Golden Man"**, which is astonishing to say the least, it dawned on me that the colour and some of the shapes from that sighting looked familiar. So, searching through some of the earlier photos, I saw the descriptive word gold and after further scrutiny was shocked at the similarity between this sighting and "**The Golden Man**".

At first glance it certainly looks like normal gold balloons, but further into the short video there is the strange appearance of two doughnut shapes, with small holes, stuck together side by side, almost like the letter B or number 8, and you can just make out what looks like a string hanging freely below. Halfway through the video the shape starts to change as the doughnut, letter B or number 8 becomes unrecognisable. Suddenly without notice it jumps back to an incredibly more perfect version of the number 8 than before.

Please note that in the video itself it is difficult to make out these changes, which only become obvious when stills are taken off the video. After the perfect figure 8, the object morphs into an indiscernible shape like a deflated balloon; but then what shocks me to the core, especially after seeing the **"The Golden Man"** video and photos, is that it slowly becomes that golden man figure and stays that way momentarily. Finally, it looks like a clump of four gold balloons tightly bonded together.

I talk about this in depth in the **"The Golden Man"**, but this video and the screen grabs tell me that it cannot be explained at all by simple logic. This object appears to be the same as the one I videotaped and photographed on 14 October 2017, and then again on 15 October. The object is morphing and takes on the shape of a human figure (**Images 15K** and **15L**), which is more clearly defined in the chapter "**The Golden Man**".

How do we explain this when it does not appear to be a vehicle of any sort, and it certainly is not a flying disc or a cigar-shaped craft but is still an unexplained aerial phenomenon, a UFO? Is it an interdimensional or extradimensional alien being of some sort? Is CERN responsible for it, perhaps? My scientific mind struggles with this because if CERN has let through these interdimensional creatures, why are there not millions of them? Perhaps I should be seeing such strange objects daily.

My religious mind also struggles with the idea that it might be a real entity from a dimension beyond our own, or a fallen angel. Such beings are common only in science fiction, fantasy and the supernatural.

The sixteen screen grabs below are taken from the short video. They are in sequence and I summarise as follows:

In images **15A to 15D** the object is beginning to transform from a rough looking letter B or two doughnut shapes stuck together, to the fully-fledged perfect looking number 8 in Images **15E to 15G**. You will also note that the tether is below the object, but in the chapter **"The Golden Man"** you can see that the tether is attached to the neck.

The object continues to morph, changing shape to a more abstract form in **15H to 15J**. The next four images, **15K to 15N,** send shivers up and down my spine as the object morphs into something recognisable only to me because I videoed that very shape some 12 days later. You can just make out the human form when you compare these to the photos in the chapter **"The Golden Man"**.

It's very interesting that in numerology the number 8 represents the concept "as above, so below", which was first laid out in the Emerald Tablet of Hermes Trismegistus:

That which is Below corresponds to that which is Above, and that which is Above, corresponds to that which is Below, to accomplish the miracles of the One Thing.

It seems like a great concept that the visible stars in the sky could be linked to life on earth in one way or another so that the microcosm and the macrocosm are connected, echoing the theories in quantum mechanics.

The writings of Hermes Trismegistus have greatly influenced Western esoteric understandings and were of great importance during the 1300–1700 Renaissance period, affirming the existence of a single, true theology that is present in all religions and that was given by God to man in antiquity. Legend has it that on an emerald tablet discovered by Alexander the Great in the third century BC are inscribed thirteen lines of which the second lines referred to the concept "as above, so below".

It is also understood that this expression (as above, so below) gave rise to and is created between the Washington Monument and Lincoln Memorial Reflecting Pool underneath the night sky filled with stars. It is also understood that there is freemasonry symbolism in this monument, such as its height of 555 feet, or 6,660 inches, which is close to the Biblical "mark of the beast", 666.

In Christianity, the number 8 is also the number of the resurrection, because Jesus rose on the eighth day. To the early Christians, Sunday was not only the first day of the week but was also symbolically the Eighth Day, the Day of Christ's Resurrection after the "new creation" was made to replace the original seven-day creation as described in Genesis. The concept of a new "eighth day" appears in the writings of many early Christian writers.

It has been proven scientifically also that people, animals, and even micro amoebas travel in the pattern of a figure 8 when blindfolded, lost in the woods or fog; and in experiments even swimmers and drivers who are blindfolded also follow a figure 8 pattern. The conclusion is that this spiral motion is a universal property inherent in all living matter.

I would like to now expand a little about CERN in more detail in the following chapters.

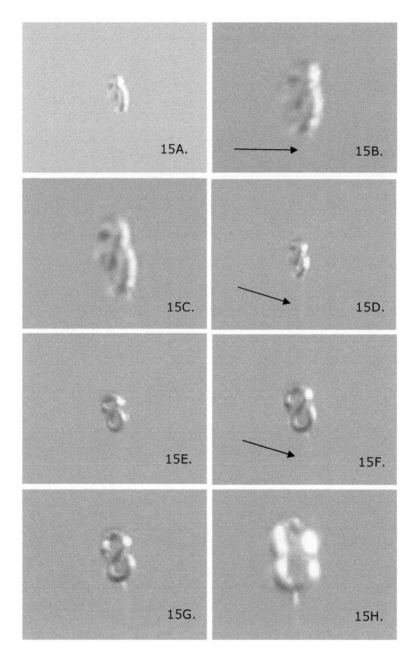

Images 15A-15D: Screen grabs showing rough looking letter B or two doughnut shapes stuck together, with fine tether hanging down.
Images 15E–15G: These images show a fully-fledged perfect looking number 8.

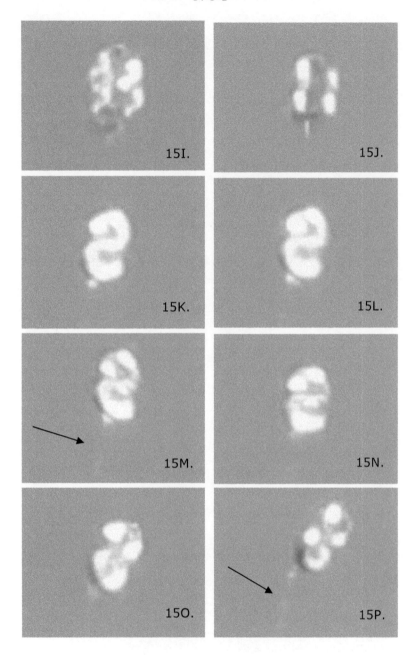

15I.

15J.

15K.

15L.

15M.

15N.

15O.

15P.

Images 15H–15J: *The object continues to morph,
changing shape to a more abstract form.*
Images 15K-15P: *The object morphs into "The Golden Man" human
form from the coiled-up S shape. Please refer to Chapter 21.*

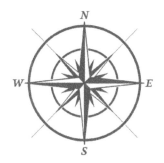

CHAPTER 14

CERN – Interdimensional Beings and Fallen Angels

As described by Wikipedia, The Large Hadron Collider (LHC) at the European Organization for Nuclear Research, (known as CERN) is the world's largest and most powerful particle collider, the most complex experimental facility ever built, and the largest single machine in the world. It was built between 1998 and 2008 in collaboration with over 10,000 scientists and engineers from more than 100 countries, as well as hundreds of universities and laboratories. It lies in a tunnel that is 17 miles (27 km) in circumference, as deep as 574 feet (175 m) beneath the France–Switzerland border near Geneva, Switzerland.

When it was first started up in September 2008, and in 2012, the discovery of the Higgs boson, the God Particle, was announced. This is the particle that makes all matter and led to the creation of our universe. We are told that the objective at CERN is to find out the fundamentals of our universe and how it was created by recreating the conditions immediately after the Big Bang.

The CERN directors and physicists have openly discussed how CERN will "open the door" from our physical universe to non-physical universes, which will allow scientists to interact face-to-face with non-physical beings. They have gone on to say that this huge machine may possibly create or discover previously unimagined scientific phenomena, or "unknown unknowns", for instance, "an extra dimension". This may come about, as there are parallel universes and parallel dimensions of non-physical intelligent beings located everywhere around us, and CERN will allow these non-Earth entities to come into our physical world and be with us.

It's hard to believe that the well-respected physicists working on the largest and most expensive experimental machine in the world would say such things as: "Out of this door might come something, or we might send something through it". Such words are more likely to be seen in a science fiction movie script.

There is an interesting belief regarding CERN and The Bible, involving Jacob's Ladder as described in the Book of Genesis. This ladder is said to be a ladder between heaven and earth, that allowed angels to come down to Earth. One strong understanding is that one of CERN's objectives is to recreate Jacob's Ladder and reopen a portal for these interdimensional, supernatural being, or fallen angels, to pass through.

It is rumoured that in 2012 CERN successfully opened a portal and witnessed such beings, which may possibly be the reason why the LHC had to be shut down; that is, to make it more powerful and fix the magnets after they broke opening the portal. As indicated, this is conjecture only.

Now to the warnings. Professor Stephen Hawking, a man considered the equal of Einstein and who died on 14 March 2018, believed that the Higgs boson, or the God Particle, could pose grave dangers to our planet. This may have been misunderstood, as what was being referred to was the fact that the precise mass needed to keep the universe from instability is 126 times the mass of a proton, which is what the boson is, about 126 billion electron volts.

Other scientists also say that the release of such tremendous energy by the LHC could cause space and time itself to collapse catastrophically. They are also concerned that the experiments being planned and conducted at CERN are a legitimate danger to the future of mankind. Whether founded in truth or not, the almost unimaginably powerful high energy collisions are aiming to produce conditions of the Big Bang, dark matter, and strange matter called quarks and stranglets. And what about the thoughts that the high energy collisions could produce the conditions necessary to bring about actual time travel?

In reading the Bible, we understand that when God created the known and unknown universe, certain aspects were kept separate. CERN's intention is to pull apart the curtain separating this world from other worlds or dimensions. Quantum mechanics has shown us that by splitting particles down to their most basic components they lack a location, or in other words are everywhere at once, which seems to go against God's principle of forbidding man to see through to other higher dimensions attributed to God only.

A British scientist at CERN was involved in the invention of the World Wide Web (WWW) in 1989. The web was originally created to satisfy the demand for automatic information-sharing between scientists in universities and government institutes around the world.

Where God forced upon man different languages to refrain from the continued construction of the Tower of Babel, the World Wide Web served its purpose in uniting people under one language again. The Tower of Babel was an attempt by man to reach God - or perhaps God-like status; its creation was due to ancient man's belief that heaven was directly above the earth, and if they built a tower high enough, they could reach the presence of God.

The people of Babel were unified in a concerted effort to work against God's intent that humanity multiply, fill the earth and glorify God in the process. Instead, they had united in one place to secure their own position and in some way raise themselves up to God. The building of the Tower threatened to be an assault on heaven, a statement saying that they could approach God on their own terms and in some measure as equals. The confusion of languages served two purposes: it kept people from uniting to overthrow God, and it forced them to scatter across the earth.

Religious internet sites do not believe in UFOs; they see them as falling under the umbrella of demons and fallen angels, and they see CERN as unlocking the gates of hell, opening a Pandora's Box which contains all the evils of the world. In my opinion, UFOs such as saucers, discs, cigars, triangles and so on, are intelligently controlled craft of alien origin, while all the rest are unexplained aerial phenomena of interdimensional beings. It's a simple categorisation, I know, but I need to keep these separated in my mind, otherwise many things will not make sense.

A fallen angel is a wicked or rebellious angel who sinned and has been cast out of heaven. The term "fallen angel" does not appear in the Bible, but in *Peter 2:4* the gospel talks about them being cast into hell and committed to chains of gloomy darkness until the judgment day on earth. It's interesting that upon review, the timeline of CERN operations seems to coincide with the increase in sightings by me from early 2015. Note that from early 2013 to the end of 2014, I believe that I only saw one object, a glowing disc. In my view this should be ringing alarm bells.

10 September 2008: CERN successfully fired the first protons around the entire tunnel circuit in stages,

30 November 2009: LHC becomes the world's highest-energy particle accelerator.

28 February 2010: The LHC continues operations, ramping energies.

21 April 2011: LHC becomes the world's highest-luminosity hadron accelerator.

4 July 2012: First new elementary particle discovery, a new boson observed.

14 February 2013: Beginning of the first long shutdown, to prepare the collider for a higher energy and luminosity.

20 May 2015: Protons collided in the LHC at record-breaking energy.

3 June 2015: Start of delivering the physics data after almost two years offline for re-commissioning.

29 June 2016: Further improvements over the year increased the luminosity to 40% above the design value.

26 October 2016: End of 2016 proton-proton collisions.

10 November 2016: Beginning of 2016 proton-lead collisions.

3 December 2016: End of 2016 proton-lead collisions.

24 May 2017: Start of 2017 proton-proton collisions.

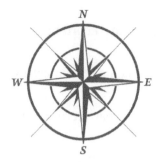

CHAPTER 15

Precursor - "The Golden Man" 2

Date: 14 October 2017   Angle: E, 60°

Time: 5:44 pm   Direction: E to E

Height: 9,842 ft (1.8 mi, 3 km) Photo: 1

Horizontal Distance: 3,200 ft (0.62 mi, 1 km)

Temperature: 61°F (16°C)   Video: 10 secs

Camera: Digital Camera 16MP   Wind: SSE, 14 mi/h (22 km/h)

Estimated Size of Object: 9 ft (2.8 m) Visibility: Sunny

(size includes long tether)

Please also refer to Chapter 15 (Precursor - "The Golden Man" 1), Chapter 19 (Precursor - "The Golden Man" 3), Chapter 21 (The Golden Man) and Chapter 28 (Return of the Golden Man).

This object was spotted in the east moving towards the east.

On this day I had many sightings but I failed to capture evidence of any of them except for one, the **Precursor - "The Golden Man" 2**. I could not focus the digital camera properly in manual mode or auto mode for most of the other sightings, and these missed opportunities disconcerted me. "Why can't I focus?", I thought to myself. "Maybe the objects are doing something to the camera." However, I did capture about 10 seconds of video of the **Precursor - "The Golden Man" 2,** about 3 hours later in the afternoon; incidentally, at the time I thought they were just balloons - more on this later. As I read over the notes I wrote at the time, I could see there were at least six individual sightings that day, and they were genuinely significant.

Most of the sightings were between 12:51 pm and 2:04 pm, mainly concentrated high in the southern sky. I recall that one object came from a southeasterly direction towards me, splitting into two objects; the first one faded away to my left, while the newer second object continued in the original direction and with the same original intensity. The objects were not glowing, and no matter how hard I tried I just couldn't focus on them as I frantically switched between manual and auto focus. Soon another object appeared to come from the southwest; it also was high in the sky but with a more prominent appearance, and again I could not focus properly.

This was the first time I had seen objects speed off at a very high rate in a southerly direction. I often read about this in UFO articles, but all my accounts to date show that I have never seen them speed off like that. It is probably indulgent to announce my impressions without providing video or photographic evidence, so I am hoping the next sighting just two hours later will do justice to the sighting. You can refer to the edited 10-second video in normal speed and in slow motion on YouTube.

At 5:40 pm high in the east I saw what looked like a glowing orb, so I pointed my camera and this time successfully focused onto it and commenced recording. As I looked through the lens I was unimpressed in the first instance, as the object appeared to be like a regular clump of gold balloons, so I ceased filming after only 10 seconds with the intention of discarding the footage.

I am so relieved that I didn't deleted it, because when you compare it to **Precursor – "The Golden Man" 1 and 3** and the **"The**

Golden Man", there are many inherent similarities. If you quickly have a look at the section of **"The Golden Man",** you will see that what I had captured the day before, and in fact also 11 days before this one, was an "undeveloped" form of the "**The Golden Man**", which I successfully videoed the following day.

I took some sequential screen captures from the video, and I will include some here. In them you can clearly see two long tethers hanging from the bottom of the object; they are independent of each other as they would be if they were strings beneath a bunch of balloons. In the **Precursor – "The Golden Man" 1,** you can see what appears to be one tether beneath the object, while **"The Golden Man"** has a more solid tether hanging from its neck. From what I can remember and from the predominant ambient sounds of birds tweeting on the video, there was not much noticeable wind at all.

From my perspective the two tethers have some significance, as they seem to have irregular sized nodules or nodes running the length of them. Over several weeks I was wondering where I had seen or heard about a similar structure, and then it dawned on me that NASA has been using something similar, called space tethers, which can be from 300 metres to as long as several kilometres in length.

Their purpose is for altitude control, propulsion and stabilization in satellites or spacecraft, making it less expensive than using rocket engines. The main idea is that the tethers carry a current that can generate either thrust or drag from a planetary magnetic field, like an electric motor. There are a few other types of tethers that perform different functions, such as electrically charged tethers that are pushed by the momentum of solar wind ions.

NASA has been deploying missions using tethers as far back as 1966, on satellites and on the Space Shuttle in the early 1990s. Is the **"The Golden Man"** object using tethers like those NASA has been using for their satellites and spacecraft such as the Challenger and Space Station? With the risk of affronting everything by lack of discretion, I will suggest that perhaps NASA invented this form of propulsion by previously observing and studying what I have seen through the eye of the camera.

With the number of high-definition cameras in NASA's possession, do you not think they already would have the most incredible footage and photos from cameras in space? Remember the adage: "Spy satellites can read a newspaper headline from space."

If you watch the video - and especially as I recall from watching this object through the camera lens - the object does not appear to be yellow, but truly gold. The gold colour itself used in painting, for instance, is the combination of yellow and orange blends to give the impression of the colour of the element gold. Gold, chemical symbol Au (from the Latin *aurum* meaning "shining dawn"), is a precious metal which has been used since antiquity. It was discovered in streams all over the world and used in the production of jewellery, coins, vessels, sculpture, statues, and as a decoration for buildings and in monuments.

Gold is dispersed throughout the geologic world so it was discovered by many different groups, and nearly every culture that found it was impressed with it. Gold was the first metal widely known to man; then came iron and copper. Gold excavated in Turkey and dated to 2450-2600 BC, has been seen in delicate jewellery and other items such as a gold boat, indicating how gold was owned by the powerful and well-connected, or made into objects of worship, or used to decorate sacred locations. The first money, in the form of gold coins, appeared about 700 BC.

For thousands of years humans (alchemists) tried to turn matter like lead into gold, as it was considered to be the highest form of matter. With all the advances in science and technology, scientists still could not understand where all the gold in the universe came from - that is, until recently. With the use of advanced telescopes and detectors, scientists and astronomers have seen it created first-hand by the collision of two stars, first detected by LIGO via the gravitational wave they emitted.

Out of the 118 elements in the periodic table, about 92 occur naturally while the rest are synthesized by man. The elements are detected in stars, nebulas, and supernovae from their spectra, as each element has its own unique atomic emission spectrum. When an atom absorbs energy, its electrons jump to higher energy levels and as they jump back down again the jump corresponds to a particular wavelength of light, hence its own unique signature.

There are many possible electron transitions for each atom, and each transition has a specific energy difference. This collection of transitions makes up an emission spectrum, so incredibly the emission spectra are as distinctive to each element as fingerprints are to man. Thus, scientists can use atomic spectra to identify the elements present in stars, for instance. While most of the elements found here on the earth are the same when compared to the rest of the universe, the ratios of the elements and their isotopes can be different.

Besides being a precious commodity for jewellery and wealth, gold is also used in electrical components and in fact almost everything that has to do with electricity, because gold is a wonderful conductor. It's soft and malleable, so it can be made into wires. And the ability to use it in small forms such as nanoparticles is going to make it an incredible technological resource for - let's go out on a limb here - any sort of intelligent life form.

So it is easy to believe that an alien race or interdimensional being with the ability to travel through space or dimensions uses gold in many of its forms. As an energy source it can be used through properties called thermoelectric effects, where it can take heat and turn it directly into electricity: this means obtaining clean and efficient energy. Gold also reflects infrared light, which we cannot see due to its longer wavelength; but we feel it in the form of heat as the radiation interacts with our molecules, which makes them vibrate faster, and then they are felt as heat. Gold can act as a heat shield for reflecting and heat protection, making it truly the only metal that is proven to last the test of time: we may even say that gold is indestructible.

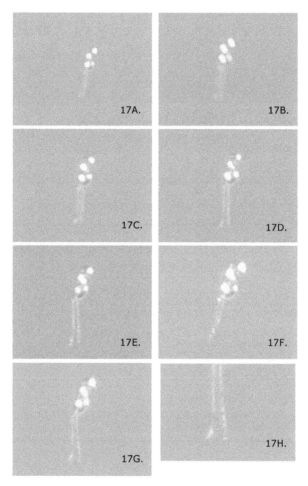

Images 17A–17C: Screen grabs of what looks like four gold balloons with a couple of strings dangling below them.
Images 17D–17G: Images showing how this object morphs into what looks a "head, with hood" and three limbs almost visible.
Image 17H: Images showing a close-up of the two tethers with the many nodules along the length of it.

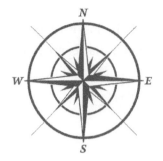

CHAPTER 16

HAQSR - High Altitude Quantum Singularity Reactor?

Morphing - boomerang shape - spinning grey top – highly erratic irregular shape, turning red then yellow and gold.

Date: 15 October 2017   Angle: S, 75°

Time: 10:12 am   Direction: S to SE

Height: 13,123 ft (2.48 mi, 4 km)   Photo: 4

Horizontal Distance: 3,200 ft (0.62 mi, 1 km)

Temperature: 66°F (19°C)   Video: 15 min 05 sec

Camera 1: Digital Camera 20MP +   Wind: S, 15 mi/h (24 km/h)

Skywatcher Telescope x 66   Visibility: Scattered clouds

Camera 2: Digital Camera 16MP

Estimated Size of Object: 7.2 ft (2.2 m)

This was a very interesting sighting indeed, not only for the sighting itself (which I am about to describe) but also the fact that over a six-hour period there were at least a further three independent and unique sightings that were all different in nature. Please refer to the subsequent chapters for details.

The first sighting, which I have called "Morphing - boomerang shape - spinning grey top" was highly erratic because that is exactly what it did by altering its shape strikingly for over 15 minutes up to a crescendo of erratic spinning, changing its shape and colour along the way. In the final moments of filming this object, my mind went into overdrive as I attempted to speculate what it was and determine its objective.

The sighting began when I noticed this bright orb to the south, high in the sky. Instinctively I grabbed the refractor telescope which I have in the lounge room, and immediately narrowed in on it using the laser scope.

What I saw was truly amazing. It was light tan in colour and I promptly noted the following details regarding the shape and motion. It was like a boomerang, "L" or "J" shape as it slowly turned and tumbled; but what drew my attention more were the two very small but intense bright lights at either end.

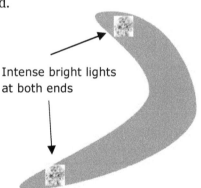

Image 18A: As I viewed the object through the telescope I saw a slowly rotating object with bright lights at either end, on top.

Intense bright lights at both ends

I recognised that I had previously seen a similar arrangement in 19 October 2016, when I saw through the telescope a bluish ring-shaped UFO with a dark underside, fluidly rotating and dynamically moving in and out of shape. But again, what struck me most was that there were intensely bright but small points of light at either end of the ring, just like this one (located on top of the object). This object was one of the "prettiest" entities I have seen and I sincerely wish it would return to grace the heavens once again.

Returning to the boomerang object, I frantically attached my small digital 20MP camera to the back of the telescope, and unfortunately, in the three or four minutes that took, the object had changed shape to a grey metallic dome with an occasional burst of light, single rod shape and dual rod, again with bursts of light. If you go to YouTube you will see in the video how it cycles several times through the same sequence. After some time, it turned slightly red, with the same cycle and bursts of light, single rod, and dual rod, again with bursts of intense light.

Have a look at the video for yourself and you will see the violent discharge and bright light exploding off the object.

What do I estimate the size of the object to be?

When I am pressed for time and want an instant idea of an object's size, I use a basic proportionality calculation. The object was hovering just below cloud height, so I estimate it to have been at 13,000-20,000 feet (4–6 km); and I estimate it to have been approximately one-quarter of the size of a light aircraft at 13,000 feet, while the smaller orbs were approximately one-sixth of the size of the larger object.

		ft	m
Average length	Light aircraft	30	9
If 1/4 size of aircraft	Object	7.5	2.2
If 1/6 size of object	Smaller orb	1.2	0.36

Still photographs may belittle and not do justice to the words outlined above, so please refer to the related videos and more screen-grab photos on my website and YouTube while I attempt to interpret and provide an explanation of what I believe was the purpose of this object's existence.

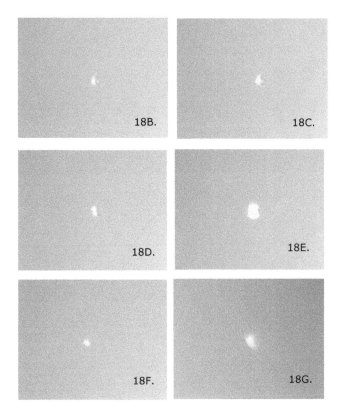

Images 18B–18G: Screen grabs taken from Skywatcher telescope of grey metallic dome with an occasional burst of light, then single rod shape and dual rod, again with bursts of light. This could be the beginning of the dematerialisation process before it moves through the portal recently created.

From all the evidence of videos and photos I have amassed to date, I am inclined to think these glowing objects are high altitude-controlled quantum singularity reactors, which I have dubbed HAQSRs (High Altitude Quantum Singularity Reactors). I am basing this purely on the fact that from the screen grabs above and especially the actual video on YouTube, the volatility, unpredictability, and the obviously colossal amount of energy expended by this object to enable it to fulfil its objective are suggestive of the quantum in the macroscopic world.

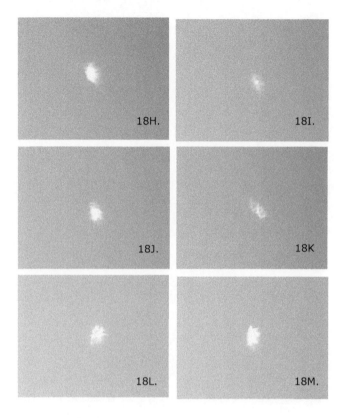

Images 18H–18M: Screen grabs of the same object continuously morphing and spinning with an occasional burst of light.

Quantum Mechanics at the Macroscopic Scale, HAQSRs - High Altitude Quantum Singularity Reactors

I wish to talk about quantum mechanics at the macroscopic scale in relation to "HAQSRs in an attempt to provide an irresistible explanation for what I experienced that day, which bordered on the realm of science fiction more than fact.

Many scientists believe that superconducting systems are phenomena on an equal footing with quantum mechanics, but at the macroscopic scale, the Pauli Exclusion Principle applies because essentially the theories that describe it are quantum theories. This principle states that electrons in a superconducting metal, with a spin of one half, such as Helium atoms of isotopic mass 4 (where *isotopic* means 2 or more forms of the same element, containing an equal number of protons but different numbers of neutrons in their nuclei, which results in different relative atomic mass but the same chemical properties), can be many particles in the same state. The same applies to photons (quanta of radiation), which are usually regarded as particles. Accelerators such as the LHC at CERN have many kilometres of superconducting magnets and detectors. Another aspect is the superfluid flow in liquid helium, which also seems to be a macroscopic quantum manifestation. The commonality throughout these systems is that at the macroscopic level they occupy a single quantum state.

If you take the case of a superconducting metal, it will obey the exclusion principle. Therefore, subatomic particles fall into two groups of classes, based on their statistical behaviour described above. Those particles to which the Pauli Exclusion Principle applies are called fermions, while those that do not obey this principle are called bosons.

Another way of describing it is the probability of interactions as a wave, and quantum mechanics can mathematically express the phases between the waves. If the waves of peaks and troughs match, then the phases are fixed and unchangeable, presenting macroscopic views of quantum effects such as superconductivity and superfluidity.

I firmly believe that what I have been observing in the fast spinning object in the sky is a quantum manifestation at the macro level, just as we see with superconductors. Physicists cannot seem to agree on what the quantum world looks like, and they are unable to demonstrate and accede a picture of reality that quantum mechanics describes. The most popular interpretation is the Copenhagen interpretation, only because it's the first and the only one a physicist is taught - but just because it's the conventional picture of quantum mechanics, that doesn't mean it's correct and applicable.

With this theory comes the acceptance that physicists just had to come to terms with the idea of the so-called wave particle duality where light was calculated, and it was "proven" in experiments that it was both a wave and a particle at the same time. Evidently it behaved sometimes as a wave and sometimes like a particle, presenting the idea of the wave-particle duality. More accurately, light is determined as a wave or particle depending on the experiment performed. Therefore it is not deemed a particle or a wave until then, even if all the while it is exhibiting particle or wave properties.

The French physicist Louis de Broglie in 1924 found that the wave-particle duality was present not only in light or radiation but in all particles, including at the macroscopic level. Even though in theory everything has a wavelength, including humans and everyday inanimate objects, they can be so small as to not be perceptible.

There are other interpretations, including with a view in the macroscopic field called pilot wave theories. Experiments have been drawn up where silicone oil droplets are placed on a vibrating bath, providing a remarkable physical realisation of pilot wave theories. This gives us a physical picture of what the quantum world might look like without the weirdness which the Copenhagen interpretation brings with it, such as the particle being in two places at once and with complete randomness, contradicting commonsense. The pilot wave theory reduces the fuzziness contributed by the conventional picture of a wave function containing all the information we know about a particle, yet in this theory only probabilities are calculated about where a particle is likely to turn up. As per the Heisenberg Uncertainty Principle, we cannot know where the particle went or where it will be at a later time.

In comparison, is the object that I saw – which resembles such weirdness - comparable to text we read about quantum mechanics? Although I did not witness a collision between objects producing new objects (as we see in the LHC at CERN with experiments in high-speed particle collisions which lead to the formation of new and exotic particles), I did, however, see a very high velocity, unidirectional, spinning display of a single object. It certainly had a measure of weirdness: it was moving in and out of existence in a very short space of time, and changing shape from a boomerang (or "L" or "J") shape with bright lights at either end to a dome shape, then tubular (single and double), then a rapidly spinning circular object, all the while changing colour from tan, grey, red to white, yellow and glowing "hot".

Was its objective to create a portal for inter-dimensional or interstellar travel? It is unfortunate that I did not capture continuous footage of the sighting from beginning to end, to show without a doubt the transformation the object went through, and the end result.

However, I am satisfied to have captured over 20 minutes of footage using two methods - a telescope with a digital camera attached and a digital zoom camera. Even though I missed the beginning and the end, I can speculate that it completely disappeared from this reality. It is very interesting to note - unnoticed at the time but obvious in the footage shot - that there are many other smaller objects flying near this object with no clear direction and seemingly trying to avoid colliding with it. It's apparent that these smaller objects are not a direct consequence of the larger one, as they do not seem to be discharged from it, but materialise off-screen.

Is the object some sort of HAQSR? The word "singularity" would suggest a point in space where physical laws break down, the same as would occur inside a black hole as matter is continuously fed into it, thereby releasing enormous amounts of energy for its use. Could I have witnessed a gravitational singularity where massive localised distortions of space and time allowed this object to launch through it?

This suggests the most fascinating and fundamental complex problem remaining in physics: how to merge Einstein's Theory of Relativity and quantum mechanics.

By its very nature, a singularity is a component of Einstein's Theory of Relativity, according to the understanding of black holes; and singularities are infinitely small, so we expect this to be essentially quantum mechanics. A theory that is yet to be complete will include quantum gravity, the Holy Grail amongst physicists for the theory of everything, which fully explains and links together all physical aspects of the universe.

Cosmic Rays, Gravitational Waves, HAQSR - High Altitude Quantum Singularity Reactor

We will now delve into the world of cosmic rays and gravitational waves in relation to "Quantum Singularity Reactors". In my final year at University, to achieve my BSc in Physics and Physical and Inorganic Chemistry, I was required to devise a unique and original experiment based on a list of suggested examples, and to provide a full detailed project report. As I had studied astrophysics, I chose to devise a cosmic ray experiment.

Cosmic rays are fast-moving particles first discovered in 1912 by Austrian scientist Victor Hess after a high-altitude balloon flight of about 17,400 feet (5,800 yards, 5,300 metres). He measured the ionizing radiation and discovered that they were three times greater at this altitude than they were on the ground. He established that this radiation must be penetrating the earth's atmosphere from outer space, which earned him the Nobel Prize in Physics in 1936.

These charged sub-atomic particles are mainly protons from hydrogen achieving speeds close to the speed of light. Fast-track to 100 years later and scientists cannot be sure where these particles come from and how they achieve such fantastic speed and energy.

While stars collapsing forming supernova may be one obvious explanation, we still cannot be certain as they are only few and far between in the cosmos, on average only one supernova per galaxy per century. Admittedly, though, using the calculation of 100 billion galaxies in the observable universe (as we discussed earlier) actually brings the figure to 1 billion supernovae per year, or 30 supernovae per second in the observable universe.

It is still unclear what effect these very distant supernovae have on the earth, and whether they are the sole perpetrators of these very mysterious high-energy particles. Most of the particles scatter in the upper atmosphere, and some manage to reach the earth in the form of secondary particles called muons. These particles became the integral component of my experiment, which comprised a huge water tank with a cover, and strategically placed sensors beneath the tank which registered a point in a graphical form and counter method.

As my degree also included chemistry, I came up with an ingenious idea of adjusting the pH value of the water slightly, using an array of chemicals available from the Chemistry Department, to see what effect it had on the data collected. So there I was, allowing the experiment to run over 24 hours a day, 7 days a week. I even attended on weekends to change the water and alter the pH value again, ever so slightly, to see what effect it had on the registered pattern of cosmic rays hitting the light-sensitive detectors.

The pH is a logarithmic scale of values from 1-14, where numbers below 7 indicate acidity of water-soluble substances (1 being the most acidic), while numbers above 7 indicate alkalinity (7 being neutral). Furthermore, pH stands for "potential of Hydrogen".

It was amusing that the only way I could empty the water tank was by a small hose stretched through an open window down a drain outside, but most spilled outside of the drain and after a few months the greenest of green moss-like formations had grown on the building walls and around the drain.

The basis of my experiment was these secondary particles hitting the tank and ultimately registering on the light-detecting sensors that formed. In comparison, there is a category of cosmic ray called "Ultra High Energy Cosmic Rays," or UHECR. They are very rare indeed and at least 60 times more powerful than anything the Large Hadron Collider (the world's most powerful particle collider), can produce. The first one detected was in 1991.

There are many arguments against suggestions that cosmic rays come from the sun or exist outside of our galaxy, based on one common fact: the intensity of cosmic rays does not change during the day or night. Interestingly, in an article published by the University of Adelaide on 22 September 2017, it is stated that: "A global collaboration of scientists including members from the University of Adelaide have discovered for the first time that cosmic ray particles bombarding Earth originate from other galaxies far outside our own Milky Way". The sole reasoning behind this argument is that over a 12-year period of collecting data of over 30,000 cosmic rays, most were coming from a direction consisting of a high density of other galaxies.

I will propose that some of these detected cosmic rays of high energy could be attributed to these UFOs, but only for detectors on earth discounting the cosmic ray detectors on the International Space Station. As I have seen so many UFOs in such a short space of time, and frequently in the same section of sky, who is to say whether this is happening thousands of times a day and night around the world? Imagine the residual traceable energy remaining for many months after the UFO disappears.

It has been estimated that 10,000 low-energy cosmic rays per square metre hit the earth's atmosphere every second, while five million ultra-high-energy cosmic rays hit the earth every year - which mathematically equates to only one particle per square kilometre every 100 years. To provide an idea of how rare these ultra-high-energy cosmic rays are, only 60 have been detected by the Pierre Auger Observatory since

2004. Their argument that the ultra-high-energy cosmic rays are the nuclei of heavy atoms (such as iron) and originate in the nearby galaxy Centaurus A, is highly questionable, especially since there are no low-energy protons from the same direction.

Obviously, my argument, if it has any basis of truth, would not only direct rays of energy down towards the ground but out towards the upper atmosphere and space. I often wonder what reading would be received by these space-based instruments if they were directed towards earth and not space.

Now, gravitational waves have been in the news recently, with headline status, following the award of the 2017 Nobel Prize in Physics to three scientists in October 2017. The scientists had successfully detected, with actual evidence, gravitational waves using the Laser Interferometer Gravitational-Wave Observatory (LIGO). The LIGO searches for stretching and squeezing in space-time that would indicate the thoroughfare of gravitational waves. A laser beam is split down two 2.5-mile (4 ks) arms containing mirrors. These gravitational waves are extremely weak and difficult to detect. Even though they were predicted in 1916 by Albert Einstein in the famous Theory of Relativity, it is believed that he doubted whether they do exist.

Einstein postulated that as large masses in space, such as planetary bodies, move they warp the so-called fabric of space and time, generating gravitational waves travelling at the speed of light. In comparison, a boat causes similar ripples in a lake and an accelerating electrical charge also produces electromagnetic waves.

Thereupon, as accelerating objects generate changes in the curvature of space-time, gravitational waves propagate outwards at the speed of light; and I will be alluding to the fact that possibly the objects I have been observing would also generate gravitational waves. Within the context of the Theory of Relativity, the speed of light in a vacuum "c" associated with gravitational waves is not restricted to light only, but it is suggestive of the highest possible velocity for any interaction in nature.

Furthermore, my reason for believing that these UFOs are a perfect candidate for gravitational wave producers is based on the assumption that there exist even larger "Quantum Singularity Reactors" moving extremely fast within the vacuum of space. As can be seen in the close-ups of some of the photos above, the erratic object is not spherically or cylindrically symmetric, so by definition it will produce gravitational waves. One would think, therefore, that it's probably fair to say that saucer- or disc-shaped objects and even cigar-shaped objects will not produce gravitational waves.

Black-Body Radiation and Colour Temperature, HAQSR - High Altitude Quantum Singularity Reactor

I would like now to talk about the transition in colour that the object went through, and whether what we know in science can be applied to the object. If you recall, besides the object changing shape in a weird display of transformation, the colour also changed from tan to grey to slightly red, yellow, and then white.

At a higher level we probably agree (it's more obvious if we examine the video) that the HAQSR is just getting hotter and hotter, thus producing the bright glow, yellow and white colour. On the other hand, nuclear reactors glow with a blue colour due to Cherenkov radiation, which is named after the Russian scientist who discovered this phenomenon in which, basically, charged particles moving through a medium faster than light, whether it's water (as is the case with nuclear reactors), or the atmosphere (perhaps as is documented in some UFO sightings).

Moreover, under normal circumstances the speed of light, c, is 186,282 miles per second (299,792 kilometres per second) in a vacuum and is universally constant. When light travels in water, however, the speed is only 75% that of the speed of light since the photons of light are interacting with the other particles in the medium, slowing it down. So, Cherenkov radiation occurs when charged particles (usually electrons) in the particular medium travel faster than light would in that medium; this occurs in nuclear reactors because high-energy particles are constantly decaying and being ejected at an enormous rate of speed, certainly greater than 75% the speed of light.

In essence, photons of higher frequencies, but shorter wavelength, give off the appearance of blue light as the charged particles disrupt the electromagnetic field in the water, by constructively interfering and increasing their energy state to achieve equilibrium.

Returning to the object that interchanged from tan to grey to reddish to yellow and white, it can analogously be described by colour temperature, where a light source of an ideal blackbody is radiating light of a particular colour comparable to that of the light source in question. A blackbody is a scientific term used for objects that emit thermal radiation and absorb all incoming light rather than reflecting light. The thermal electromagnetic radiation can be within the object or surrounding it and a blackbody at normal room temperature appears black because most of the energy emitted is infrared, which is not perceived by humans.

I believe that this is what happens when UFOs use a cloaking device and are only photographed or videoed using infrared cameras. Even though the object I saw looked like a flickering orb with the naked eye, in the telescope it was tan in colour (boomerang, "L" or "J" shape). Then as I commenced filming it was more a grey colour, which is what actually happens when the human eye cannot perceive colour at low light and at great distances - as I assume this one was.

The eye is more sensitive to black and white at low light intensities (or great distance), hence the appearance of a grey colour. As it gets hotter it becomes dull red, yellow then white, and as the temperature increases further it finally becomes blue-white. Colour temperature, on the other hand, is a characteristic of visible light for light sources that correspond closely with the radiation of a blackbody. This will be the case for reddish-orange to yellow and white to bluish-white, but does not apply to green or purple.

Colour temperature is expressed in units of kelvin, "K", where absolute zero (0 K) is equivalent to –459.67 °F (–273.15 °C).

Kelvin	Colour
1,000	Red
1,500	Reddish-Orange
2,000	Yellowish-Orange
2,800	Yellow
3,500	Yellowish-White
4,500	Warm White
5,500	White

This was the last time I have filmed via the telescope with a small compact digital camera attached at the back of it. I regret that I chose that option for this sighting rather than the digital zoom camera, which would have perhaps captured the initial boomerang shape with the intense small lights at both ends and closer detail as the object progressively morphed and changed colour. I did manage to record about eight minutes an hour later using this zoom camera, with incredible results.

As mentioned earlier, this day (15 October 2017) was the most UFO-filled day to date, in which I observed the Boomerang-Shaped UFO that kept morphing and spinning at **10:12 am**; the return of this yellow object still morphing and spinning at **11:32 am**; the strange Cluster Balloon Formation at **4:39 pm**; the incredible Golden Man at **5:06 pm**; and Multiple Orbs in Formation at **5:33 pm**.

There are incredible similarities in the last stages of this yellow object seven hours later. The facts so far are that the object morphs many times and spins at an incredible rate of speed; and it glows and turns yellow, which even at these initial stages appears to be the beginnings of the "Golden Man". The object seems to disappear and then return one hour later in the same section of sky, to almost continue where it left off (refer next chapter).

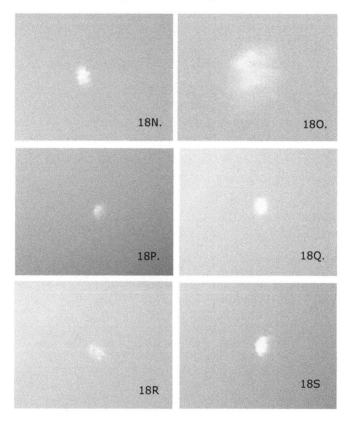

Images 18N–18S: Screen grabs showing continuous morphing of the object with an occasional burst of light; predominant colour is yellow, reminiscent of the "Golden Man". The object soon disappears only to re-emerge one hour later continuing as before with the same volatility but glowing yellow, again reminiscent of the "Golden Man".

UFO 1

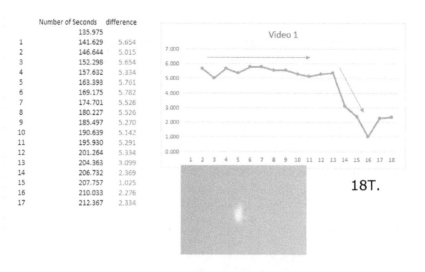

	Number of Seconds	difference
	135.975	
1	141.629	5.654
2	146.644	5.015
3	152.298	5.654
4	157.632	5.334
5	163.393	5.761
6	169.175	5.782
7	174.701	5.526
8	180.227	5.526
9	185.497	5.270
10	190.639	5.142
11	195.930	5.291
12	201.264	5.334
13	204.363	3.099
14	206.732	2.369
15	207.757	1.025
16	210.033	2.276
17	212.367	2.334

Image 18T: *The number of seconds taken to cycle through 17 grey metallic dome shapes, where it repeats as a cycle. Downward trend and smaller peaks mean it's speeding up.*

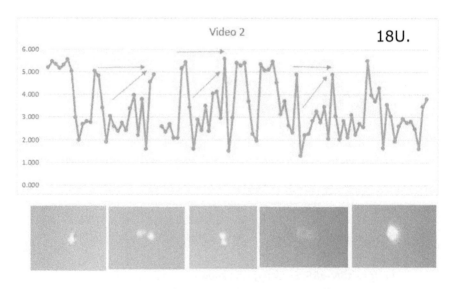

Image 18U: *The number of seconds taken to cycle through 97 stages pictured above, where it repeats as a cycle. Downward trend and smaller peaks mean it's speeding up.*

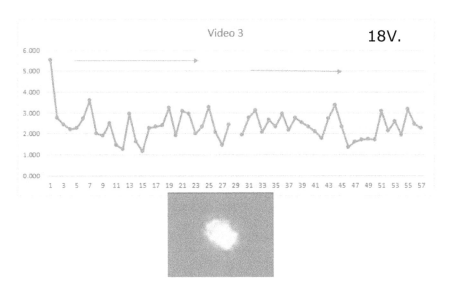

Image 18V: The number of seconds taken to cycle through 56 stages pictured above, where it repeats as a cycle. Downward trend and smaller peaks mean it's speeding up.

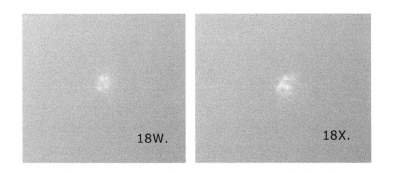

Images 18W-18X: There are many similarities between this object and the "Golden Man". Please refer to the video.

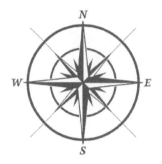

CHAPTER 17

Precursor - "The Golden Man"3

Date: 15 October 2017   Angle: South, 75°

Time: 11:32 am   Direction: S to S

Height: 9,842 ft (1.8 mi, 3 km) Photo: 0

Horizontal Distance: 6,561 ft (1.2 mi, 2 km)

Temperature: 61°F (16°C)   Video: 8 min 32 sec

Camera: Digital Camera 16MP Wind: ESE, 5.5 mi/h (9 km/h)

Estimated Size of Object: 8.8 ft (2.7 m) Visibility: Scattered clouds

While finalising the chapters in this book, on more than one occasion I missed the fact that this sighting and the third video in the previous chapter was the "Golden Man" once again. The "Golden Man" has been documented in this book for a total of five times, which is amazing. Furthermore, the most surprising thing about this footage is the fact that more than one hour later, the HAQSR in the previous chapter completed the "portal" construction and disappeared towards the south; this object emerged in virtually the same location.

The object's yellow-golden colour was unmistakable as it became larger; and it was more erratic in its motion and spin, which seemed to be anti-clockwise. Finally, the shape became extremely irregular without any symmetry whatsoever, although it momentarily displayed a disc shape for some reason, even though I believe that within five hours it would evolve into "The Golden Man". Have a look at the video for yourself on YouTube, and you will see the violent discharge and bright light emanating from this yellow object.

The sighting of the HAQSR at 10:12 am and again at 11:32 am is very special because it provides a platform where a beginning, middle and end sequence of events transpires. Following on from this at 5:06 pm was the amazing "Golden Man" formation. Unfortunately, the video ends abruptly, but it is evident that the object is moving further away from the camera (further south), since it is fading somewhat. The "Golden Man" returns about five and a half hours later high in the east (refer to the next chapter). The spinning is very erratic, and when viewing at normal speed it is difficult to see if it is spinning in a uniform direction.

We have all heard stories about how a traveller was driving his car in the English countryside, only to find himself being transported, as if through a portal, to a bygone era, as seen by people around him wearing period costumes and old motels with original antique décor. It is widely accepted that other realities and dimensions exist beside our reality. It is understood that these other realities are very close to our own. The "fictional" account of the traveller seemingly transported into the past could be explained by the fact that some physicists believe that all time exists at the same time, past present and future. Time is no longer thought of as a river flowing in one direction but, just as eastern philosophy and religion have taught us and new theories in physics suggest, the past, present and future coexist in the universe.

If we believe for one moment that a portal to and from another dimension was created on the morning of 15 October 2017, then we can use our knowledge of black holes and make comparisons. On the assumption that the object had passed through into our reality, why was it behaving like this near the "newly created portal" in the south? If this object is to reappear as the formed "Golden Man" at 5:06

pm, then perhaps the only way it could move through the portal is to disassemble itself into an energy pattern in order to de-materialise, beam through the portal, and then reconvert itself back into matter, re-materialising. Does all this sound familiar? You are correct if you think it sounds like an episode from *Star Trek*.

As for black holes, if we got too close to one we know that we would encounter spaghettification (the process of being pulled apart) due to the massive gravitational pull. So it appears that this interdimensional being may have travelled through a portal created earlier, then returned into our reality, and was in the process of re-materialising. It would have been fascinating to see whether this is exactly what happened by continuing filming, but we will never know for sure.

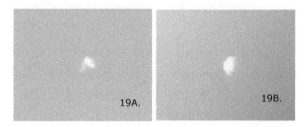

19A.

19B.

Images 19A–19B: The continuous morphing of the object with an occasional burst of light; predominant colour is yellow.

But before the re-emergence later of the fully formed "Golden Man", a large cluster of balloons can be seen exactly where this and the previous sightings were (discussed in the next chapter). To add to the confusion, why did the object supposedly disappear through the portal the same way as it had re-appeared one hour later, only to coalesce into the humanoid-looking "The Golden Man" five hours later? It can be very confusing indeed to try and understand why the object transformed from a grey spinning object of many forms to a yellow "heated" continually spinning form; disappeared for an hour; emerged at the same location as before in the south, still yellow-golden in appearance and glowing hot; and five hours later reappeared high, towards the east, as "The Golden Man".

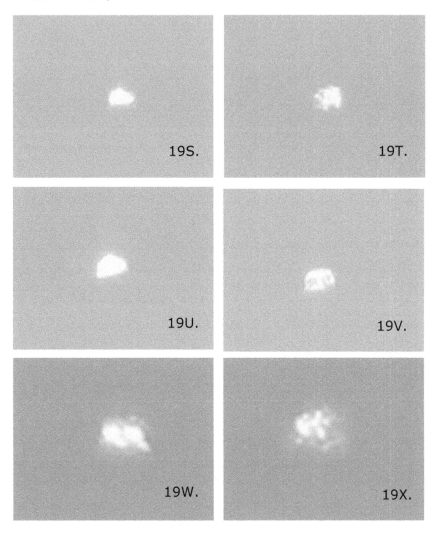

Images 19S–19X: It appears that the yellow object is in the process of re-materialising, to become "The Golden Man" five and a half hours later.

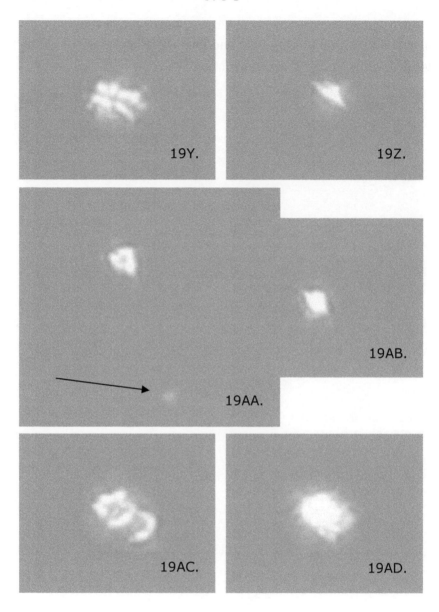

19Y.

19Z.

19AB.

19AA.

19AC.

19AD.

Images 19Y–19AD: The many shapes of extreme irregularity
without any symmetry whatsoever, and momentarily
displaying a disc shape as indicated in Image 18Z

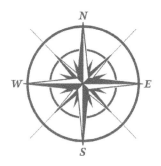

CHAPTER 18

Cluster Balloon Formation

Date: 15 October 2017   Angle: South, 75°

Time: 4:39 pm   Direction: S to S

Height: 13,123 ft (2.48 mi, 4 km)   Photo: 0

Horizontal Distance: 3,200 ft (0.60 mi, 1 km)

Temperature: 66°F (19°C)   Video: 5 min 49 sec

Camera: Digital Camera 16MP Wind: SSE, 15 mi/h (24 km/h)

Estimated Size of Object: 21 ft (6.4 m) Visibility: Scattered clouds

As has been the case many times after a prominent sighting, a balloon formation is sighted either immediately or some hours later; and I will include this as an interesting sighting regardless of the mundane appearance that at first, understandably, may well have just looked like a bunch of ordinary balloons.

I have now learned that rather than discard and delete videos and photos just because the objects they show do not resemble the classic saucer/disc shape UFO, I should include them in this book even as I try and justify why I do so. Yes, I can hear the laughter already, be it friendly or cynical; but I trust that the goodness of man will prevail as the appetite to understand the mysteries around us from the metaphysical, spiritual, supernatural to plain science is the carriage which will take us forward.

Just on the basis alone that the strikingly coincidental sightings of "balloons" occurred soon after the appearance of strange aerial phenomena documented in this book, they require some serious scrutiny. These sightings did not occur in any random section of the sky, but at virtually the same spot where the previous sighting occurred. I regard this as a new (although small) discovery. I will put forward that whenever I see a balloon formation in the sky with no unusual aerial phenomena prior, then I will conclude that a prominent sighting had probably preceded it.

The length of time between a UFO sighting and the balloon sightings may vary from minutes after the initial UFO sighting to four and a half hours, as this one was. So how high can normal helium-filled balloons travel? Well, it depends of course on the material used in the balloon's construction, together with one scientific principle: that the pressure of the surrounding atmosphere drops as the balloon ascends higher, while the opposite occurs to the helium as its pressure increases.

The air in the earth's atmosphere becomes thinner with higher altitude; thus the balloon can only ascend until the atmosphere surrounding it becomes the same weight as the helium within the balloon. Thereafter, normal household party balloons burst at an altitude of approximately 32,808 feet (6.21 mi, 10 km); and at 98,425 feet (8.64 mi, 30 km) if they are professional balloons used for meteorology, military defence, aerial photography or transportation, which are made from materials such as rubber, latex, polychloroprene, or a nylon fabric.

Having said that, I prefer joyful agreement at times and so for the non-believers I wholeheartedly agree that it's extremely easy to inadvertently confuse shiny balloons for a UFO, whether or not a string is dangling beneath it. The continual mass release of balloons at ceremonies is considered harmful to the environment and animal life

- particularly birds and marine animals - even though biodegradable latex balloons are used in most cases. There are balloon laws in the USA which make it illegal to mass release balloons, and similar laws are being considered in some states in Australia.

Russian writer Leo Tolstoy, regarded as one of the greatest authors of all time, wrote his first great novel, *War and Peace*, in 1873. A famous quote by Tolstoy says: "I know that most men, including those at ease with problems of the greatest complexity, can seldom accept even the simplest and most obvious truth if it be such as would oblige them to admit the falsity of conclusions which they have delighted in explaining to colleagues, which they have proudly taught to others, and which they have woven, thread by thread, into the fabric of their lives."

At first glance, I agree that the photos in this chapter are unimpressive. You may say they just look like an array of children's party balloons, but if you look closely you will see there is no string below the balloons, which may not amount to much since many balloons are released without a string, or if there was one it may become loose and fall off as the wind blows it around. It does not have a tether, but nevertheless something long is dragging beneath the object.

What I find truly perplexing is that in a matter of minutes the many "balloons" start changing around the upper section, from a blue semi-circle formation to a full white glow converging into one large formation (refer **Image 20D** and the video). As it becomes consumed by a massive glow, the upper section is now unrecognisable from when the video first started, while the rest of the object still has the familiar agglomeration of "balloons". Whether it's an optical illusion or not, I cannot be certain, but the small curved tether-like structure beneath the object seems to become larger and circular in shape, with a pulsing effect. I will pause here while sexual innuendoes subside.

I sincerely wish that the equal exposure I have given these "balloons" on this journey will not detract from the subject at hand, as presented in the previous chapters. All I am doing is bringing forward a subject that is of less interest than the public's favourite sightings deemed as the classic UFO. And maybe these "balloon" UFOs are so extensive that they fall in the category of "hidden in plain sight" – a phrase which generally refers to secret government agendas.

It's almost laughable, actually, to think that if (as we are implying) alien intelligence is controlling objects such as HAQSRs), they would make a futile attempt to cover up their tracks by revealing soon after, in the same location, earthly looking "balloons".

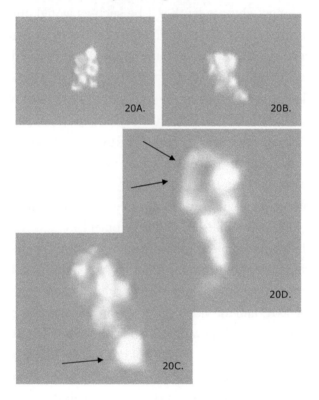

Images 20A–20D: Screen grabs of strange balloon formation seen 6 hours after HAQSR sighting in exact same position in sky.

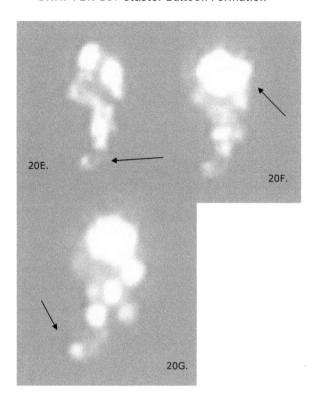

Images 20E–20G: *Images of strange balloon formation structure beneath the object; it seems to become larger and circular in shape with a pulsing effect.*

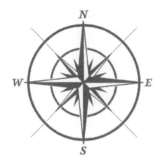

CHAPTER 19

The Golden Man

Date: 15 October 2017   Angle: East, 60°

Time: 5:06 pm   Direction: E to N

Height: 9,842 feet (1.8 mi, 3 km)   Photo: 6

Horizontal Distance: 3,200 ft (0.62 mi, 1 km)

Temperature: 66°F (19°C)   Video: 11 min 27 sec

Camera: Digital Camera 16MP Wind: S, 15 mi/h (24 km/h)

Estimated Size of Object: 6.52 ft (1.99 m) Visibility: Passing clouds

Please also refer to Chapters 15 (Precursor - "Golden Man" 1) and 17 (Precursor - "Golden Man" 2), Chapter 19 (Precursor - "The Golden Man" 3), and Chapter 28 (Return of the Golden Man).

This object was spotted in the east moving towards the north.

With almost every sighting, I get the feeling that these objects somehow detect the optical camera zooming in. Whether it is by obvious visual means or detecting human consciousness, they invariably give me the feeling that they know I am observing them.

Just 30 minutes after the Cluster Balloon Formation, I stumbled into the twilight zone, paranormal, metaphysical, and supernatural, all amalgamated into one complete package. I don't know where to begin with this one, except to say that I will never ever forget it for the rest of my life. What I saw through the camera lens that day was absolutely spellbinding, and I hope the essence of it all is captured in the still grabs from the videos (a massive 11 minutes in total) at the end of this chapter. You will be amazed at what happens at the end, but as I always say, check out the videos for yourselves.

When I saw this object, my mind was filled with conflicting thoughts, from distrust, enjoyment, and curiosity to quite a lot of humour. I was confused. "Was it a balloon?" I thought. "It has to be, as it's just hanging there". I continued observing with distrust and disbelief as the details became more pronounced as it ever so slowly rotated clockwise, from my perspective, and nonchalantly bobbed up and down as if suspended on an invisible string.

It all started while I panned the sky after the "Cluster Balloon Formation" sighting in the south. My eye caught a yellow glow towards the east. For a moment I contemplated the colour, as it wasn't the ordinary yellow I was familiar with; and curiously it was shinier in nature, though not glowing like an orb. Then as I pointed my camera in its direction I was exceptionally surprised at how quickly I was able to narrow in on it, so I thought it must be moving closer. This was verified when I was able to focus on it instantaneously; and as can be seen in the first of nine videos, very clearly and without a doubt the letter "S" came into view as I began to zoom in. As I looked through the camera I was captivated by its golden colour because it immediately reminded me of my favourite coffee cup, which is gold in colour, given to me by my niece for Christmas a few years ago. I hadn't known at the time, but even though it is porcelain it is not microwavable, as I learned the hard way when I blistered my fingers and hands by reaching into the microwave to remove the coffee cup.

This was odd, I thought, as I continued zooming in with the letter "S" becoming ever more prominent. In a way, I tried to remain unaffected by this projection in the sky before me, still pondering the balloon theory and projecting in my own mind how someone could release such a beautiful balloon. However, around 44 seconds into the video the appearance of the object suddenly took a human form, and I could recognise what appeared to be a head and then a face protruding ever so slightly from what had the shape of a hood.

At that point that I immediately zoomed in further, and by the 46-second mark my secular thoughts on the matter impetuously dissolved into thoughts of the extra-terrestrial, supernatural and the spiritual. Additionally, at this point I was able to distinguish two legs dangling beneath the form, and my immediate impression of its demeanour was one of sitting down and crouched or hunched over. Moreover, by the 50-second demarcation I was uncertain whether my observation that it seemed to be moving its left knee in an upward direction was correct or not, because by the 58th second it progressively turned in a clockwise direction.

Consequently, it relinquished the human form to become just a goldish indiscernible figure. In fact, the two previously discernible legs became one; and as it turned 180 degrees to the left profile, from a perfect "S" form on the right profile, it lost all the familiar human features as it still managed to retain the "S" shape in the left profile. Upon closer scrutiny, though, the left profile leg area occasionally looks like an open human left palm. By the one-and-a-half-minute mark it was pointing away from me, and by the two-minute mark of the first video, it had completed one full turn and was again at the right profile and showed the perfect human form. Zooming in made it difficult to focus, perhaps due to the sun glaring off its shiny surface; so I stopped filming to gain my composure, and re-commenced filming soon after.

By now it was already into its clockwise turn, and I was beginning to notice something tether-like dangling beneath it. This, too, seemed to be shining, although its reflectiveness was not due to the shiny golden lustre of the object above it; from my perspective it was more "organic" in nature, while my impression was that the object was more inanimate. When you watch the videos for yourselves, not only will you see this unusual figure dangling in the sky but you will also hear a crow and other birds in the background, and it certainly was not a windy day. I smiled to myself at the one-minute point of the second video, when the detailed human figure at the right profile could clearly be seen again, the legs, head and face visible past the hood; but this time it seemed to be bowing down further.

Two things suddenly dawned on me: the figure had no visible arms; and I remembered seeing something similar the day before when, after 10 seconds of filming I thoughtlessly tossed the footage aside, thinking that I was just seeing a bunch of balloons. If you have a look at that video **Precursor - "Golden Man" 2** and the associated screen grabs, you will come to the same conclusion: without hindsight, without noticing detail such as the tether beneath it, and without this one to compare it to, it can easily be passed off as nothing of significance. But hell, was I wrong - and so glad I had not deleted that video. Hopefully you will agree that it seems to be a precursor to a fully formed human figure, minus the arms of course.

Notwithstanding the large distances involved, it is a shame that it's not as crystal clear as when I was observing it through the eyepiece or viewfinder. The object looked like pure gold, and as I write this I am convinced that this is something from virtually out of this world due to the mass of video evidence at my - and your – disposal; so I won't take offence at some of the cynics that may make comparisons to a Hollywood award, for instance. With the amount of negative publicity surrounding Hollywood, I couldn't care less; so yes, let's hit that ball out of the park, and compare it to a statuette. But I am positive that when I describe what this object did during the final stage of filming, you too will think differently. So keep in mind first and foremost how far away I believe the object was at the time - 3,200 feet (1 km).

Before I do that, I wish to paint a picture of the detail that I saw through the viewfinder, in particular the gold texture. Several years ago, I took my mother to a country town in Victoria named Ballarat, which in its heyday during the mid-1800s was famous for gold mining. There is a tourist area called Sovereign Hill, where actors are dressed in clothes from that era and tours inside gold mines are provided. I also recall a demonstration where 6.6 lbs (3 kg) of gold was melted down, shaped into a gold bar, cooled and then handed to members of the audience so they could touch and feel 99.99 % pure gold.

There were, of course, jokes amongst the audience about running away with the gold. I remember that as it was passed to me I noticed it was not as smooth as I expected it to be. What struck me was the roughness and the imperfections, especially around the edges. As molten gold is poured into a bar-shaped mould and left to solidify, it can often lead to improperly formed bars with uneven surfaces. Although this makes the bars imperfect, it also makes each bar unique and easier to identify, and sometimes more appealing to buyers. These bars are also cheaper to produce compared to those that are minted, because minted bars are identified by their smooth and even surfaces as they are made from gold blanks cut to a required size from a flat piece of gold.

This is what the object looked like through the camera in the left profile, where it no longer had most of the human features, especially in the lower leg area section. On the other hand, the additional incredible features were the detail in the trousers coupled with creases and what I believe are shoes. No facial features can be distinguished, except for the outline of a face beneath the hood covering the head area.

Another striking feature of this object was the tether dangling from around the neck area. This tether had a natural movement of its own, swaying in an independent motion as the object swung around clockwise. Some questions to ponder, besides the obvious: What the hell was it?; why was it in the human form, and why only the right-hand side?; was its method of propulsion the tether and bulb-like formations hanging from it?.

After experiencing what I have seen, and with the distinct impression that the object knew I was looking at it, I have learned to abandon all notions that life is too dull. Every easy life fact leading to boredom and apathy needs to be replaced with at least 10 difficult and challenging thoughts, ideas, and actions - the old term "think outside the box" comes to mind – thereby forming new connections between your brain cells, which communicate by sending chemical messages in the form of neurotransmitters or electrical signals via the synapses. I am in no way implying that I know for certain what this was, but I would certainly like to know.

Moving on, I have left till last the best part about this phenomenon. Two very strange incidents transpired, and they were recorded on video. But before I talk about them, I would like to put something out there regarding the question of: why the human form? As you may have noted at the beginning of this chapter, the object was first seen at a low angle in the sky, and not as high as other sightings, before it moved a little higher.

I have walked many times in the easterly direction and stood beneath the general area where I think the object was first sighted. I could be mistaken by hundreds of metres, but nevertheless I will convey that this is a heavily cosmopolitan area with seven-floor high-rise apartments amongst established homes, and dotted with small- to medium-sized garden parks. Public transport is key here, and most stops have an uncovered bench area for commuters as they wait for the electric trams or buses.

What if this object took on the appearance of someone sitting on a park bench or tram and bus stop, perhaps? This would explain why only the right profile was human in appearance, as this would have been the only part visible to the object at the time. Imitating someone below it would also explain, perhaps, the hood and the crouching demeanour.

I capitulate - you can be forgiven if this seems like a Hollywood movie, where the villain is a morphing golden man from a movie franchise (hence the twilight zone referenced earlier).

Can this be an alien drone perhaps, with its levitation, antigravity and propulsion *modus operandi* based on the tether-like substance hanging from the left-hand side of the neck area? Was this a futile attempt to veil itself by attempting to take on the persona of someone on the ground?

If you look at video number 6, in the first few seconds you can clearly see what looks like a spherical object on the left-hand side of the screen, replicating every move the camera is doing as I struggle to keep the object in frame. Admittedly, this suspiciously looks like a sun dog (or sundog), which in meteorological terms is called parhelion - an optical illusion of a bright spot resembling a fake sun. I have a problem with the sun dog explanation, as these spots tend to occur on either side of the sun, especially when the sun is near the horizon. This sighting was in the east, and the sun was setting at 7:37 pm (daylight savings time) on that day, so at the time it was still high in the sky, directly behind me at about 60-degree angle.

Having watched this video many times, I genuinely doubt that this is a human-made device. How can such a disproportionate vehicle not only bob, rotate clockwise then anticlockwise, and then suddenly catch me by surprise as it accelerates in my direction?

You can see by the footage in the remaining two videos how I struggle to regain focus in the final stages as it crosses over my roof. I was drawn despite my disbelief, and I ran to the side of the house but could not locate it. I opened the rear sliding door and ran through to the front of the house and stepped onto the road in my frustration. I still could not find it. Did it just vanish or did it speed away in the distance beyond the buildings across the road? For many weeks afterwards, I searched on the term "strange gold man in the sky", but nothing came up, and I could find no other witnesses.

What size do I estimate the object to be? Well, I used the following high-level formula:

Estimated Size of Object

*Object size in image = object size * focal length/object distance from camera, or*

*Object size = (Object size in image * object distance from camera) / (focal length).*

The Pythagorean Theorem to calculate distance from me is

$a^2 + b^2 = c^2$ or (vertical distance)^2 + (horizontal distance)^2 = (distance from camera)

(3000 m)^2 + (1000 m)^2

(9,000,000) + (1,000,000) = √ 10,000,000 = 3,162 m (distance from camera).

Digital Camera 16MP

Sensor size = 6.2 mm x 4.6 mm

Average = 5.4 mm (0.0054 m)

Size on image = 35 mm (0.035 m)

Vertical height of screen = 150 mm (0.15 m)

% of screen taken by object = 23

% of above compare with sensor size = 1.26 mm (0.00126 m)

(focal length used ~ 2,000 mm) = 2 m

To calculate size of object (m) = ((0.00126 x 3,162) / (2))

= 6.5 ft (1.99 m)

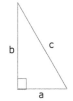

I am privileged to have witnessed an interdimensional, golden humanoid at the point it exited our world through a portal, return into our world to consolidate into a human-size being, inanimate looking yet alive and thinking. There are many stories and pictures of humanoids on the internet, but few compare to the clarity of this sighting.

It defies logic, and brings the additional challenge of trying to make sense of it. What is this creature that seemingly knows that I am observing and filming it? There is much data collected that eventually I would like to review and analyse further.

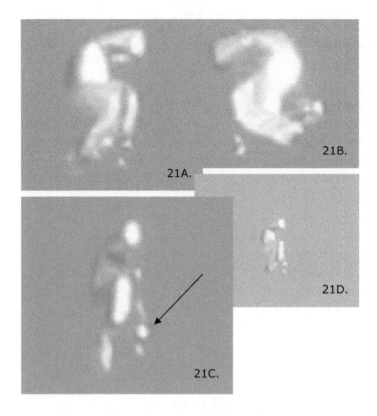

Images 21A–21D: "The Golden Man". Right profile shows a somewhat human form; left profile is less discernible. The tether is clearly visible, with metallic looking nodules along the length of it. The object clearly looked metallic - in fact, like pure gold. It seemed to be suspended in the air rotating slowly, mainly clockwise.

It's interesting to note that the tether hanging from the object may be of a significance to the object, yet to an observer it seems to be just hanging there and moving with the object, exactly as something hanging from an object would. If it wasn't for the strange golden appearance, one could be excused for seeing it as nothing but a human-shaped balloon, with a rein in the place where a horse would have it, except on the side.

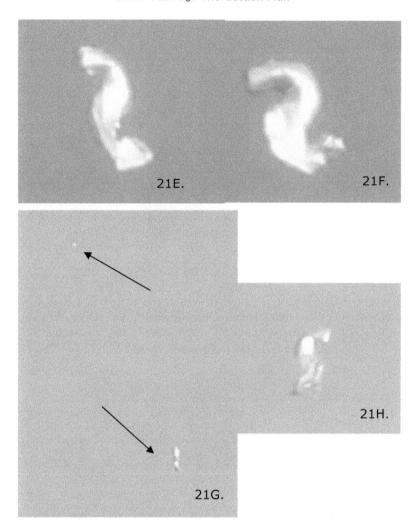

Images 21E, 21F & 21H: Screen grabs of right and left profile. Notice the lower left profile: does this resemble a right thumb on an open left palm? Image 21G: You can clearly see what looks like a spherical object on the left-hand side of the screen, moving with the "Golden Man". Images 21I–21J: Rear view of "The Golden Man", clearly showing the tether hanging from the left side of the "neck" or "head".

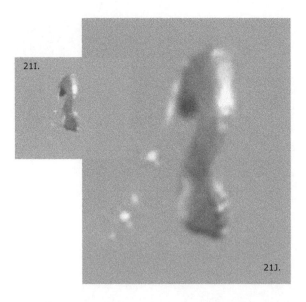

*Image 21K: This is the moment "The Golden Man" was racing towards me. The wide white diagonal line is the clothesline in my backyard.
Images 21L–21M: Right and left profile again.*

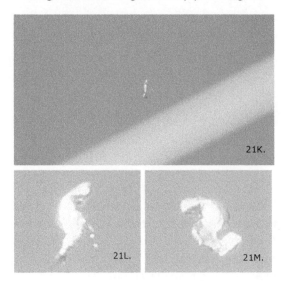

In Image 21K, you can see how the object caught me by surprise, as from a hovering position it starts to pick up pace as it moves towards me (west). On the video the tether seems to be moving in the direction of the object, not behind it as one might expect.

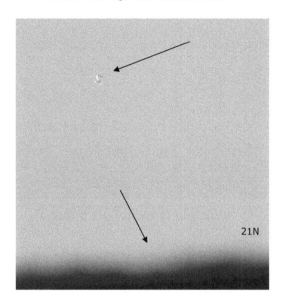

Image 21N: This is the moment "The Golden Man" flies over my roof (heading north), which is the dark image below the blue sky.

In a very short amount of time the object was over my roof from about 1,000 m, as I struggled to focus on it. I estimate its speed to have been about 37–50 mi/h (60–80 km/h).

This was truly an amazing experience , one that will remain with me forever. If this object was seen by a mass of people but lower in the sky, they would be forgiven for thinking that they were seeing an apparition.

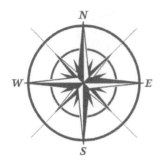

CHAPTER 20

Multiple Orbs in Formation

Date: 15 October 2017   Angle: East, 90°

Time: 5:33 pm   Direction: E to SE

Height: 13,123 ft (2.48 mi, 4 km)   Photo: 4

Horizontal Distance: 3,200 ft (0.60 mi, 1 km)

Temperature: 62°F (17°C)   Video: 4 min 44 sec

Camera: Digital Camera 16MP   Wind: S, 13 mi/h (22 km/h)

Estimated Size of Object: 4.9 ft (1.5 m) Visibility: Passing clouds

This was the final sighting for Sunday 15 October 2017. Not only was I fortunate enough to witness many UFO sightings that day, but they were all unique and extraordinary. My mind celebrated decisively and thoroughly at the prospect that the seeming escalation in quantity of sightings showed no signs of waning; and to add further strangeness to the mix, without fail, I sighted balloons after major sightings.

Just to recap, as "The Golden Man" flew over the roof I ran through the house to the front yard and onto the street, but it had disappeared. I looked across the sky from west to north to east and I could not believe my eyes. High in the sky towards the east were several orbs in formation. I tried to contain myself but letting out a war cry I ran back inside and through to the backyard again.

At first it was a little difficult to scan the sky in the easterly direction where I thought I had seen the objects, only because they were not reflecting any light off the setting sun behind me in the west. I finally located them. With my thoughts in overdrive, I counted eight objects moving slowly, independent of each other. As I have said, the prominent and peculiar sightings are almost always followed by the appearance of balloons in very close proximity to the original sightings. "Is that what they are?" I thought as I tried to focus in on them, "Just balloons?" There were so many that I could not zoom in close to see any detail with all of them in frame, so I picked only one to zoom in on. I thought perhaps they were the Chinese lanterns we have all heard about; but I immediately ruled this out as I have never seen such a thing in my area, and also they were not luminous, flickering, pulsating or shining.

At first, I must admit, they did look like normal whitish balloons. And as I have said, I would not have included them here, but I have learnt never to dismiss anything. There had been multiple sightings that day, and I thought that my luck would continue straight after "The Golden Man" sighting, so I was determined to capture as much video and as many photos as I could. They were very high in the sky – 10,000–20,000 feet, which helium filled balloons can easily fly to. They may well be proven to be just balloons, and I may well have mistaken the small string hanging from them as smaller orbs. In any case, I have documented here the fact that almost straight after any prominent sighting there are normal balloons seen close by.

One strange fact, though: of the initial eight objects, only three remained in their original visible intensity, while the other five faded away. In some of the zoomed-in screen grabs, it appears that either there is a protrusion on the end of one of these objects or it is emitting very short-lived smaller orbs and is rotating. In extreme close-up, it starts to resemble the shape of a Christmas ornament or bauble.

As these smaller orbs are released, after a short distance they seem to dissipate and fade away, leaving a small darkish trail. To me this conjures up an image of propulsion, or method of levitation, perhaps. Another interesting fact is that as soon as a helicopter comes into view flying below the objects from south-east to north, they disappear and then re-appear as soon as it passes. Again the questions persist, because they look like mundane balloons with nothing really captivating about them except for the few anomalies pointed out above.

In their own way these objects have succeeded in hiding the true treasures that lie behind the door to a reality hidden from us. Look at all the evidence that abounds on the internet, along with the equal amount of ridicule triggered by the speaker or writer. These **Multiple Orbs in Formation** are not your typical alien-looking metallic spacecraft, but they could well be an interdimensional object of which we are only seeing a small component within our reality. I wonder what magic this balloon-shaped object can weave; but in the videos and screen grabs they look very basic, and whether they are interplanetary or interdimensional objects or creatures that have lived for millennia in the atmosphere, we may never know.

Images 22A and 22B: About the time when three of the eight orbs remained, a helicopter comes into view from right lower screen, heading north. Assuming that the helicopter is unaware of the orbs above it, they can be seen "turning off" one at a time as the helicopter gets closer.

Image 22C: The three orbs in formation

Images 22D–22G: A close-up of one of the orbs, clearly showing the release of smaller orbs which do not venture any distance and are quickly diminished in intensity.

Images 22H–22O: Close-up of one of the orbs again, showing the discharge and the residual effect as it reduces in intensity until the discharge finally disappears.

The discharged smaller objects seem to always be present in most of the sightings of this type. This was seen in the H-Shaped Metallic Object, the Cross Metallic Object and the Bright Yellow Orb 1, 2 & 3. The three remaining objects slowly faded and disappeared as did the other five.

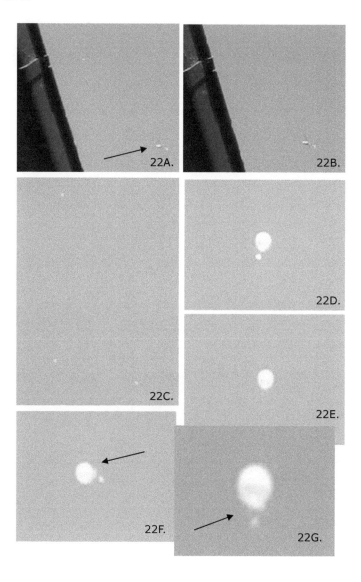

171

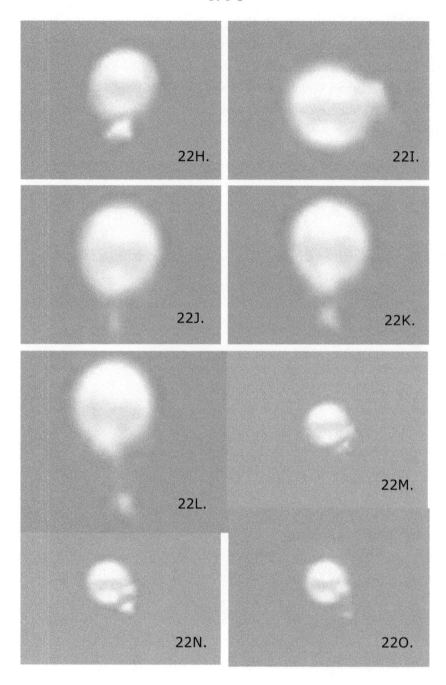

22H.

22I.

22J.

22K.

22L.

22M.

22N.

22O.

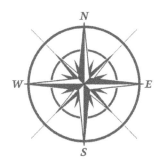

CHAPTER 21

Two Rectangle Shape – Grand Prix

Date: 19 November 2017   Angle: West, 20°

Time: 9:05 am   Direction: W to SW

Height: 54 yds (50 m)   Photo: 0

Horizontal Distance: 109 yds (100 m)

Temperature: 71°F (22°C)   Video: 0

Camera: N/A   Wind: NNE, 6.8 mi/h (11 km/h)

Estimated Size of Object: 6.5 ft (2 m)   Visibility: Partly sunny

I felt obliged to include this sighting even though it was only for about 15 seconds, with no photographic or video evidence. It had a profound effect on me, mainly because the sighting was so close, and no one else noticed it even though there were many joggers and walkers nearby.

The location of the sighting was above none other than the Australian Grand Prix, home to the motor race held annually in Melbourne, and currently under contract to host Formula One until 2023. I was on my way to church in the city. To avoid the traffic I tend to take the scenic route around the Albert Park Lake, which is used as the Formula One racing track every March.

Only seconds after turning into Lakeside Drive, in between the palm trees thinly lining the surroundings of the lake, I clearly saw what looked like two rectangular objects side by side, about 54 yards (50 metres) about the centre of the lake. They can be described as tan in colour, extremely fluid – almost like horizontally placed flags flapping in the wind - and both had very bright horizontal lights running all the way along the front of them.

It was very clear that there were two objects, and what was very striking was that they seemed to be scanning below using the bright "headlights", so to speak. I call them "head lights" not only because they were in front of the objects, but also because they do indeed look like the headlights of most new cars, which illuminate the bottom length of the rectangular head lamp component.

I know it sounds amusing when I say I saw such objects above the water and especially with the racing track so close, but it's the truth. The objects were heading in the opposite direction to where I was heading and as there was a car behind me I could not just stop and turn around, especially as it's a narrow road. In the next 20 or 30 seconds there was a section on the opposite side of the road where I was able to do a U-turn. This track has a restricted speed limit, but I just had to try and catch up to these objects, mobile phone at the ready, to verify what I had tried to assimilate with difficulty in such a short amount of time.

I would say about 50 to 60 seconds transpired between when I first saw them and the second time, travelling a distance of about 0.93 miles (1.5 km) and calculated speed of 50 mph (80 km/h), when they came into view just ahead, and again hovering at the tree line. The objects were making up some ground and heading towards the beachside suburb of Saint Kilda, the long glowing "headlights" visible in the front as they turned side to side. The objects were still doing the same thing. They appeared to not be solid, and they were assessing the situation below them. I waited at the traffic lights but quickly lost sight of them.

My main concern throughout this ordeal was how everyone seemed to be oblivious to these objects just metres above their heads, so nothing made sense as I turned around. I know what I saw, as they say. They were not drones - there were no visible rotors and they were not suspended by helicopters above them.

Images 23A–23B: White arrows indicate height and direction the two objects were travelling in. They were over the lake at tree level travelling right to left (W to SW). Yellow arrow is the direction I was driving towards.
Images 23C–23D: White and black arrows show how much distance the objects travelled, still at tree height - 0.93 miles (1.5 km). They were heading towards the coast.

CHAPTER 22

Vertical Blue – Plasma 1 and the Cartoon Characters

Date: 26 November 2017   Angle: South, 80°

Time: 5:01 pm   Direction: S to E

Height: 13,123 ft (2.48 mi, 4 km)   Photo: 0

Horizontal Distance: 9,842 ft (1.86 mi, 3 km)

Temperature: 81°F (27°C)   Video: 3 min 12 sec

Camera: Digital Camera 16MP   Wind: SSW, 4 mi/h (7 km/h)

Estimated Size of Object: 11.8 ft (3.6 m) Visibility: Sunny

This strange, blue, vertical four-tiered object was heading east from a southerly direction, and strangely enough - or not - the winds were also from SSW. Sometimes it's a difficult decision to include something in this book, with the fear that it may just be a balloon or bunch of balloons. It's difficult, but careful checking of the sightings before or after the one in question provides a better decision-making process, as was the case with **The Golden Man.**

In this situation, I decided to keep it due to an incredible sighting just one hour later in the exact spot as this one was last observed (please refer to **Vertical Blue – Plasma 2)**. Additionally, there are some compelling similarities between this object and the one in the next chapter, which was sighted one hour later. The object did not float around aimlessly as balloons would do, and it maintained a vertical composure that would prove to be difficult if it were a group of balloons.

On the other hand, admittedly, there does appear to be some connectivity, ever so subtly, between the "head balloon" and the "body balloon". There do not appear to be any solid connections between them, so if these were helium-filled balloons one would expect them to be twirling around themselves in a horizontal fashion. I had taken a video recording of exactly that some time ago. I videoed what at the time looked like four circular objects moving from north to the east quite erratically. Scrutinising the video, once it was uploaded to my computer, quickly revealed the mundane explanation that they were only four balloons tied together by strings. I will add this video to the end of the book, in the section about how easily anyone can be fooled into thinking that they have captured UFOs.

One further point to note is that for the time I was watching this object, it did not seem to be rising higher as a helium-filled balloon would, but moved horizontally. We know from Archimedes' principle that a body immersed in fluid experiences a buoyant force equal to the weight of the fluid it displaces. Since the balloon will rise when released, this buoyant force must be greater than the weight of the helium-filled balloon. So the weight of the helium-filled balloon is less than the weight of the volume of air it displaces and therefore is less dense than the air it displaces. There is an upward net force on the balloon, equal to the difference in weight between the balloon and the volume of air that it displaces.

The first and second "balloons" remained blue in colour, while the third and fourth continually flashed and changed colour from gold to a purple-like colour. There are some great videos on YouTube where people have let go of mylar metallic helium-filled balloons and recorded them as they reach a great height.

I certainly understand how easily one may be fooled and report balloons as UFOs - not only because of the number of different shapes, but also the shimmering and flashing as their surface reflects the sun. It gives the impression of plasma or electric discharge, but there is nothing sinister about it at all, and this is one of the biggest problems I face; I have been fooled many times. Even after recording with zoom for a close-up, before it's analysed on the computer I have been certain that I have captured some strange aerial phenomena, but analysing the captured object on the computer by studying it frame by frame reveals its true origin. Unfortunately, we must be more vigilant than ever and not take anything for granted. Please refer at the end of the book for some examples.

Even components of normal balloons, such as the colourful tethers below or the curved surface of a metallic balloon giving off flashes as it reflects the sun, contribute to the impression of a plasma discharge. Key things to watch out for are wind direction in relation to the object, although this is not always accurate, as the direction of the wind provided by the meteorological bureau is measured at 33 feet (10 metres) above ground; so when we talk about objects 10,000–15,000 feet above the ground, we can soon see why it can't really be all that accurate.

Watch out for tell-tale signs such as string beneath the balloon, neck and lip of the balloon, creases around the balloon where it's shaped. There may be small raised extensions on the surface of the balloon used to tie it together with others. The biggest ticket item for me is the behaviour of the balloon-like object. Besides having the feeling that it knows I am observing it, in many cases, I have seen an object fly directly over my head, as had occurred with three prominent sightings in December 2017 and January 2018. In the December the "Golden Man" returned yet again, flying directly over my head; the same occurred in January, when the blue-coloured version of what appeared to be the H-shaped object also flew directly over my head; and also in January in a suburban street of Melbourne, what looked like a hooded man flying under a thin veil of clouds, flew directly above my head.

I have called this sighting **Vertical Blue – Plasma 1** only because that is the impression I had when watching the video. On the other hand, when I slow down the video and watch some of the frames, ready to paste the screen grabs into this book, something very strange happens. I will play devil's advocate and suggest that it could be pareidolia, a psychological phenomenon in which the mind responds to a stimulus such as an image and perceives a familiar pattern where none exists. This happens when we look at the unusual shapes of clouds and see images of animals, faces, people and objects in cloud formations. Pareidolia can cause people to interpret random images, or patterns of light and shadow, as faces, but what concerns me is that I can see so many cartoon-like characters in the short video clip.

Please have a look at the video yourself in YouTube, pause it where you want, and see if you have captured one of these caricatures (shown below) yourself. We all have seen caricatures in newspapers with the purpose of insulting, serving a complimentary political purpose, or simply drawn for entertainment. Caricatures of politicians and movie stars are popular as they are rendered images showing the features of its subject in a simplified or exaggerated way through sketching, pencil strokes, or colour.

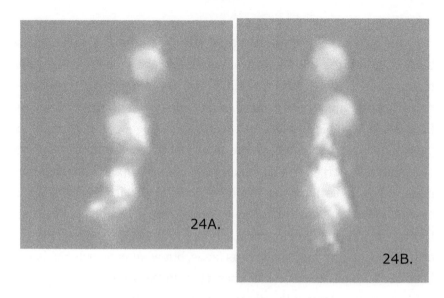

Images 24A–24B: I see a duck with a helium balloon above it, and a little old lady.

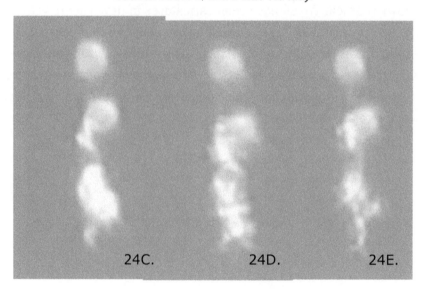

Images 24C–24E: I see a Disney-type character and two little old ladies, each with a helium balloon above.

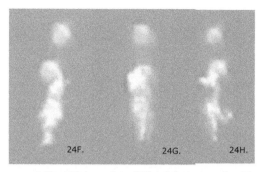

Images 24F–24H: I see two little old men and a Disney-type character, each with a helium balloon above.

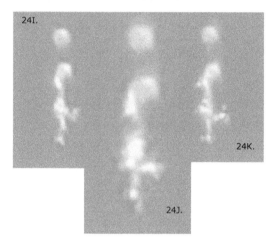

Images 24I–24K: I see a chef kicking up his right leg, someone jogging with left leg cocked up, and a Disney-type character with a large tail, each with a helium balloon above.

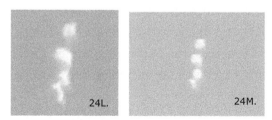

Images 24L–24M: This is how it all started before the flashing: four vertical objects that remain in vertical composition throughout.

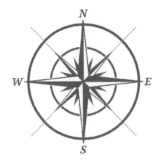

CHAPTER 23

Vertical Blue – Plasma 2 and the Cycles of Life

Date: 26 November 2017　　Angle: East, 80°

Time: 6:13 pm　　　Direction: E to E

Height: 13,123 ft (2.48 mi, 4 km)　　Photo: 0

Horizontal Distance: 9,842 ft (1.86 mi, 3 km)

Temperature: 81°F (27°C)　　Video: 6 min 05 sec

Camera: Digital Camera 16MP　　Wind: SE, 7 mi/h (11 km/h)

Estimated Size of Object: 4.4 ft (1.35 m) Visibility: Sunny

This object was in the same vicinity as the **Vertical Blue – Plasma 1** filmed one hour earlier, but moving further east. I am certain that this is one and the same object. Some of the stills look like the previous object, but overall it envelops and consumes the underlying bluish yet transparent object with a heavy yellow glow. In my original notes I had written that this and the previous object (even if they are not the same objects) may still have come through the "portal" located southwest.

If this is the case, then the object's behaviour had drastically changed from flashing and electrically discharging in a haphazard manner at the lower half of the vertical object, to this bluish oblong object that after initially also discharging, was completely enveloped in a bright yellow glow. The incredibly strange thing is that this second object followed a predictable cycle from the time the bluish transparent oblong object was present, to when the enveloping yellow glow or plasma returned to the bluish transparent object.

If you recall, plasma is considered to be the fourth state of matter, due to its unique properties. It's a gas where the atoms are ionised, which means there are free negatively charged electrons and positively charged ions. These charged particles can be controlled by electromagnetic fields, allowing the plasma to be used as a controllable reactive gas. Plasma is used in many high-tech industries, for instance in making microelectronic or electronic devices such as semiconductors, and in making features on chips for computers.

It's very interesting to note that scientists tell us plasma is the most common state of matter in the universe, as stars, lightning, the auroras, and that some flames consist of plasma. Plasma is used in television, neon signs and fluorescent lights.

Two videos of this object were filmed four minutes apart and the annoying thing is that I feel pressured to occasionally provide a reference point for perspective, such as a tree. Many people write comments on the internet about UFO footages being filmed in close-up only without a reference point that will determine direction and speed. The problem with this is that - as was the case in this video - I panned out to provide perspective, but as I zoomed back in I lost sight of the object, forcing me to start again, and losing valuable time. The object was moving away from me and therefore getting smaller, so it was difficult to relocate.

There are many cycles in the world and universe: **planetary cycles** - climate and weather cycles, geological cycles; **organic cycles** - agricultural cycles, biological and medical cycles, brain wave cycles; **physics cycles** - mathematics of waves and cycles, electromagnetic spectrum cycles, sound wave cycles. There are other secular cycles such as military and war, social and cultural cycles, religious, mythological, and spiritual cycles, music, and rhythm cycles, and also economic and business cycles.

In summary, I have timed the cycle related to this object, and there is undeniable evidence that the object is speeding up over several minutes by 66.66%, which is strange. A wave is periodic motion where the particles of the medium oscillate back and forth about a fixed position. The period for such a particle to complete one full cycle is also the time which it takes to complete the cycle, in seconds, minutes, hours, or a fraction thereof.

The number of complete cycles during a given period of time is the frequency of a wave. The mathematical relationship between the frequency (f) of the wave and the period (T) of the wave is $f = 1 / T$. So what is speeding up in our object, as is evidenced by the lesser time taken to complete one cycle? As we discussed previously, it's almost as if we are seeing quantum mechanics in the macro again.

Even though we are not seeing the classical sine wave here, the effect over time as per the graph below is a periodic wave. We see a strict transpiration of a periodic cycle, as far as timing is concerned, for the two distinct visual appearances. One has a bluish, oblong, and transparent appearance; and the other has a completely enveloping yellow plasma type of effect, returning to its original appearance where the cycle repeats at a faster rate.

There seems to be a strong resemblance between this sighting and the earlier chapter, **HAQSR - High Altitude Quantum Singularity Reactor**, although the position of the earlier sighting seems to be where most sightings enter and leave from in the south-western portal location, but this one was nowhere near that area. I believe there is a second portal to the northeast, some distance from where this object was sighted high in the east, and this gives me the impression that it's probably not a **HAQSR**. I am currently investigating whether this also might in fact be a portal, which would make sense as it follows a straight line and is dead centre from the one in the southwest connecting to the one in the northeast. I will require more sightings in this eastern area before I present my findings.

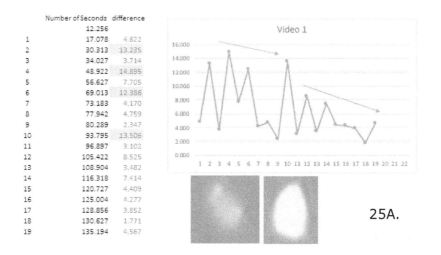

	Number of Seconds	difference
	12.256	
1	17.078	4.822
2	30.313	13.235
3	34.027	3.714
4	48.922	14.895
5	56.627	7.705
6	69.013	12.386
7	73.183	4.170
8	77.942	4.759
9	80.289	2.347
10	93.795	13.506
11	96.897	3.102
12	105.422	8.525
13	108.904	3.482
14	116.318	7.414
15	120.727	4.409
16	125.004	4.277
17	128.856	3.852
18	130.627	1.771
19	135.194	4.567

25A.

Image 25A: The number of seconds taken to cycle through blue transparent form until end of the plasma state where it repeats the cycle. Down trend and smaller peaks means it's speeding up.

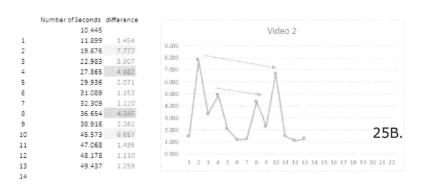

	Number of Seconds	difference
	10.445	
1	11.899	1.454
2	19.676	7.777
3	22.983	3.307
4	27.865	4.882
5	29.936	2.071
6	31.089	1.153
7	32.309	1.220
8	36.654	4.345
9	38.916	2.262
10	45.573	6.657
11	47.068	1.495
12	48.178	1.110
13	49.437	1.259
14		

25B.

Image 25B: The second video shows the high peaks at a cycle of around 7-8 seconds, while in the first video high peaks were in a cycle of about 14 seconds. This equates to about a 66% speed increase in the cycle after about 6 minutes.

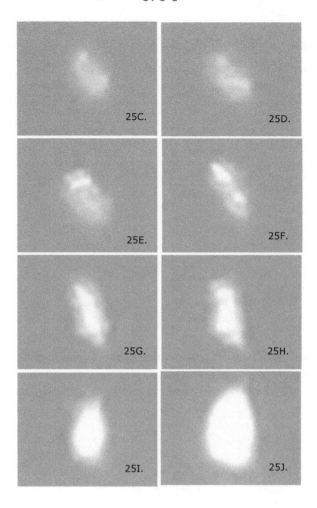

Images 25C–25F: Object transformations through one cycle showing the initial blue transparent object.
Images 25G–25J: Object transformations through one cycle showing the final yellow glow enveloping the object.

Please have a look at the videos as these photos alone do not provide the full convincing story, tempering the delight with a grain of salt. After watching the videos slowed down and at normal speed, I found it difficult to be certain that there is any spinning, although there certainly is substantial morphing during the recurring cycle.

Are we again observing quantum physics at the macroscopic level? In 2011 a unique experiment was devised to see if quantum properties can survive into the macro level. For over 100 years quantum physics was concerned with and related to the world of the infinitely small. Researchers from the University of Geneva had successfully entangled crystals, therefore crossing over from the atomic dimension into our dimension. Since then two optic fibres have also been entangled, which until now has only been unique in the world of quantum mechanics.

Quantum entanglement is when pairs or groups of particles such as photons are generated or interact physically, where a laser beam fired through a certain type of crystal can cause individual photons to be split into pairs of entangled photons. The quantum state of each particle cannot be described independently of the others, even when the particles are separated by a large distance.

Experiments to prove quantum entanglement have been devised by physicist John Bell. They involve entangling particles, then separating them, moving them off in different directions, and measuring to see if they maintain that so-called "spooky" connection or "action at a distance" even while physically separated.

If scientists can successfully entangle not only miniscule objects, but also macroscopic crystals visible to the naked eye, then the object discussed in this chapter may well be emulating something from the atomic dimension yet to become visible to us. Was it preparing to launch itself inter-dimensionally through an existing portal or an existing wormhole as a theoretical passage through space-time, creating shortcuts for long journeys across the universe? Wormholes have been predicted by the Theory of General Relativity; but as far as our calculations and mathematics indicate, the wormholes bring with them the dangers of sudden collapse, high radiation, and dangerous contact with exotic matter.

We have previously discussed NASA's confirmation of the existence of magnetic star-gate portals in many locations above earth. These portals are deemed to be in the vicinity of 40,000mi (65,000 km) to 56,000 mi (90,000 km), where the geomagnetic field bumps up against the passing solar wind, resulting in a direct pathway between the earth and the sun; but as mentioned before it's my belief that these portals may also occur closer to earth.

Whether true or not, the Bermuda Triangle is regarded as one of the famous portals to another dimension or interstellar space. First acknowledged in the early 1950s, it's a vast, mysterious area off the Florida coast where huge military ships and planes have been "lost" without any plausible explanation from the government or the military as to why.

The Philadelphia Experiment was an alleged military experiment reported to have been carried out by the US Navy at the Philadelphia Naval Shipyard in Philadelphia, Pennsylvania, sometime around October 28, 1943. It was an attempt to render a ship invisible to enemy radar. This was to be accomplished by strategically placing electromagnets around the ship with the intention of absorbing or deflecting radar waves. When activated, the electromagnetic field would extend out from the ship and divert radar waves around the ship, making the *Eldridge* invisible to radar receivers.

When the actual test was conducted, several unexpected and bizarre effects occurred. As the electromagnetic field increased in strength, it began to extend as far as 100 yards out from the ship in all directions, forming a large encapsulating area around the ship. Within this field, the ship became fuzzy and a greenish haze formed around the vessel, obscuring it from view. Eventually, the only visible object was the outline of the hull of the *Eldridge* where it entered the water. Then, to the amazement of onlookers, the entire ship vanished from view.

To the amazement of all involved, the *Eldridge* vanished and the true power of the electromagnetic field that had been created became apparent. The *Eldridge* had not only vanished from the view of observers in Philadelphia, it had vanished from Philadelphia altogether. The ship had been instantly transported several hundred miles from Philadelphia to Norfolk, Virginia. After a few minutes, the ship once again vanished, to return to Philadelphia.

To the Navy, the test had succeeded beyond their wildest dreams. Not only had they rendered a ship invisible to radar, they had made it optically invisible as well, not to mention causing the vessel to teleport hundreds of miles in a matter of minutes. For the crew, however, it did not end too well as when the power was eventually turned off they were found to have been fused to the bulkheads, decks, and railings of the ship.

As has been the case many times, I zoomed out from the object and eventually lost sight of it as I attempted to zoom back in. It is impossible to say whether it vanished or just moved to another section of sky.

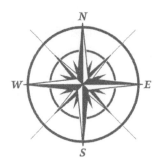

CHAPTER 24

Bright Yellow-Orange Orb 4

Date: 7 Dec 2017   Angle: West, 80°

Time: 4:29 am   Direction: W to SE

Height: 9,842 ft (1.86 mi, 3 km)   Photo: 0

Horizontal Distance: 0 ft (0 mi, 0 km)

Temperature: 50°F (10°C)   Video: 4 min 13 sec

Camera: Digital Camera 16MP   Wind: N, 6.8 mi/h (11 km/h)

Estimated Size of Object: 2.6 ft (0.8 m) Visibility: Clear

On this Thursday morning I was on my way to work when for some strange reason I was drawn to look at the sky. I reduced my speed and I was compelled to pull over and focus my attention towards the sky - nowhere in particular, just towards the black velvet sky. Pulling down the window, I noticed a bright yellow light in the sky so I jumped out. I knew straight away that it was not a helicopter or a light plane, not only because there were no strobing lights but also because there was no noise at all. I grabbed my trusty camera (which I now take with me everywhere), removed the lens cap, manually focused, and started shooting.

I had stopped on a generally busy road but fortunately at the time not even one car was in sight, so it was very quiet except for the zooming mechanism of the camera. If you did not notice this light moving slowly, you could easily mistake it for a star or even Venus. I certainly could see it moving, and it was moving in my direction. At one point it continued directly overhead, as has happened for me on many occasions with prominent sightings. I recall that when the object had passed overhead I could just make out what appeared to be a green and red light below it.

If the mathematical estimate I used is correct, then the size of the object must only be about 3 feet (1 m). Looking back at the video on my computer, I could not see what I had thought were green and yellow lights below when I was looking through the camera viewfinder. Correspondingly, additional observations are noticed during playback; for example, halfway through the video there appears to be a second object flying from below screen to the right.

It's incredible that such a small object as this can still be seen so high in the sky. How can I tell the distance and height in the sky? It's obviously just a best guess, where I mentally compare the object to some small light planes, especially the ones used by parachute jumpers flying at 13,000 feet (4,000 m) which I have seen many times. It's difficult to see in the video, but the object just followed a straight path with a slight curve from west to south-east, maintaining the exact same height. The speed also seems to be the same, at approximately 9 mph (14 km/h).

I find it incredible to think that if this object is bright enough to be seen from such a great height (as if it was only 50-100 feet away), then it must be giving off an enormous amount of plasma energy. Is it under intelligent control? It seems so. Being so small, could it be a living glowing organism such as we see in the oceans of the world? Probably not. I say that only because of the occasional disc shape appearance, although changing shape to something else is common - in this case from circular to rectangular.

Just on the subject of strange marine creatures that are self-luminous, namely bioluminescent: the luminescence is used in defence, as the light temporarily stuns a potential attacker. Some creatures that we know of are masters of luminous disguise; they use light as a cloak to evade predators, but appear to be see-though.

If the object's size is only 2.6 feet (0.8 m), other than an alien investigative probe, what else could it be?

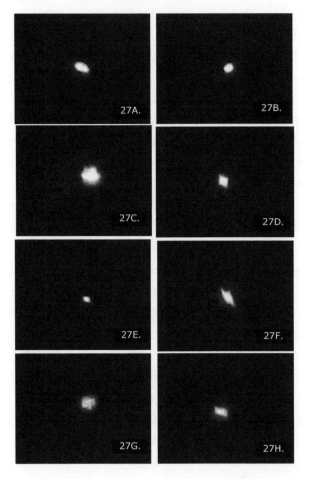

Images 26A–26H: The object seems to initially appear white in colour, then become more yellow-orange in colour. The orb also constantly morphs from disc, circular to rectangular shapes.

Most reports of this type of orb describe them as orange only in colour, and I would tend to agree, but I do feel that there is some yellow present. Reports of bright, glowing orange objects in the sky have been growing over the years, with no explanation of what they are and what they are doing.

The questions often asked are: What the hell are they? Why are they orange in colour? Where do they come from, and what do they want? As mentioned before, the orbs are somewhat different to the solid metallic UFOs I have presented in this book, such as the H- shaped and disc-shaped ones. As seen clearly in the stills and slowed down video, they have the ability to morph easily in size and shape, and apparently some even split into multiple secondary orbs.

Unlike those seen by other witnesses, a high percentage of the UFOs I have seen, whether metallic or orbs, follow a direct path and do not perform erratic movements. My calculations indicate that they are small; and the only facts that I have so far are that they appear with a general high frequency in similar areas to where they were last seen, giving the impression that they have a role as observers.

Conversely, there are long periods of inactivity where they are not sighted for a while, giving the impression that they have moved onto another area or that their task has been completed and they are not required until a later stage. Hold onto this thought, as I believe that I have discovered a pattern to explain why their appearance wanes during certain times of the year and increases at other times.

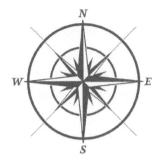

CHAPTER 25

Bright Yellow-Orange Orb 5

Date: 22 December 2017   Angle: SW, 45°

Time: 4:20 am   Direction: SW to NE to SE

Height: 9,842 ft (1.86 mi, 3 km)   Photo: 0

Horizontal Distance: 6,562 ft (1.2 mi, 2 km)

Temperature: 55°F (13°C)   Video: 4 min 15 sec

Camera: Digital Camera 16MP   Wind: N, 3.7 mi/h (6 km/h)

Estimated Size of Object: 1.9 ft (0.6 m) Visibility: Passing clouds

There is an interesting aspect to this sighting, and I kind of wanted to have fun with it. This time I tried to see if these yellow-orange orbs are predictable to such a degree that I can sit and wait for them at one destination; and secondly, I wanted to see if I can jump in my car to go to the second destination about 1.7 mi (2.7 km) away where I have also seen them repeatedly.

I thought that I might be able to determine whether I am seeing the same object or a different one, but mathematically rather than by a visual method. If it continued at the same pace from the first destination, I thought I could probably work out how to outpace the object with my car, and will catch it at the second destination.

I estimated the object's usual speed over a short distance with one easy calculation, using the time taken to travel about 50 metres, from my backyard to the street, which I estimated to be about 5-6 seconds. In this case the speed is about 19 mi/hr (30 km/hr). At this speed it would take approximately six minutes to reach the second destination 1.7 mi (2.7 km) away. Unfortunately, this is not be enough time for me to reach the second destination, when you take into consideration 40 km/h speed limits and traffic lights.

So, judging purely by the times the object was seen at Destination 1 (approximately 4:20 - 4:25 am when travelling south to north), and the times seen at Destination 2 when travelling also from a southerly direction (also being 4:20 - 4:25 am), I would suggest that there is a high possibility it is the same object, especially since it would only take about six minutes.

Another interesting fact is that the yellow-orange orbs always seem to arrive in and depart from a section of sky in the southwestern area that suspiciously appears to be a portal. I say that because (as you will see if you refer to the sighting documented in the chapter on HAQSR) I believe the highly energetic and erratic nature of that object in the exact section of sky in question had the objective to create a portal for inter-dimensional or interstellar travel.

My other evidence is that I have seen objects appearing exactly like a star, moving north to south and disappearing just as they reached that part of the sky in the early hours of the morning. Not only that, it is my belief that as these orbs travel a short distance to Destination 2, they bank and turn towards the southeast.

So, back to this yellow-orange orb. I drove to Destination 2 at 4:00 am and waited patiently. It was a very still and cool morning with just a hint of cloud in the distance. Jupiter was rising in the east and was very bright indeed as I pulled down the window and stared intently at the southwestern sky, at the same time glancing at my watch. The only sign of life was a white cat wandering around, and the occasional fox, which we tend to see across Melbourne's metropolitan area.

I could not believe my eyes when it appeared right on time, just before 4:20 am, and slowly moved in my direction. It was very surreal knowing that I predicted this object's appearance to the exact time. I quickly grabbed my camera and jumped out of the car. It did not take long for me to manually focus on the object and commence filming.

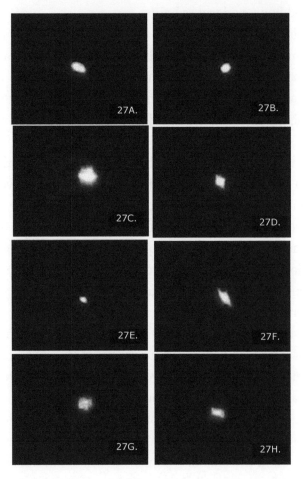

Images 27A–27H: Stills from yet another yellow-orange orb. These objects always seem to fly at the same height, same speed, and on the very same predictable paths.

Date	Location	Time	Direction	Chapter
4/06/2017	Destination 1	5:59 PM	from S	12
2/07/2017	Destination 1	5:36 PM	from E	13
3/07/2017	Destination 1	6:19 PM	from W	14
31/07/2017	Destination 1	6:37 PM	n/a	N/A
7/12/2017	Destination 2	4:29 AM	W to SE	28
9/12/2017	Destination 1	4:30 AM	W to SE	N/A
10/12/2017	Destination 1	4:25 AM	NE to SW	N/A
15/12/2017	Destination 1	4:27 AM	NE to SW	N/A
16/12/2017	Destination 1	4:27 AM	SW to N	N/A
17/12/2017	Destination 1	4:27 AM	N to SW	N/A
19/12/2017	Destination 2	4:15 AM	N to SE	N/A
20/12/2017	Destination 2	4:25 AM	SW to NE to SE (arc)	N/A
21/12/2017	Destination 1	4:25 AM	SW to NW	N/A
22/12/2017	Destination 2	4:20 AM	SW to NE to SE (arc)	29
6/01/2018	Destination 1	4:05 AM	SW to N	N/A
3/02/2018	Destination 1	5:59 AM	W to SE	36
4/02/2018	Destination 1	5:07 AM	W to SE	37

The above table shows some of the yellow-orange orb sightings which I have documented in 2017. Highlighted in yellow is the predictable nature of the object moving south to north on 5 separate occasions. Unfortunately, N/A refers to the unsuccessful attempts at filming the object. Please take note of the dates, as I have something interesting to disclose later.

I remember that I caught the object early as it was coming in my direction, when it slowly banks ever so slightly into a right arc or turn. It came from a southwesterly direction and continued in a southeasterly direction, maintaining the same height and speed of 10,000 feet (3 km) and about 19 mi/hr (30 km/hr).

These strange balls of light seem to continually morph and change shape when slowed down and magnified. They seem to travel at very similar speed and height, following predictable paths and times. Picture this: it's a clear sky with stars all around and there's a marvellous view, then out of nowhere one of the stars is noticeably moving. When you are lucky enough to first see these things in the late afternoon or early hours of the morning, you too will react by shaking your head in disbelief.

These orbs appear as spheres to many people until they are magnified, revealing their true shapes; and they have been around for years. When I look at old grainy videos on the internet, I find it difficult to conclude whether they are the same kinds of objects that I have been observing. Some look solid and metallic, while the objects I have seen are nothing like that, but glowing. Others have observed the orbs change direction mid-flight like an aircraft, while the ones I have seen remain steady on course with only a slight bend in their path, similar to what happens as an aircraft banks when changing direction.

The consistent explanations over the years have been that these unexplained luminous objects in the sky could be glowing plasmas resulting from natural configurations of electromagnetic fields. Even the military has been interested in incorporating such a phenomenon into their cache of weapons. The suggestion that these plasmas could be used for novel military applications stems from the idea that since charged masses can appear as visual, infra-red and radar targets, they could be useful as decoy targets.

The British and the Russians have shown interest in plasma technologies for radar signature reduction or control, amongst other potential uses such as passive electromagnetic spectrum energy-absorbers and weapons with very high-power energy generation. There are theories that the technology is so far advanced in the military that it is well beyond the public domain, hence similar theories (which I do not participate in) that some of the discs, triangle and boomerang objects sighted are advanced man-made technologies. The objects I have seen and documented in this book are alien; they are not of this world. Whether they are interdimensional beings and objects accidentally or deliberately released at the hand of man, which I will discuss later, they are interstellar objects that are here for a reason, and we still need to find out.

As I was filming the object in this chapter I was faced with the prospect that a large gum tree 40 feet away would soon obscure the object; after 30 seconds you can hear me frantically repositioning myself until I re-located the object again and resumed filming it in frame. As usual, the object seemed to be on a mission and wanted to go somewhere, but at the same time I sensed that it was observing the surroundings.

The term "orb" used freely throughout this book is not used by the Mutual UFO Network (MUFON) under the banner of UFOs. Nor will they classify them as Unidentified Aerial Vehicles (UAVs). Field investigators use the label "Unknown Others" when reporting these phenomena or circles and spheres. The MUFON sighting database has reports filed daily from around the world with some very good video evidence backing up the sightings.

The question remains. Are they technologically advanced craft, some sort of biological entity, or interdimensionally related? The essential point is that these silent yellow-orange orbs seem to be objects of advanced technological capability, and they have faint outlines and auras, as can be seen in some of my stills from the videos. The feeling one gets is that there is an overall, possibly mechanical, aspect to them, yet it is not directly obvious.

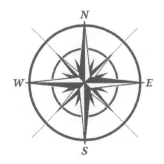

CHAPTER 26

The Return of the Golden Man

Date: 26 December 2017   Angle: W, 65°

Time: 9:54 am   Direction: W to NE

Height: 9,842 feet (1.86 mi, 3 km)   Photo: 0

Horizontal Distance: 6,562 feet (1.2 mi, 2 km)

Temperature: 66°F (19°C)   Video: 9 min 11 sec

Camera: Digital Camera 16MP   Wind: N, 4.3 mi/h (7 km/h)

Estimated Size of Object: 6.2 ft (1.9 m) Visibility: Passing clouds

I could not believe my eyes when I noticed this reflecting object in the west with the all-too-familiar golden shine. Surely it cannot be, I thought. Has the Golden Man returned? As I zoomed in closer I was immediately satisfied that it was the Golden Man, but it was not in the recognisable human form I had witnessed back in October. The human form seemed fleeting this time round, as it morphed in and out of the human form.

It was only late 2017 when I read about an Italian-American nuclear physicist dismissed by mainstream scientists as instigating fringe science theories. I admire how he stands his ground and does not budge as he accuses them of conspiracies against novel science.

The claims are that there is a conspiracy to suppress or not investigate novel theories which may conflict with established scientific theories, such as Einstein's Theory of Relativity. According to the physicist, many institutions have an effective conspiracy in place, and institutions receive funding and have established entire departments dedicated to long-established theories. These same institutions refuse to challenge the current well-established scientific theories with new theories.

He argues that some theoretical physicists, who have received the Nobel Prize in Physics for their contributions to the study of unification of the weak force and electromagnetic interactions between elementary particles, have conspired to stop him from conducting research which might have led to the inapplicability of part of Einstein's Theory of Relativity while he was at Harvard. Some of his complaints were that published papers he submitted to peer-reviewed journals were rejected because they were controlled by a group of physicists.

Lawsuits alleging the suppression of his scientific ideas have been filed. Some of the so-called "crackpot" ideas and theories may be supported by sections of this book. It was reported in January 2016 that an optics, nuclear physics and energy company claims to have detected "invisible entities" living in the earth's atmosphere. Pictures were published that scientists say prove that "invisible alien entities ARE here on Earth".

The claim is that while searching for evidence of anti-matter in space they stumbled across an "invisible life form" in the earth's skies above, that was possibly studying us. The nuclear physicist used a modified telescope developed to try to prove the existence of theoretical anti-matter galaxies, anti-matter cosmic rays and anti-matter asteroids, and inadvertently discovered invisible entities instead.

It is documented that the telescope has been able to pick up a life form which cannot be seen by the naked eye, binoculars, or traditional telescopes. He explains that he is unsure what these biological entities are as they become visible only through cameras attached to his telescope.

The strange **Golden Man** was clearly not only seen by the camera but also by the naked eye. I believe that all objects related to ufology - from discs to glowing orbs to entities such as the **Golden Man** - are interdimensional objects, but that there are differences between them. As you will see later, I believe that most of the objects in this book have appeared because of man's intervention, while the familiar UFOs such as metallic discs and other vehicular craft may also be interdimensional but only as a method of traversing the huge distance between galaxies.

Are these entities, then, visitors from other "realities" or "dimensions" that coexist separately alongside our own? Some paranormal researchers believe this is a multidimensional para-physical phenomenon that is largely indigenous to planet Earth. People consider that the correct explanation of UFOs is in terms of spiritualistic phenomena, but I believe that there is confusion when encapsulating all UFOs under the one banner. I have narrowed these into two distinct categories: first, the extremely rare cases of metallic craft such as discs; and second, orbs and the like, which are more common.

The more scientists push the notion that interstellar UFOs do not really exist due to the vast distances between stars, the more confusion will exist that all UFOs must then be interdimensional objects – and therefore we do not have to explain impossibilities such as faster-than-light travel, anti-gravity, and other methods of propulsion. They are comfortable in thinking that UFOs are not spacecraft, but rather devices that travel between different realities. Another popular reasoning is that reports of the appearance and disappearance of UFOs by witnesses or radar operators are due to the UFOs entering and leaving our dimension. The "Glyfada, Athens (Greece) Red Orb", anyone?

The commonality between all four separate sightings involving the Golden Man in this book (not including the fully formed being with the long flowing tether attached to the side of the neck in Chapter 21) is that they are all morphing shapes, sometimes with clear repetitious cycles, occasionally displaying the letter B or number 8; and it seems to repeat by collapsing into a globule of either pure golden self-luminosity of varying intensity or reflecting off the morning sun whose ecliptic path is to the right side of camera.

Please refer to the baffling footage and photo extracts on YouTube. In some of the footage you can make out what appears to be a small length of tether beneath the object, but it was rather difficult to frame the object properly in a very short space of time; and the fact that it. flew directly overhead increased the difficulty as I strained to keep it in view then lost it completely in the glare of the sun. At times - as can be seen in the video and extracts - when the object collects into itself as one large globule that reflects off the sun, it then begins to look very similar to some of the other objects outlined in this book such as the High Altitude Quantum Singularity Reactor (HAQSR), which seem to be self-luminous rather than reflecting the sun.

The occasional spinning and erratic behaviour of the object, and the occasional tubular formations, are very peculiar; they can also be seen in other objects discussed in this book, including the HAQSR. The other matter of peculiarity is that, as happens most of the time after these major sightings, a strange looking balloon also becomes visible. In this case there were two. One was nine minutes later and another, even stranger, one was 30 minutes later at the exact same spot.

I believe that I have discovered a distinct correlation between CERN and these objects, but not the usual metallic disc type UFO (more on this later). As three-dimensional beings, we cannot visualise four-dimensional space, or the higher 9, 10, 11 or even higher dimensions hypothesised by physicists. How would we then directly visualise an object or being that is present in these dimensions?

We can see the result of their existence, but only as a cross-section of the reality they exist in. For instance, if a four-dimensional object was about to pass through three-dimensional space (our world), we would see a three-dimensional object that keeps changing shape and size, as I have seen with the Golden Man in this chapter. In some sections of the video and stills taken from it, where I remain at the same level of zoom, the object noticeably changes not only by shape but by size as well. We can see this readily when a three-dimensional object passes through a two-dimensional space.

Imagine a pyramid (three-dimensional) passing through a flat plane like a table top (two-dimensional). From our point of view, as we are living on this table top or two-dimensional world, we would see a point that grows larger and into a square.

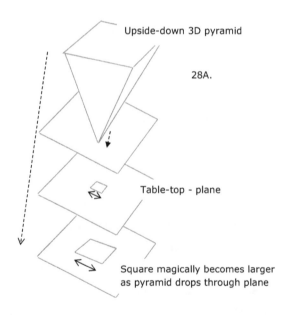

Upside-down 3D pyramid

28A.

Table-top - plane

Square magically becomes larger
as pyramid drops through plane

Image 28A: As the upside-down pyramid enters the table top, the two-dimensional beings on the table top will suddenly see a square mysteriously appear and grow larger, then disappear as it goes right through the plane.

Our imagination will not allow us to project our consciousness onto a world so very different from ours - our imagination gets in our way. Visualising uses three-dimensional features in our brain that prevents us from allowing our imagination to construct reality in a higher dimension. However, the understanding is that we can train our brain to fill in the blank, just as we do all the time when we look at photos or watch images on our computer screens. We see a picture which is two-dimensional, and with the help of visual cues and our imagination we reproduce it as three-dimensional. Our minds reconstruct the three-dimensional world all around us as our brains combine the two-dimensional images passing through our eyes.

We can compare the tesseract to a three-dimensional cube. A tesseract is a four-dimensional hypercube, a cross formed by cubes when folded, and represented in our three-dimensional world by a cube. The three-dimensional cube is represented in the two-dimensional world as a square. When you are looking purely at an image of a cube it is only two-dimensional, but with all the intuitive and different techniques utilised by your brain, you reconstruct the three-dimensional nature of the object from the simplified image. The exact same analogies apply for projecting 4D objects into 3D space, and then of course into two-dimensional space to make an image out of it as seen by two-dimensional beings.

For so many years scientists and science fiction writers have contemplated the possibilities of higher dimensions and their evil inhabitants which on rare occasions appear in our realm, as in the writings of the early 20th century horror writer H.P. Lovecraft.

	Number of Seconds	difference
	5.612	
1	10.075	4.463
2	19.514	9.439
3	38.885	19.371
4	49.894	11.009
5	5.207	
6	18.968	13.761
7	48.410	29.442
8	55.570	7.160
9	60.000	4.430
10	66.177	6.177
11	86.000	19.823
12		
13		
14		
15		
16		
17		
18		
19		

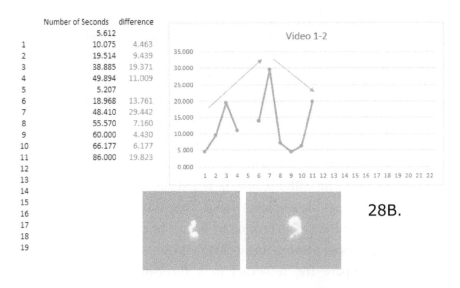

28B.

Image 28B: The number of seconds taken to cycle through repeating shapes, from Image 30C to 30D; earlier in the video, uptrend indicates it is slowing down, while towards the end of the video downtrend and smaller peaks mean it's speeding up.

We understand that the universe has three spatial dimensions and one time dimension (not to be confused with the four spatial dimensions we have discussed thus far), but we only see in two dimensions and feel in three dimensions. The brain uses clues such as motion, relative size and so on to provide impetus to "visually see" the third dimension. The point is that if we were able to see in three-dimensions we could see through objects and around them, just as we do by feeling around objects.

What chance have we then to visually understand true four-dimensional objects, let alone the fourth dimension? How did the "Golden Man" progressively shift into our realm of awareness? Was it just an extremely realistic hologram that only in appearance was a three-dimensional object projected from a higher dimension? In the short segments of video, why does the object cycle through repetitive shapes?

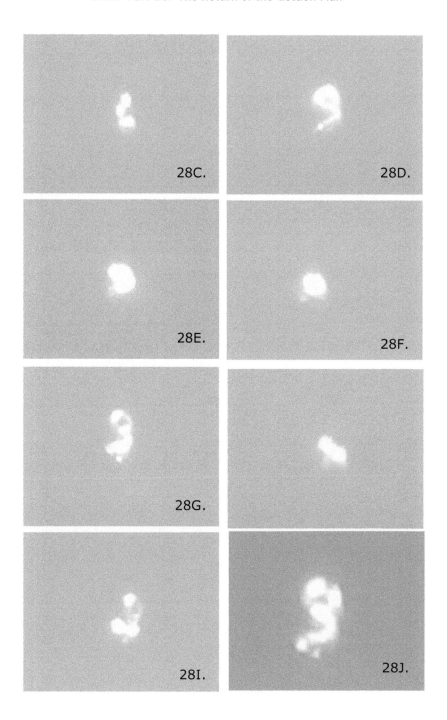

28C.

28D.

28E.

28F.

28G.

28I.

28J.

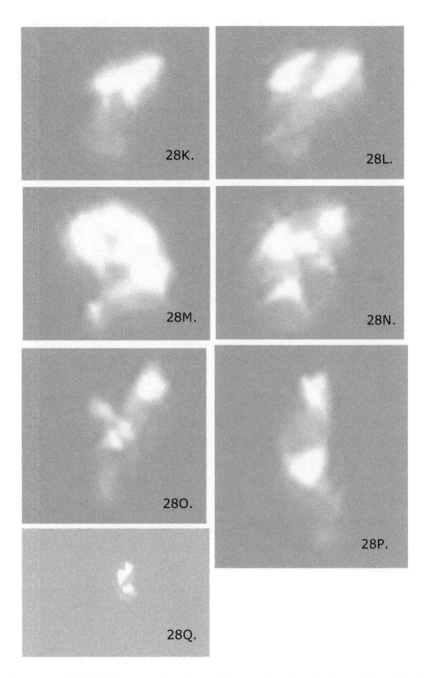

28K.

28L.

28M.

28N.

28O.

28P.

28Q.

Images 28C-28P: *The many transformations undertaken by the golden object.*

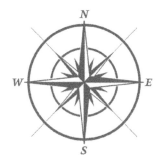

CHAPTER 27

Greetings from the Fourth Dimension

In this section I would like to discuss what I have come to believe the Golden Man was and where he came from. If this is not a science fiction movie played out in real life, then I don't know how else to describe it. I have worked on the premise that the Golden Man is a four-dimensional being appearing in our three-dimensional world, witnessed over six days, and that there were six distinct stages in its appearance.

Chapter 15: Precursor - "Golden Man" 1. This sighting comprised morphing events of a figure 8 with a small thin tether below it, gold nugget or cluster/blob, S-shape and finally, four sectioned nodes.

Chapter 17: Precursor - "Golden Man" 2. **11 days later**, this was mainly four sectioned nodes with larger dual tethers below it. Object disappears through portal.

Chapter 18: HAQSR. **One day later**, after multiple transitions from a solid grey spinning object, it turns glowing yellow and disappears through portal.

Chapter 19: Precursor - "Golden Man" 3. **One hour later**, object re-appears through portal in our reality.

Chapter 21: "The Golden Man". **Five hours later**, in the right profile this was a "fully" formed human figure, except for arms, with a heavy tether from its neck area.

Chapter 28: "The Return of the Golden Man". **9 weeks later**, this was a heavily morphed sighting comprising the familiar nodes, but in the vertical this time; the occasional S-shape appearance; and finally the gold nugget or cluster/blob type appearance.

To me there seems to be a logical progression to these six stages, as Stages One and Two are where the object suddenly appeared in our third dimension as a solid object, from a fully formed figure eight to one where four sectioned nodes are prevalent. These nodes appear to be possibly the two legs, body and head, all the while retaining a tether. The important element in all this is what I believe will turn books like *Flatland: A Romance of Many Dimensions* (first published in 1884), and other books like it, on its head. The focus of this book is a two-dimensional world occupied by geometric figures, and their visit to the one-dimensional world where they try and convince the occupants about the existence of the two-dimensional world. Throw a three-dimensional sphere in the mix and a well-written book gets very interesting indeed.

As we are three-dimensional beings, it is virtually impossible for us to visualise four-dimensional space or beings and objects within it. However, science tells us that we can see the effects of their cross-sections as they move in and out of the lower dimensions. As previously describe, an upside-down three-dimensional pyramid moving in a two-dimensional plane will magically appear to someone in that world as a point which gradually grows into a square, progressively increasing in size, and then disappears. The same would apply to a hand from a four-dimensional creature which, with five fingers protruding into our three-dimensional space and then withdrawing, will appear as five separate spheres growing in size (depending on how far the invasion extends in our space) and then getting smaller as the hand is withdrawn.

I get all that and it makes sense to me. But if indeed I have witnessed a being from a higher dimension such as the fourth dimension, then I have a problem in that it did not remain as an indiscernible shape for long. On the fifth sighting, there was a distinct human figure in the sky that looked like a solid gold three-dimensional object. Perhaps this "living" interdimensional being somehow has the ability to do the impossible and manipulate space to fully appear as a solid three-dimensional object in our world, literally leaving its own world behind. I will disclose later where I think these aerial anomalies are coming from, as they fit a distinct pattern that I still find hard to believe.

Remember that the Golden Man looks like pure gold and is a solid form, as it slowly rotates and reflects the sun off its surface. We may never know what these strange objects look like in their four-dimensional world, or whether the transformation into jellyfish-type objects, yellow-orange orbs, possibly the H-shaped objects and so on, is due to instant full teleportation into our world. With its disappearance and reappearance, the "Glyfada, Athens (Greece) Red Orb" from an earlier chapter displays similarities in behaviour to objects described in the book *Flatland*. The same goes for the morphing "Golden Man" in the first, second, third, fourth and sixth sightings, as it moves from a higher dimension to ours.

If it's not a real solid object that moved through our reality from the fourth–dimension, then, due to the many planes of differing time it could be evolving as one moving object with a natural time progression, like a movie reel. A four-dimensional object may appear as three-dimensional, as it moves in our reality in sections like a movie or the familiar flip book with cartoon images that seem to come alive as you flip the pages.

There is a possibility that the universe is four-dimensional, but we are only aware of three of those dimensions. So when a four-dimensional object crosses over to our three-dimensional space of perception and existence (cube-shaped space) we would only perceive the three-dimensional component of the four-dimensional object. As it moves in the four-dimensional space, we will suddenly see the appearance of the three-dimensional component of the object move through our realm until it disappears back into the fourth-dimension.

The possibility may then exist that two sets of life have evolved in parallel over multiple dimensions, with different evolutionary appearances. It is good to suggest such unproved theories and bring them to the forum; but I believe that I have evidence, whether circumstantial or part thereof, that the appearance of these objects has a direct link with the activation and deactivation of CERN, the Large Hadron Collider.

The current quantum mechanics theory mathematically proves that our universe has four spatial dimensions and one dimension of time. The string theory, superstring and ultimately the M, membrane, theory of the universe, predict these higher dimensions, while Einstein's Theory of Relativity predicts only three spatial dimensions and one time dimension. The three-dimensional universe can only allow large black holes to exist, while the four-dimensional (or more) universe allows very small black holes to exist. If this becomes conclusive in experimentation, as may be the case at CERN, then it will prove that the universe is indeed of a higher dimension. Beyond that it may prove the existence of multiple universes.

Witnesses lucky enough to see solid metal UFOs notice the accompanying morphing ability, amongst other feats such as dramatic speeds and change in directions. Surely it's logical to assume that these extra-terrestrials are so technologically advanced that they have found a way to bend space to enable the ability to traverse between the stars. This is what we call interplanetary travel, but there is a problem with this if we do not also take inter-dimensionality into account due to the huge distances involved.

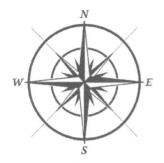

CHAPTER 28

H-Shaped Blue

Date: 1 January 2018 Angle: W, 75°

Time: 11:24 am   Direction: W to E

Height: 9,842 ft (1.86 mi, 3 km)   Photo: 0

Horizontal Distance: 6,562 ft (1.2 mi, 2 km)

Temperature: 70°F (21°C)   Video: 0 min 51 sec

Camera: Digital Camera 16MP   Wind: SW, 6.6 mi/h (9 km/h)

Estimated Size of Object: 4.2 ft (1.3 m) Visibility: Passing clouds

In the previous chapter we learnt that to enable space to be bent, beings need to traverse an extra dimension, piercing through higher dimensions. Bending space, creating wormholes, or utilising natural black holes, will require an enormous amount of matter-energy, making it unlikely that we can visualise this in our comparatively simple minds. Nevertheless, some of the objects I have witnessed, along with their behaviour in the sky, show that they have been doing something that resulted in them appearing and disappearing in a particular section of the sky as well as their morphing abilities.

Following on from the previous chapter, the popular mindset is that none of the limitations in Einstein's Theory of Relativity will apply when we utilise the more probable and simpler explanation that these beings are extra-dimensional beings.

If this "H-Shaped Blue" object was trying to cloak itself by matching the colour of the sky, it did not do a very good job, as the shiny flashes or reflection of the sun drew me directly towards it. The first thing I tried to establish was why the objects are all now coming from the west. It is not clear in the very small footage I took, but I distinctly recall that through the viewfinder I saw what looked like the H-Shaped object in late 2016. The only difference this time was that it did not appear metallic, reflecting off the sun. It was producing light shows that seemed to be headlights or rear lights on the craft. Granted, if the estimated size of 1.3 m is correct, then it is awfully small to be manned, but what's not to say that it is a surveillance craft or drone of some sort, or of course only part of a three-dimensional object entering our three-dimensional space. The spectacular footage from late 2016 quite clearly showed a metallic object reflecting the sun and releasing small orbs. It seems to me that if the yellow-orange orbs I have been seeing are between 1.5 and 2 metres, then the H-Shaped object from late 2016 should be 10 to 15 times as large, but of course this is not the case in my estimate.

Like previous sightings in this book, this object morphs from an H-shape to a single rod shape. I have wondered what the letter H would look like in the fourth dimension if it were not fully in the third dimension. No human as far as we know has ever perceived what the fourth dimension looks like, so we can only interpret and perceive the fourth dimension through projections. I will try to illustrate how to draw the H-shape in the fourth dimension similar to the tesseract, a four-dimensional cube, all the while understanding that our three-dimensional brains will not let us picture them because the idea is inconceivable. We cannot leave the realms of quantum physics if we are to understand what the higher dimensions, starting with the fourth, look like.

If I fail to do so, in some eyes, then at least it will become evident how complex the object will look to be in the fourth dimension.

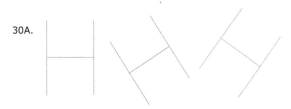

Image 30A: Draw three H-shapes at 45 degrees to each other

Image 30B: Overlay the three H-shapes to form a Hexagram or six-pointed star.

Image 30C: Extend the three outer sides

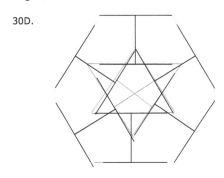

Image 30D: Add six H-Shapes around the perimeter along the lengths and extend the diagonal lines between the corners.

Basically, I was hoping to show what three pairs of H-shaped objects in three dimensions, perpendicular to each other and connecting their vertices, would look like. We can never truly imagine what the fourth dimension (perpendicular to our three dimensions) would look like, but we can create a two-dimensional projection of it.

New Year's Eve and New Year's Day came and went but this sighting will be one that I will never forget. I say that so much these days, that writing the words does not strike an impact any more.

Small UFOs are quite commonly witnessed by the public. Some of the dimensions quoted in reported sightings are even smaller than some of those presented in this book. Some are discs the size of 18 x 12 x 4 inches, almost like silent sophisticated drones, while others are about four or five feet in size. In mid 2017 I believe I saw a small grey disc speeding in front of me above the power poles while I was walking during the day. It was a moderately windy day, so initially I thought it was something picked up by the wind, but the disc shape soon became clear enough for me to grab my mobile in an attempt to take a video of it. I remember its speed was much faster than the wind as it moved in an arc or semi-circle in front of me. Unfortunately, the very short video came up with nothing. I estimated the disc to have been 18 inches (45 cm) across.

The important thing to take from this is that UFOs not only come in all shapes and sizes, but sometimes seem to be inanimate intelligently controlled craft (either manned or remote) and at other times biological living entities. Several layers below this are the descriptive categories of extra-terrestrial inter-dimensionality and extra-dimensionality for UFOs.

The fascination with UFOs has been with us for decades, and apart from videos and photos, hard evidence is still elusive.

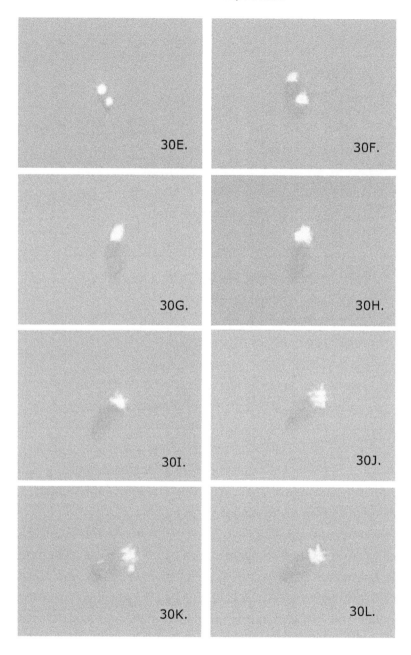

30E.

30F.

30G.

30H.

30I.

30J.

30K.

30L.

Images 30E-30L: The self-luminous "H-Shape", and at times morphing, UFO seemed to be cloaking against the blue sky, making it very difficult to focus.

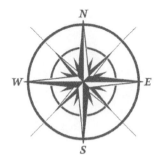

CHAPTER 29

The Hooded Man

Date: 2 January 2018 Angle: SW, 75°

Time: 08:41 am   Direction: SW to N

Height: 16,404 ft (3.10 mi, 5 km)   Photo: 0

Horizontal Distance: 6,562 ft (1.2 mi, 2 km)

Temperature: 64°F (18°C)   Video: 1 min 37 sec

Camera: Digital Camera 16MP   Wind: S, 08 mi/h (13 km/h)

Estimated Size of Object: 9.5 ft (2.9 m) Visibility: Partly sunny.

As always, when concluding any of my observations about any sighting, I refer to my first impressions. With the "Hooded Man" sighting, I was overwhelmed with feelings that I was looking at a hooded individual, and therefore this description stuck. Who needs the Hooded Man Ritual? This hypothetical supernatural ritual circulating the internet since November 2014, involves a lengthy preparation and cleansing process leading to a "Black Cab" magically appearing outside your residence and being driven by a hooded man. As I said, who needs it, when I saw in the sky what looked like a very tall slowly spinning hooded man heading towards me.

I had some idea of its height above the ground (approximately 15,000 feet) due to the type of sparse clouds around at the time. Using this figure and the field of view, focal length and so on, I was able to estimate the size to be quite significant, at over 9 feet. "The Hooded Man" was slowly spinning about the centre point, and was in a vertical position as with most sightings. This object had a definite counter-clockwise spin from my perspective; but the other absolutely profound - and always shocking - climax was how the object seemed to fly exactly overhead to the point that it was nearly impossible to continue filming.

It was just one day after the beautiful blue "cloaked" H-Shaped object first appeared, and from the time I went to sleep to when I got up, I so wished I would see it again. I made a note that whatever I did today I would ensure that I returned to the same site at the same time that I first saw it, which was late in the morning. Early the next morning I thought I would take the opportunity to visit a large hardware store located to the south-east, to buy some paint to freshen up my picket fence, which was in a bad state of disrepair.

Since it was the day after New Year's Day, everyone was still in holiday mode and sleeping in, so the roads were quiet that morning. I purchased the paint but as I walked to my car I was wondering why small cans of paint can be so expensive, while it makes much more economical sense to buy a larger can, as whatever is unused (usually three-quarters to half if you are lucky) will be stored in the shed in the hope that it will see the light of day once again, before it dries up and is hard.

It was a beautiful morning and there I was standing beside my car parked inside a massive carpark with unhindered views of the sky above. I hope that I am believed when I say that something made me stay and gaze at the sky just that little bit longer than the usual sideways glance at the beautiful blue sky before jumping back in the car and going on your merry way. No, I stood there for a good few minutes, whether motivated by the sighting the day before, or perhaps even subconsciously influenced. It is important that I point out that for a high percentage of my sightings, I have an accompanying feeling that the object knew I was observing it. I have considered this recognition to somehow be a consequence of the camera focusing onto the object, or of my own consciousness or the full attention I directed towards it. But in this particular case, I just had a feeling that something was there, and that is when I saw it.

This object was far away to the southwest, yet I could see the bright white dot against sections of the blue sky when not obscured by the faint whiff of high cloud. I quickly unlocked the car to take out the camera, which I keep under a dash reflector shield on the rear floor or in the boot, or trunk. If you jump on the video linked from my website to YouTube, you will see how small the speck of light was as I lost it out of frame, and then in one continuous shot you will see it coming back into frame as I zoomed in. It's not long before the hooded figure comes into view, as well as the noticeable counter-clockwise rotation from my perspective, at a calculable rate as displayed on the graph in the following pages. As seen elsewhere in this book, the object slowed down (trend arrow upward direction), then dramatically sped up (sharp downward trend), while the spin began to slow once again.

The object was moving in one direction with what appeared to be a steady speed as it moved just in front of or behind the clouds. Hopefully, during the video close-ups it is obvious that the object is spinning in the vertical position and at the same time travelling along a straight line. Towards the end of the video I am hoping that you will see that the object is seemingly changing shape - but it is not. As it spins or is directly overhead, as expected, you only can see the bottom of the object with a hint of the hood as it comes into view again.

I timed the number of seconds it took to make one complete revolution, and this is what I found. In the small footage I captured, you can see that it revolves about eight times and each time it slows down, but after the fifth rotation it suddenly speeds up only to then commence slowing down again (please refer to the basic graph in the following pages). It is a shame that I could not continue filming after it was directly overhead, as a tree obscured my view and running around the tree did not help as the clouds were somewhat thicker and the morning sun was reflected in the cloud, so I was forced to stop filming.

With a head position similar to that of the "Golden Man", this one seems to be looking down towards the ground. But the head area showed no facial features at all, while the "Golden Man" does show possible facial features in very few positions. One other point of interest is that the bottom section of the "gown" reveals what appears to be folds, or how you would expect to see a long gown flowing down to the ground and covering the feet. Not only is this what I feel I observed, but the bottom of the object is reminiscent of the bottom section of the "Golden Man", but on the left profile where the legs are no longer visible. Please refer to the photos towards the end of this chapter.

This was not a balloon of any sort, as it retained its strange head and body shape in the vertical position throughout. If my estimated distance of the object when first sighted is correct, and I know the time taken for it to be directly overhead, then a simple calculation reveals that the forward travelling speed of the object was about 46 mi/h (74 km/h).

I am not afraid to be the first to point out that it was going in the same direction as the wind; both were coming from the south, although the speed of the object was over 5.5 times faster than the wind measured at a lower level by the weather bureau. Again, this of course will not amount to much, since it's common knowledge that wind speeds increase dramatically at higher altitude. Another observation that I have made is the shimmering, or halo effect, around the object, which is clearly seen in the video and the screen grabs from the video.

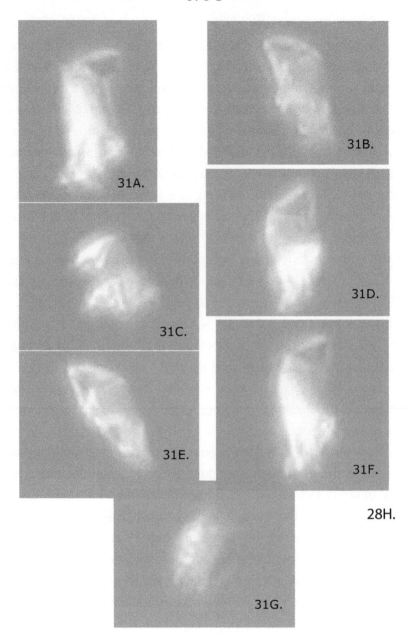

31A.

31B.

31C.

31D.

31E.

31F.

28H.

31G.

*Images 31A-31F: The Hooded Man rotates in the vertical position.
Image 31G. The Hooded Man is directly overhead.*

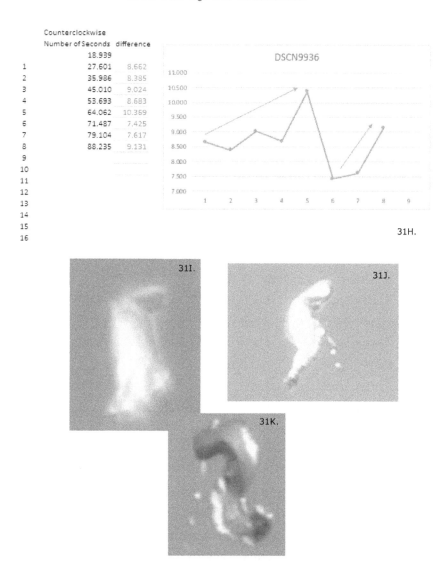

	Counterclockwise	
	Number of Seconds	difference
	18.939	
1	27.601	8.662
2	35.986	8.385
3	45.010	9.024
4	53.693	8.683
5	64.062	10.369
6	71.487	7.425
7	79.104	7.617
8	88.235	9.131
9		
10		
11		
12		
13		
14		
15		
16		

31H.

311.

31J.

31K.

Image 31H: The number of seconds taken to cycle through a single rotation; upward trend indicates is slowing down earlier in the video, while halfway at the fifth rotation it drops, meaning the object speeds up, with another developing upward trend meaning it is slowing down again. *Images 31I-31J:* The Hooded Man and The Golden Man with similar head positions, looking towards the ground. There seem to be more facial features on the Golden Man's face. *Images 31I-31K:* The Hooded Man and the Golden Man with similar lower features - of folds and creases.

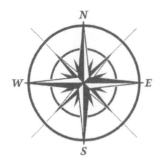

CHAPTER 30

Bring on the Chemical Trails

Date: 4 and 5 January 2018   Angle: W, 45°

Time: 03:54 pm and 5:00 pm   Direction: W to N

Height: 20,000 ft (3.78 mi, 6 km)   Photo: 16

Horizontal Distance: 6,560 ft (1.24 mi, 2 km)

Temperature: 84°F (29 C)   Video: 0

Camera: Digital Camera 16MP   Wind: S, 16 mi/h (26 km/h)

Estimated Size of Object: N/A   Visibility: Sunny

Since late December 2017, there has been a shift, from sightings towards the east or objects travelling towards the east, to sightings prevalent in the western sky. Normal aircraft emit contrails (or condensation trails) behind them, while modified aircraft -knowingly or unknowingly part of a conspiracy - emit chemtrails (or chemical trails). One is fleeting while the other remains in the sky, slowly spreading in the upper atmosphere and giving the appearance of thin clouds, leaving no other trace of the original trail.

Someone is spraying chemical or biological agents at high altitude for various top-secret reasons. The most suspicious trails remain visible for a very long time, eventually dispersing into cirrus-like cloud formations. Most prevalent in the United States are seriously crazy formations where the trails cross each other in the sky, as I saw for the first time in June 2013 following a major sighting.

I was overcome with feelings of anger during this observation as my initial thoughts were of government conspiracies to hide something, although there are many theories circulating the internet.

Images 32A-32B: Chemtrail towards the west quickly spreads.

There are many theories as to why this is occurring, from controlling global warming to the most sinister - that the Government's goal is human population control. Remember the infamous Georgia

Guidestones - a granite monument erected in 1980 in Elbert County, Georgia, in the United States? In a similar vein to the Bible's Ten Commandments, these also cite ten guidelines, inscribed in eight modern languages, and a shorter message is inscribed at the top of the structure in four ancient language scripts.

The first message is: "Maintain humanity under 500,000,000 in perpetual balance with nature". Hmmm, I wonder how they propose to do that. It has been widely accepted that chemtrails are to blame for health problems and respiratory illness. This has always worried me, as I have stopped drinking tap water over 12 years ago, and boil filtered rainwater collected in a large water tank. But am exploring other options - who knows what hard metals settle on my roof and ultimately flow into the rainwater tank?

I had wonderful sightings leading into the New Year, and was absolutely disgusted to be greeted by such a disgraceful sight as these chemtrails. Mother Nature did her utmost best to please me, though, because within two hours the wind slowly blew it away from my area, leaving a beautiful clear sky once again.

The internet has many articles on the relationship between chemtrails and UFOs, for example describing how they always appear during chemtrails and even magically dissipate some of the trail. As for the chemtrails documented in this chapter, I did not witness anything else, such as chemtrail-eating orbs.

I wonder why they started to spray the western sky just after the latest sightings? I am 50-50 on this one, as it could have been just a planned schedule to chemically spray that section of the sky as the winds were southerly and the trail was running south to north, ensuring maximum spread and effect.

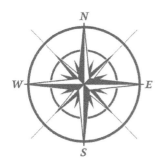

CHAPTER 31

CERN and the AAAs
Aerial Anomaly Activities

It's important to point out that I have had many more sightings than I include in this book, but for many there was little or unclear footage, or they were missed opportunities altogether. I began to get very strange feelings after the early January 2018 sightings, although they were fleeting as far as documenting the event goes. They were feelings of a sense of loss, like when the Hum had disappeared from my life. There seemed to be an eerie silence, more than usual during the day or the night.

At least three weeks had passed when there were absolutely no objects in the skies, not even a balloon, and no orbs. Having said that, I did see some very strange balloons, not after prominent sightings, but by themselves. For fear of ridicule I have not included them here as aerial phenomena, but I may include them in a section at the end of the book to show how difficult it is to determine what is just a normal balloon, even when you zoom in. The only reason I say "strange" balloons is the behaviour that they exhibit. I have seen them spin in a distinct predictable manner, like a slow version of a spring in a wound-up wrist watch, and not aimlessly blowing in the moderate wind. The other strange aspect is that as I film these "balloons", I have a feeling that they know I am observing them and from a distance of some miles they follow a distinct single file path until they are directly overhead and then continue on.

The silence in January 2018 was more noticeable because the regular appearances of orbs to which I have become accustomed had been reduced to zero. Further to the frustration of the decline in sightings, in January the summer weather was not in my favour. For the last few summers, the Southern Hemisphere summer between the months of December and February has included many sunless days, and this time heavy clouds rolled in a few days after New Year's Day and remained for over three weeks with only intermittent sunshine or starlight lasting for a few hours at a time. Regardless, the sense of loss was overwhelming and I was sure that something was wrong.

Even though, as I say, there are many sightings I have not included in this book, since 2012 I have documented them the best I can by date and time in text files saved on my computer. In looking through my old notes in preparation for this book, I found that on a few occasions I penned comments such as the relationship - if any - between CERN activation dates and my level of frequency in sightings.

Throughout the internet there are articles about the negative consequences of experimenting at CERN with the Large Hadron Collider, for example, articles titled: "CERN to unlock the bottomless pit of Revelation 9"; "CERN has unleashed absolute hell on earth"; "Plans to use LHC to open portals to other dimensions"; "LHC to help contact parallel universes"; and the list goes on.

It may be different in other parts of the world, but the majority of what I have found does seem to apply in my location, as far as I can see with the small amount of data I have collected thus far. In my reality, from my perspective, there appears to be a direct correlation between my sightings and CERN's LHC activation and deactivation dates (which have been hiding in plain sight), that is especially noticeable during the extended shutdown period between 2013 and 2014, when I only had one sighting. But how do you make sense of this when there have been many UFO sightings worldwide during this period? With just one database alone, if we include metallic discs, triangles, and orbs - basically all aerial phenomena over the period 2013–2014 - there were 7,790 sightings in 2013 and 8,647 in 2014, at a rate of approximately 684 a month worldwide.

If anything, there has actually been a 40% increase on average, with 8,200 sightings a month over those two years 2013-2014, compared to the following three years 2015-2017, when there were 5,700 sightings a month. Not only that, but on average there was a huge 69% increase in sightings from the previous seven years - from 2005 to 2011 - when there were 4,800 sightings a month. So in my reality there were no sightings over the two years when the LHC was turned off, but in everyone else's there was an increase in sightings. Additionally, it seems that the increase in sightings of 69% commenced from 2012 and ended in 2014, where it plateaus at 4,800 sightings a month. This is extraordinary. I look up to the skies all the time, and just by the law of probability there is absolutely no way that for 730 days and nights I would miss many aerial phenomena.

The European Organisation for Nuclear Research (CERN) built its Large Hadron Collider between 1998 and 2008. From March 2010 to early 2013 it ran at an energy of 3.5 to 4 teraelectronvolts (TeV) per beam (7 to 8 TeV total), which is about four times the previous world record for a collider. The accelerator was then upgraded between 2013 and 2014, and was restarted in early 2015 for its second research run, when it reached 6.5 TeV per beam, 13 TeV total, the current world record.

I know that I used the throwaway line "from my reality, from my perspective" seemingly to make my theory fit, but who knows what the LHC is capable of? As explained earlier, even esteemed physicists - and some are allegedly working on the project - have warned or openly boasted about other dimensions, doorways, portals, and other realities.

I have mentioned how huge the LHC is and how deep - as much as 574 feet (175 metres). But I would also like to talk about the significance of the site where it was constructed. It is interesting to note that CERN's LHC is built on the same spot where (it is believed) a temple in Roman times existed in honour of Apollo, the son of Zeus. The town in France where CERN is partly contained is called "Saint-Genus-Pouilly". "Pouilly" is from the Latin word "Appolliacum". The people who lived there in Roman times believed the site to be a gateway to the underworld.

On the other hand, it is stated that the CERN location was chosen purely for the ground stability and its situation in politically neutral Switzerland. All that is well and good, but why do CERN scientists fuel speculation by making comments, as stated above, regarding portals and the potential discovery of parallel worlds and their inhabitants? There are just too many strange facts and common threads throughout, for them to be denied.

Many of CERN's experiments have acronyms that rival any book about Greek mythology. For instance, Cerberus, the name of a triple ionization chamber system at CERN, is also the name in Greek mythology of the three-headed dog that guards Hades, the underworld. What about the detector used to study di-electron production in heavy ion physics? It is called the High Acceptance Di-Electron Spectrometer, and its acronym is HADES. CERN was involved in the initial prototype development of the HADES, and in the 2008-2009 experiments. Hades is best known as the ruler or God of the underworld so I cannot help but wonder why these acronyms have been chosen.

There are many more Greek Mythological related named acronym experiments but we can discuss further symbolism with none more talked about than the two-metre-tall statue of the Indian od Shiva Nataraja, the Lord of Dance, which was installed outside CERN in June 2004. We are told that the statue symbolises Shiva's cosmic dance of creation and destruction, and it was given to CERN by the Indian Government because of its long association with India.

I do not have a problem with the actual statue. It does make sense because the concept of creation and destruction lines up beautifully with quantum field theory, which is the basis of the very existence of matter. We now know that every subatomic particle performs the energy dance and is the energy dance at the same time, encapsulating the process of creation and destruction.

Just out of university, one of the very first books I bought was *The Tao of Physics* by Fritjof Capra. It's a beautifully written book exploring the parallels between modern physics of subatomic particles and Eastern religion. There are symbolisms throughout, starting with the book's cover image of the yin-yang symbol. Neils Bohr was the famous Dutch physicist who had contributed to the understanding of the atomic structure and quantum theory, for which he received the Nobel Prize in Physics in 1922. He chose the Taoist yin-yang symbol for his coat of arms because he saw that the polarised states of matter and the wave-particle duality are beautifully described by the yin-yang symbol, which eternally describes how seemingly opposite or contrary forces may actually be complementary, one and the same.

The problem I have is that when strange dark videos emerge over the internet depicting a faked "human sacrifice" in front of the Shiva Nataraja statue, posted by scientists as a prank, it does nothing to subdue the internet's chatter about CERN's ulterior motives.

Strange symbolism leaning towards the dark side is not only confined to CERN. There is a telescope at the Vatican Observatory linked to other organisations and aptly named "LUCIFER". It was built by the Max Planck Institute for work in extra-terrestrial physics. Lucifer stands for **L**BT Near **I**nfrared Spectroscopic **U**tility with **C**amera and **I**ntegral **F**ield Unit for **E**xtragalactic **R**esearch. The mind boggles. Firstly, why would the Vatican allow such an acronym; and secondly, why choose that acronym when there are so many other letters that can be arranged into something else? Apparently, this has indeed been addressed and the acronym has been changed to LUCI, by just dropping off three letters at the end.

Now we come to CERN's logo, where everyone's imagination fires up wildly. For most people, the mind easily recognises the image to be 666, the mark of the beast. We cannot blame the non-scientific and non-technically minded for this, even though apparently, as disclosed by a CERN insider, it's just the stylised representation of a synchrotron particle accelerator similar to the SOLEIL synchrotron facility in Paris. Regardless, we can safely say that the logo developers surely knew the conspiracy theories would dominate the internet with that one.

CERN's previous large accelerator, called the LEP, was dismantled in 2000 and the current accelerator was built in its place. It proved economically wise to remain underground rather than displace a wide region's population by building above ground. Having said that, it would be much safer underground anyway, just in case of radiation leaks from beam control loss of the accelerated particle collisions, as the earth's crust would provide some shielding against radiation.

Where am I going with all this? An idea or theme has been consistently present amongst most of my sightings - not only the virtual zero sightings during the extended shutdown period between 2013 and 2014, but also the direction the objects are coming from and going to, in most cases. As I have said before, from my reality, from my perspective, most of the day sightings, other than the bright yellow-orange orbs at night and mornings, have appeared to be coming from the east. Strangely enough, towards the end of 2017 and early in 2018, suddenly they were coming from the west.

In geography the **antipode** of any place on earth is diametrically opposite that point in latitude and longitude. It can be easily calculated using simple mathematics once you have the initial coordinates selected. In this case I was interested in finding the antipodal point on the other side of the world from CERN, Switzerland.

Basically, if you were to drill straight down the ground from the longitude and latitude you have selected, you will end up coming out of the ground (or ocean) directly on the opposite side of the world.

What I have found is that the antipodes (antipodal region) of CERN is about 621 mi (1,000 km) SE of New Zealand or 1,988 mi (3,200km) SE of Melbourne, Australia.

The *search from* location is CERN SWITZERLAND —
Coordinates: 46.234032, 6.052951 (46° 14' 2.5" N, 6° 3' 10.6" E)

The *antipodes* location is 621 mi (1,000 km) SE of New Zealand —
Coordinates: -46.234032, -173.947049 (46° 14' 2.5" S, 173° 56' 49.4" W), or 1,988 mi (3,200km) SE of Melbourne, Australia.

The calculation:
The *search from* location is **CERN SWITZERLAND:**
The latitude and longitude of the first location requiring the antipodes for Coordinates (CERN-Switzerland): **46° 14' 2.5" N, 6° 3' 10.6" E**

1. The degrees latitude does not change but the N to S changes to the opposite of what it was.
2. The latitude coordinates become: **46° 14' 2.5" S**
3. Subtract 180 degrees from the longitude and flip the E to W. The longitude coordinates become: **173° 56' 49.4" W**

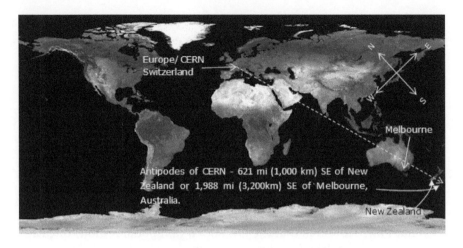

Image 33A: Arrow indicating the antipodes of CERN Switzerland is 2,174 mi (3,500km) SE of Melbourne. Could a portal have opened here over the ocean for these anomalies to enter our reality?

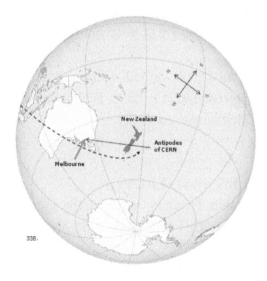

Image 33B: Could some of these aerial anomaly activities be directly related to CERN's activation dates? There seems to be an inherent correlation with CERN's extended shutdown period between 2013 and 2014, when I did not sight many aerial anomalies at all.

You will see in the final chapters that some sightings continued, although infrequently, so I can safely say that the predominant objects that seem to have disappeared completely are the translucent jellyfish-type objects and the yellow-orange orbs, towards the end of 2017 and early in 2018. Like many things in life, when you turn something off there is the residual effect where the item in question continues until it dissipates completely.

For many years there has been the fear that, during the many experimental particle collisions, physicists may accidentally create a black hole and destroy earth. If they are not successful creating microscopic black holes with this Collider, they may well produce them with the next one, LHC 2.0, or the Future Circular Collider (FCC). Plans and discussions for the LHC replacement are already well under way but will take decades to come to fruition, as the current LHC took about 30 years to construct.

From the already massive LHC nearing 17 miles (27 km), the FCC's circuit would measure between 50-62 miles (80-100 kilometres) and would be located not far from the current one. The expected power is to be seven times more than we have today, up to 100 teraelectron Volts. The gravitational pull of particles trapped when they smash into one another means that the possibility of creating a mini black hole when two quickly merge into one after they collide, is very real indeed.

As far as we know, no one has made or observed a microscopic black hole, but suffice to say that Stephen Hawking, the world-renowned physicist, developed a theory that even if a microscopic black hole formed inside the LHC, it would instantly break down completely, posing no threat to Earth. Most physicists deny that a mini black hole could ever open a portal to another dimension, let alone have any influence on the weather, asteroids, or earthquakes as many of the conspiracy theories dictate.

The earth's atmosphere is continually being bombarded with energies far greater than the fleeting energies experienced with CERN's LHC, but I am not so sure we are comparing apples with apples here.

Well, I will be adding one of my own conspiracies to the mix and I will be the first to agree that it is far-fetched. But I cannot help wondering why not seeing any objects for nearly 24 months coincides with the extended shutdown period 2014-2015. Also, why were most of the objects sighted coming from the southeast or going towards that direction? If scientists are yet to observe the creation of a microscopic black hole during collisions that will ultimately reveal extra dimensions, then something else may be created below the LHC which could pass through to the other side of the world.

Even neutrinos, the lightest of all known subatomic particles, pass through the earth and all planets and stars at nearly the speed of light, hundreds of trillions of times a second. These particles are not to be confused with cosmic rays that do not penetrate the earth, but only the atmosphere. Neutrinos are unlike other subatomic particles as they do not have an electric charge; so they are neutral, impossible to see, and very difficult to detect, because electric or magnetic forces cannot be used to interact with them.

There are over 800,000,000 collisions per second in the LHC, so at the LHC an automated process has been developed where the large detectors use software to signal and identify when a collision of significance has occurred and retain the record for later study. From that huge number above, perhaps only 1,000 will be amongst the huge amount of data already accumulated to be examined further. You can imagine the incredibly painstaking work required for these scientists to sift through all the results, looking for traces of new and exotic particles and indeed quantum black holes.

There is a measurable effect of the dosage of radiation in the underground areas around the LHC and inside the tunnels, when protons collide with nuclei from the remaining gas beams or the other microscopic particles surrounding it. It's been measured that the radioactive decay, which can last for as long as days, continues even after the circulating beams have stopped in most of the surrounding areas.

On CERN's website, there is a "nominal cycle document" indicating that it takes about 95 minutes to get the beam back up to full energy and intensity. The collisions and data collection can then take place continuously for over 10 to 20 hours. Days and months of data is collected during the continuous beam time as some signals are too small to be instantly detected.

Protons and lead ion particles are accelerated in the LHC, where the source of the protons is hydrogen gas, and an electric field strips hydrogen atoms of their electrons to yield protons (positively charged particles), while lead ions are produced from vaporised lead.

As we have seen, there is some radiation surrounding CERN during experimentation and no doubt very high standards in safety are considered for all involved.

Everyone is focused on the collisions themselves, so we must step back a bit and see the whole picture. What if a different unexplained force is at play here as the proton field is accelerated to just below the speed of light? We remember how, during a live physics lecture at the University of Copenhagen in 1819, Professor Hans Oersted discovered the magnetic field being produced from a current in a wire, as his compass close by went haywire. The same of course happens when we move a magnet along a wire to produce electricity.

We have seen throughout this book the duality of nature: wave-particle duality, electromagnetism, space-time, eastern religion's yin-yang - these are all two sides of the same coin. The protons circulating in an accelerator produce both an electric field and a magnetic field, where either or both fields can be used to determine the number and position of protons. The LHC dipoles with focusing magnets keep the protons in the vacuum chamber, bending them around the ring at ever-increasing speeds just below the speed of light, thereby increasing the weight of the proton by 25%. The magnetic fields are huge, made possible by superconductivity kept at very low temperatures - colder than outer space - to conduct electric current without resistance and power loss, and therefore produce high magnetic fields.

The two opposing beams cross over at several points where they are made to collide, and the resulting traces are recorded by detectors and the data recorded on computers. Collisions aside, without knowing technically how and physically why, the actual rotation of protons and heavy ions (such as lead) for long periods in opposing directions may be causing something to occur at the opposite side of the world, and perhaps this may be where the portal has opened.

I sincerely hope that by saying this I will not lose anyone. If you think I have been talking absolute nonsense, then please stop reading this section and continue on to the next chapter.

What I am saying here has nothing to do with the resulting event of the multiple collisions at CERN's LHC, where short-lived sub-atomic particles are being examined with the hope of discovering new ones, and especially with the hope of finding the evidence for short-lived micro black holes that will prove the existence of extra dimensions. What I am talking about is the possible creation of high-energy electromagnetic fields that may interact with the earth's own magnetic fields, or an exotic field that travels right through the earth and comes out at the antipodes point which has been shown to be just southeast of New Zealand.

I have also discovered that there is a strange ratio between the circumference of CERN's LHC accelerator and the earth's circumference. CERN's LHC is in a 26.658 km long tunnel, which is the exact circumference of the giant ring through which the beams of protons are fired, about 100m underground. If you compare this to the earth's circumference, you obtain the exact ratio 0.000666 to six decimal places (refer to the calculations below).

Work is underway to design the next accelerator, which will supersede this one; it's expected to be 80-100 km in circumference. Using the same ratio calculation, I expect it more than likely to be

89.2 km due to the fact that the ratio returns a value of 0.002230 to six decimal places, which is the reverse of 322, the number of significance for the globalists Skull and Bones. Skull and Bones was a secret society formed in 1832 at Yale University in New Haven, Connecticut, United States. Some famous members of Skull and Bones have been alleged to have been Senator Prescott Bush (Bones 1916); George H. W. Bush (1948), 41st President of the United States; John Forbes Kerry (1966), 68th United States Secretary of State (2013–2017); George W. Bush (1968), grandson of Prescott Bush, son of George H. W. Bush, 46th Governor of Texas, 43rd President of the United States.

It is alleged that the skull and bones refer to the theft by the bones men of an actual skull and two bones from the grave site of Geronimo (famous leader and medicine man of the Apache Indians), to be a permanent feature on display in the group's headquarters. It is believed that the sole purpose of this secret organisation is world domination. Other related secret societies are the Illuminati (founded 1776), The Freemasons (founded 1717), Bohemian Grove (founded 1872) and Bilderberg Group (founded 1954).

The Calculations

Note that the equatorial circumference of the earth is about 24,900 miles (40,070 km). However, the circumference from pole-to-pole, the meridional circumference, is only 24,812 miles (39,931 km) around. This is due to the flattening at the poles, which makes the earth an oblate spheroid. I calculated the ratio for each value of the earth's circumference to CERN's circumference, then obtained the average.

Current diameter for the LHC is 26.658 km (24,812 mi)

26.658 / 40,070 = 0.000665

26.658 / 39,931 = 0.000668

Average of above 2 results is 0.000666 (Chapter 13 of *The Book of Revelation*, The Number of the Beast – "666")

The future accelerator diameter will be 80 to 100 kilometres

89.2 / 40,070 = 0.002226

89.2 / 39,931 = 0.002234

Average of above 2 results is 0.002230 (The reverse of "322")

So why the significance of the number 322? There have been many interpretations, one of which is that it is paying homage to the Greek philosophers and scientists Demosthenes and Aristotle, who died in 322 BC. Another theory is that this is the centre room number in the tomb or crypt (the headquarters of the famous Yale society), as revealed by the original second level floorplan, where strange ceremonies are undertaken.

But one theory gaining traction is that it is related to Genesis 3:22 (in the King James Bible): "And the LORD God said, Behold, the man is become as one of us, to know good and evil: and now, lest he put forth his hand, and take also of the tree of life, and eat, and live for ever". This basically intends to refer to the secrets that are hidden in plain sight from us mere mortals, while those in the know can see through the darkness, hence the owl symbolism associated with Christianity.

It is eagerly anticipated that the construction for the FCC (Future Circular Collider) will start in around 2025, with a possible completion date of 2035. This will ensure that the scientific progress continues unimpeded, subject to funding. It is difficult to imagine the future LHC, which is to be three times the current size, will be built in just 10 years when the current LHC took between the mid-1980s and 2008 (23 years).

There seems to be a sense of urgency to put in place the infrastructure required to see the goal of a 2035 completion. As there is still life left in the current LHC, with the hope of the first supersymmetric particle discovery, it is expected that something revolutionary will be discovered over the next few years, heralding in new theories in the worlds of relativity and quantum mechanics.

There is a downside for me, as it may mean the cessation of the current LHC while the future LHC is constructed; but this would also mean the loss of a generation of international scientists, engineers, and experts.

There we have it. The strange ratio for the current LHC to six decimal places is 0.000666; very strange indeed, yet if the published circumference was just a little smaller or larger it would not have returned such a result. As for the FCC, it is expected to be seven times more powerful, and three times the size at 80-100 km in circumference. As I have said, I expect the circumference to be 89.2 km, which returns the ratio of 0.002230 to six decimal places, the reverse of the Skull and Bones symbolic number of 322. As the LHC took over 24 years to be completed, it's expected that the development of the FCC will also take decades to complete.

So, from my perspective, my reality, if these objects and beings appear through a portal opening on the other side of the globe then an explanation is required as to why they would move in a northeasterly direction towards Melbourne, Australia, maintaining a similar constant height and mostly never closer (except for the Grand Prix sighting and one or two others to be revealed in UFO 2). How does the timely appearance of objects I have seen compare with CERN's LHC Schedule and CERN's Injector Schedule from previous years?

It is impossible to determine that they only take the direction towards Melbourne, as one would think they have a multitude of directions to choose. Perhaps they follow partly the clockwise or counter-clockwise direction of the initial ion paths within the accelerator. This may explain why these objects always seem to be rotating when observed on video, either at a steady rate or decreasing and increasing in speed. Perhaps they follow some invisible magnetic fields or ley lines which are associated with spiritual and mystical theories around alignments of landforms. Apparently, there are alignments of landforms and ancient religious sites of significance, which often include man-made structures. Ley lines are ancient, straight lines in the landscape which are believed to have spiritual and metaphysical significance.

I know that there is no basis in science for what I have been suggesting here, but nevertheless something is going on. I sincerely feel that what is going on at CERN and what I have been seeing are related in some way. I am not sure if anyone has noticed, but in my view these shiny/mirrored glowing daytime orbs never existed before. I have always looked up at the sky most of the time, and have never experienced such aerial anomalies until recent years.

I have therefore taken the little amount of collected data for the sightings I have witnessed since 2012, and I have cross-referenced it with CERN's LHC Schedule 2012-2018, including the Injector Accelerator Schedule for the same period, with the understanding that there was an extended shutdown period between 2013 and 2014. What I have found is fascinating when you look at the witnessed objects by date and the type of experiment performed at the same time or seven days before that date.

I have attempted to obtain approval to reproduce CERN's LHC Schedule and Injector Accelerator Schedule here in this book, as it is available to the public on the CERN website, but have not been able to do so.

At a very high level of observation, when the LHC is shut down over Christmas and winter I have seen some of the most incredible sightings, possibly due to the special physics runs a few weeks earlier in November. Having said that, over the period from January to March there is still the odd sighting, but they have not been as significant in terms of frequency. Things start picking up when "Start Beam Commission" commences, and for 2018 this was scheduled for early April, weather permitting from my perspective.

As can be seen in Image 35B, the exit point or antipodes is 689 mi (1,110 km) SE of Christchurch/New Zealand, so why isn't there a comparable high number of UFO sightings in New Zealand?

I would suggest that as these objects fly over New Zealand, at the most southern point, they probably continue in a northwesterly direction towards Melbourne, Australia, maintaining a steady height of 2-6 km.

period		LHC Shedule / Injector Accelerator	Object sighted
2012	mid-late Feb	Start Powering tests	Glowing Orb
2012	early & late Apr	Special Physics run	Glowing Orb
2013	early Jun & Jul	Shutdown	Glowing Orbs
2014	n/a	Shutdown/preparation tests	n/a
2015	Mar	Argon Physics	Glowing Orb
2015	Jun	Beam to AD, Injector to MD	Glowing Orb
2015	Jul	Injector to MD	Glowing Orb
2015	Aug	Injector to MD,W30 LHC MD	Glowing Orb
2015	Sep	Injector to MD	Glowing Orb
2015	Oct	Injector to MD	Classic Disc
2015	Nov	Injector to MD	Multiple Orb
2016	Jan	Technical Stop	Glowing Orb
2016	Feb	Technical Stop	Glowing Orb
2016	Sep	Recommsssion with Beam	Glyfada, Athens RED orb
2016	Oct	Special Physics run, Injector MD	Ring shape, S shape, Glowing Orb /
2016	Nov	Special Physics run,Proton-Lead run	H Shape
2016	Dec	as above then Technical Stop	cross shape, doughnut shape, Glowing Orb, disc, Orange H Shape,
2017	Jan	Technical Stop	Large orange object, masked balloons, large silver orange disc
2017	Jun	Recommsssion with Beam	Glowing Orb
2017	Jul	Injector MD, Ions to SPS	Glowing Orb, masked balloons
2017	Sep	Scrubbing run	Glowing Orb, masked balloons, star like Orb
2017	Oct	Scrubbing run/Injector MD/XENON Ion Physics	Golden Man, masked balloons, HAQSR, Multiple Orbs, Disc
2017	Nov	Special Physics run	Jelly fish orb, Bright star Orb, Rectangle UFO
2017	Dec	Technical Stop, Scrubbing Run, Special interventions	Bright Orb, White Sphere, Yellow Orange Orb, Golden Man
2018	Jan	Technical Stop	H-shape Blue The Hooded Man
2018	Feb	DSO tests, Re-commissioning with beam	White-Yellow-Orange Orb 1 White-Yellow-Orange Orb 2 Alien/Demonic Face Red object concealed Biological Entity
2018	Mar	Re-commissioning with beam	refer UFO 2

33C.

Image 33C: LHC Schedule / Injector Accelerator Schedule compared to sightings witnessed by myself over the same period. During the CERN shutdown periods, sightings occurred due to the delayed effect.

For the period late December 2017 to February 2018, CERN's technical stop or shutdown period was from 18 December 2017 to 18 February 2018 (additionally, from 3-4 February there were DSO tests - safety tests for personnel). So far, the pattern has been that I have not sighted any more "jellyfish" objects (Chapter 25) since 26 November 2017. There was a reduced number of sightings of yellow-orange orbs during this period: on 22 December 2017 (leftover from early December Xenon experiments), 6 January 2018 (leftover from early December Xenon experiments), 3 and 4 February 2018 (DSO tests LN2 &4 were conducted on the same dates).

For the duration of the experiments, the portal through which the objects enter and exit probably remains open, but during the technical stop periods (as indeed happens from December to March), the portal closes and these objects remain trapped in our world until the portal reopens. In this book I have documented how it appears that some objects create their own portals, as was seen with the HAQSR. This may explain why I only see a very small percentage of objects during the shutdown period compared to otherwise. I do not recall ever seeing the very same object more than once, but only variations as in the case of the "Golden Man". Well, the objects probably float around looking for a way out until the portal re-opens, which may explain why I never see the same objects again.

If you recall, Project Blue Beam is a conspiracy theory in which it is postulated that NASA is developing a plan to usher in a New Age religion with the Antichrist at the helm, and to commence the "much anticipated" New World Order using an advanced technologically simulated Second Coming, either by a well-projected hologram or some other possible hidden technology. I would like to ask why would you would want to risk a fake projection with whatever technology, when you can release a real three-dimensional creature through the portal, be it by design or by accident?

Releasing something over the Christmas period, or even Easter for that matter, may be the best opportunistic time for this, so I wait patiently for the release of a CERN schedule one year that will indicate CERN will not be shut down over December and January.

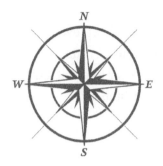

CHAPTER 32

Mandela Effect, From My Reality, From My Perspective

Since 2010, theories have abounded that when the CERN experiments were first activated in September 2008 they caused the world to shift in alternate realities. The "Mandela Effect" is the name given to a phenomenon in which a group of people collectively recall something in a totally different way to how it is to others, or how you recall it was. Believers are recalling the original reality that diverges, in most cases ever so slightly.

The original questioned reality that started all this first emerged in 2010, when many people believed that Nelson Mandela died in prison during the 1980s, despite the fact that in reality he was freed in 1990 and died in 2013, and people remembered his funeral being shown on TV at the time. There are many other examples since then, including the collective misremembering of logos, book titles, quotes, and lines from movies.

I don't really want to harp on this too much, other than to say that it is interesting that the *We are "Happy" at CERN* video released by CERN in November 2014 shows a physicist holding up two signs, "BOND1" and "MANDELA". It is understood that the first person to play James Bond was Barry **Nelson**, hence a subtle reference to Nelson Mandela. As always, my concern is the fact that CERN seems to like to fuel conspiracy theories rather than dispel them.

I am not sure what to make of it, as it is very difficult to prove because the argument is that the whole timeline changes, so all references to the previous reality are wiped away from videos and books as if the new reality has always been here and we have just misremembered.

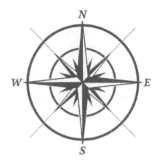

CHAPTER 33

White-Yellow-Orange Orb 1, 2018
and the Portal Entry Above New Zealand

Date: 3 February 2018   Angle: W, 45°

Time: 5:59 am   Direction: W to SE

Height: 9,842 ft (1.86 mi, 3 km)   Photo: 0

Horizontal Distance: 6,560 ft (1.24 mi, 2 km)

Temperature: 55°F (13°C)   Video: 33 secs

Camera: Digital Camera 16MP   Wind: S, 16 mi/h (26 km/h)

Estimated Size of Object: 2 ft (0.6 m)   Visibility: Passing clouds

Well, I thought, I did not expect to see anything until March-April, especially the yellow-orange orbs. What if this is one of the remaining orbs that had not escaped through the portal near New Zealand before CERN closed for Christmas and winter during the technical stop period? If you recall, "the Golden Man" was observed in five stages with three evolving stages, a fully developed stage, and again in the final stage it was breaking down as when it was first seen. Perhaps as "The Golden Man" entered our world from the portal it was in sections, only to collect itself into a humanoid appearance and disassemble itself again, all from early October to late December 2017 as it found its way beck through the portal.

I often think that the obvious location in which a portal should open is above the CERN LHC, and not 40,000 km on the other side of the world in the southern hemisphere. Perhaps the same thing does occur directly above the CERN LHC. Perhaps another portal opens but no one has noticed strange lights and orbs because the opening is at a greater height.

Standing by what I have said, I do not recall ever seeing these bright objects in the night or morning skies. They only seem to have come about over the last few years, since CERN's activation. The first sighting for 2018 was at 4:05 am on 6 January, although the footage was not clear enough to document it in this book. This sighting was the second yellow-orange orb for 2018.

I have called this orb White-Yellow-Orange, because without the camera it looked white, like a bright star, but with the aid of the camera it looked more yellow-orange. It can often be confusing when witnesses describe orange spheres or orange balls of light, but zooming in (as I have done) shows that they are anything but spheres.

Another interesting fact is that most of the time when other witnesses sight these yellow-orange orbs, they are flying silently in multiple formation, and only a few hundred feet up in the sky or very close to the ground. I have only ever seen individual orange orbs and although it is difficult to estimate their height in the dark, they appear to be much higher than that - at least over 2 km - and when magnified they are certainly not balls, but have many shapes, such as glowing discs surrounded by an aura.

These are the facts with regard to the yellow-orange lights that I have witnessed:
- They are always seen as single objects
- They always have similar luminosity and intensity
- They travel in a straight line, never diverting from it, and occasionally move in a wide arc

- Most maintain the same altitude and slow speed and, on a few occasions, have moved at approximately double the speed
- On at least one occasion shining a small torch in its direction made no difference: there was no response.

Compare this to the bright star-like orbs. On one occasion there was a distinct response when I pointed a small torch in its direction and turned it on and off, as it was flying overhead. It instantly diverted in response to the numerous times I flicked the torch on and off.

Looking at my notes, I find that I documented a similar occurrence on 26 September 2017 at 4:15 am. As I was driving to work, I took the opportunity to stop the car in an area where there were no obstructions, to gaze at the sky. It was a very still night, with many stars and no clouds. Directly above me a very bright star caught my attention because it was moving but was very high. I stood there fixated on the object, and as soon as it reached the right shoulder of the constellation Orion it diminished considerably in intensity to such a degree that it was difficult to continue observing it. My eyes continued to look in the direction it was travelling towards, and for a short time I could still see it, even though by now it was a dark figure with no luminosity about it. The belief has always remained with me that it knew at that point that I was observing it, because it instantly dimmed.

I have documented another similar instance but failed to note down the date. It was about 4:45 am when again a very bright light with the same intensity of a bright Venus caught my eye. It was not moving at all, but as I was standing there staring at it I subconsciously thought it looked out of place. There should not be any stars in that southern area other than the familiar Southern Cross constellation. Then just as suddenly as it appeared, it disappeared, and yet again I had the feeling that it knew I was conscious of it and cloaked itself as if someone flicked the switch to off.

I do hope that this clearly shows the difference in my view between the yellow-orange orbs and the bright star-like orbs. The star-like orbs seem to be intelligently controlled and respond to consciousness, but the yellow-orange orbs seem somewhat different. Without a portal opening, extra dimensions are unobservable from our reality; but they may extend into our dimension, producing effects such as apparent weakness of gravity in our reality compared to the other elementary forces, which may be stronger in the other reality. The LHC is trying to find evidence of extra dimensions by the resulting collisions of particles that may carry detectable momentum into the extra dimension.

I know it sounds mortifying that 40,000 km away the LHC is performing experiments in the hope (amongst others) of proving the existence of extra dimensions, black holes, and dark matter, yet I am saying the doorway to that other dimension is already here in the Southern Hemisphere during CERN activation times. This is where objects of all sizes and shapes have come through, and possibly exit once again. My theory is evolving as I am waiting to see what types of objects increase in frequency from April 2018 as CERN ramps up. Once the LHC shuts down over Christmas and winter, the remaining objects fly around the world until the LHC commences experiments again around April.

Is the LHC aware of this? One would think so, with the best minds in physics and billions of dollars' worth of equipment. One would also think that the area around New Zealand would be swarming with research vessels and planes, with cameras and detectors viewing the skies above the exact antipodes area easily identified by GPS.

During the time of writing this book I have identified at least two portals close to where I live, which seemed to have been created by these objects as described with the **High Altitude Quantum Singularity Reactors**. Whether I am correct or not, objects do seem to enter from and disappear into the southwest and east sections of sky. I can understand that the possible portal near New Zealand is in a fixed position relative to the earth (because it is the antipodes of its original CERN LHC location), but I struggle to understand why the two identified portals near my place would remain in the same fixed positions in the sky as the earth rotates and orbits the sun. Physicists have always said that once the results of experiments at the LHC prove the existence of extra dimensions, then further discoveries may find very exotic underlying phenomena. This is downplayed with comments that it will still be consistent with what physics has to offer by way of calculations and explanations. All it suggests, they say, is that the universe is more diverse than we think.

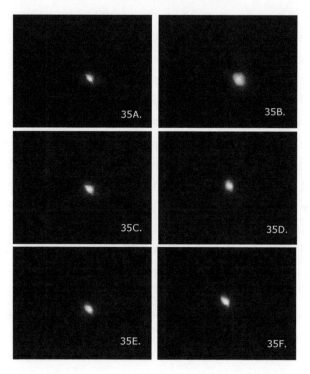

Images 35A-35F: This orb looked white with the naked eye but looked more yellow-orange in the camera and digitally. Notice the definitive disc shape with the familiar angled position as it moved from W to SE, or right to left from my point of view.

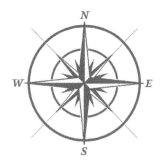

CHAPTER 34

Yellow-Orange Orb 2, 2018

Date: 4 February 2018   Angle: W, 45°

Time: 5:07 am   Direction: W to SE

Height: 6,560 ft (1.24 mi, 2 km)   Photo: 0

Horizontal Distance: 6,560 ft (1.24 mi, 2 km)

Temperature: 57°F (14°C)   Video: 46 secs

Camera: Digital Camera 16MP   Wind: W, 8 mi/h (13 km/h)

Estimated Size of Object: 1.6 ft (0.5 m) Visibility: Clear

It is interesting that on two consecutive days I have seen two yellow-orange orbs which seem to contradict the hypothesis that they should appear from around April. But the definitive answer remains that as the last of these orbs disappear, if the portals created by the HAQSRs are still actively open, then there is a lengthy pause until the CERN LHC starts up again. As I write this chapter we start entering the final week of February 2018 and I am yet to see another yellow-orange orb.

Even though I estimate the size of the two yellow-orange objects to be quite small (this first one was just over one and a half feet), they are quite impressive because even at a considerable altitude their luminosity is significant, rivalling the sodium-vapour street lamps.

When magnified on the computer, this orb moved through three or four distinct shapes and then faded twice, only to completely disappear from view. The shape appears to be disc-like, then a rectangular shape, to abstract, back to rectangular shape; and finally the object begins to dim, only to go slightly brighter for a very short amount of time and then fade from view completely.

It is my perception that these yellow-orange orbs are the most common UFOs I have seen to date. This complies with the witness accounts documented around the world. I have seen article after article about the mystery of how these orbs came about and what their purpose is. I believe that I have found the correlation between the CERN LHC and the sudden appearance of these objects, but I am now trying to find the purpose of these alien interdimensional objects or probes while they are here in our reality. If these objects only appear here on earth as a result of the portal opening because of the LHC, then are we saying that these objects have never appeared in our reality before then?

If this is correct, then it contradicts the sightings of Foo Fighters from WWII, and even the many reported witness accounts of "lights in the sky" since records began. It's important to understand that when we eliminate all the non-UFO related lights and orbs such as planes, blimps, stars and planets, and other natural phenomena, we are still left with numerous varieties of UFOs, so of course there will be a multitude of different orbs and lights. The metallic disc and triangle- and cigar-shaped UFOs are some of the few objects that do not fall into the category of interdimensional travel due to the CERN LHC.

Astronomers will go so far as to say that they agree it's mathematically impossible that there are no other intelligent life forms amongst the immeasurable number of stars, planets, and galaxies; but they throw in that, even so, it's impossible to travel between stars due to the immeasurable distances involved. Physics tells us about the limitations of travelling faster than the speed of light, especially for objects with mass.

Their argument is that even for a technologically advanced civilisation it will prove futile. The current best feasible human concept that we have to achieve extremely fast space travel is the ion propulsion system, but even if that was achieved tomorrow it would take us something like 75,000 years to travel to the nearest star.

I believe that these vehicles use a method of space travel that we can never comprehend, while the interdimensional travellers have come to us via a door opening that we have provided via CERN's LHC. I also believe that these objects enter and leave through the same portal while some others (HAQSRs) have created their own portals as a method of exiting this reality.

I realise that this all sounds like science fiction, but even astronomers and physicists grew up watching science fiction movies and reading science fiction books. They want to believe much more than anybody else when it comes to the unknown, but they have been trained to view nature with scepticism and caution because in their highly competitive fields reputations are at stake.

Possibly as a result of the many years of virtually zero solid evidence, the biggest problem faced by professionals and the public is the failure of everyone to be constantly enthused by the subject to the degree that a huge amount of funds (private or otherwise) is poured into this type of investigation. So the best we can do is document the occasional sighting of lights in the sky that mostly eventuate to nothing.

Not to take anything away from what man has discovered thus far, the ultimate in all of this is that there may be more to physics than we understand today, and CERN's LHC and the LHC 2.0 may reveal it to us in all their glory if we do not destroy ourselves in the meantime with mutually assured destruction (MAD). The warning rang out in January 2018 when *The Bulletin of the Atomic Scientists* moved the doomsday clock closer to midnight, currently set at two and a half minutes to midnight. This serves to warn the world that it is as close to catastrophe in 2018 as it has ever been.

The threat of nuclear annihilation hangs over us every single day, and we hope that MAD continues to act as a deterrent, but the biggest threat of all is that an error in judgement may be the key which sets it all off.

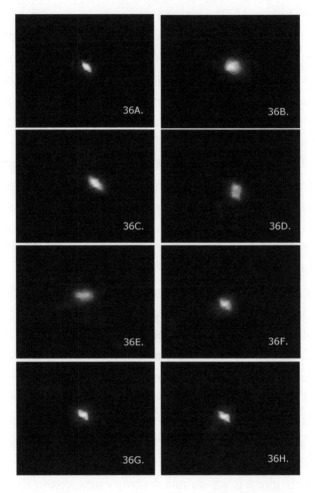

Images 36A-36H: *Stills from the Yellow-Orange Orb showing the many shape shifting transformations. The changes are disc, circular, and rectangle.*

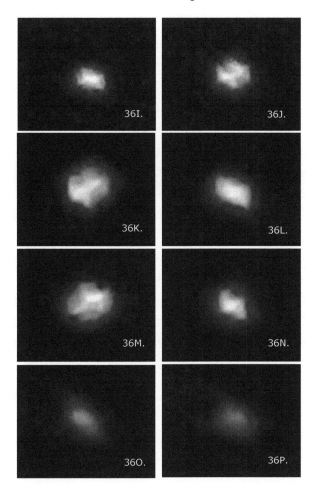

Images 36I-36P: The shape change continues but is more abstract until it fades, returns momentarily, and then fades completely.

I say, enough with the theories of government scientists, and the military experimenting with plasma ball lighting for weapons using bursts of energies from lasers. I say enough with the Chinese lantern arguments. Because when you see these beautiful flying objects for yourselves, all will agree that they are none of the above.

All witnesses report these orange orbs as spheres, which I agree is exactly how they look unaided. But zooming in with the camera and on the computer reveals much more, as the morphing ability of these objects is outstanding. There is no doubt about it, these Unidentified Aerial Phenomena do exist; and it has even been suggested that they are extra-terrestrial beings slowly acclimatising humans to their presence in preparation for full disclosure.

This could be a possibility if a multitude of these objects are coming through the portal because of the CERN LHC activation: then it's only a small jump to announce disclosure, especially when their release could be in a controlled manner by key dates such as Christmas or Easter.

It is strange that across the globe the common colour of these sighted orbs is orange, and at the same time popular streetlights around the world are also orange sodium vapour lamps. The sodium gas tends to emit more photons in the long wavelength (yellow, orange and red), which is the spectrum leading to the yellow/orange colour you see.

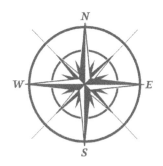

CHAPTER 35

Alien/Demonic Face in the Sky

Date: 13 February 2018   Angle: S, 75°

Time: 11:41 am   Direction: S to E

Height: 9,842 ft (1.86 mi, 3 km)   Photo: 0

Horizontal Distance: 6,560 ft (1.24 mi, 2 km)

Temperature: 73°F (23°C)   Video: 8 min 32 sec

Camera: Digital Camera 16MP   Wind: NE, 5.6 mi/h (9 km/h)

Estimated Size of Object: 10.4 ft (3.2 m) Visibility: Passing Clouds

This sighting shook me to the core for two reasons: I almost feel that I wished it into existence, and the moment I uploaded it onto my computer, I could see a head and faces of strange beings from within the object or from its surface.

It was a nice day with the occasional cloud but still mostly clear. I sat down in a quiet park where I have a full, unhindered view of the sky, surfing the web on my mobile phone and occasionally glancing at the sky. I had befriended this magpie (a black and white bird native to Australia) and I was annoyed with myself that I had forgotten to bring some bread to feed it.

It looked older and seemed to be comfortable around me as it jumped onto the park bench just a few feet away from where I was sitting. I was making funny noises and laughing at its reaction as it stared at me with that menacing beak and reddish eyes tilting its head slightly. Eventually resigned to the fact that I had no food, it slowly walked to the edge of the bench and jumped down as it searched for food amongst the short grass. Looking up I could see a large section of the sky was clearing towards the south. I remember thinking to myself how great it would be if I could see something now. It was an unconscious passing thought.

I did not even have time to look away when I noticed a round white object, balloon-like with a small thick tether below it, just slightly to the right of where I was looking. How good is that, I thought. What great luck... although it dawned on me later that perhaps I had somehow wished it into existence. This is quite a common ability with some witnesses, where through their consciousness and thought orbs and UFOs seem to appear as if by magic.

So can we telepathically make contact and communicate with UFOs? Consciousness is peculiar in that it might transcend time, space, vast distances, and even dimensions in the multiverse of which we are a part. Mixed feelings are prevalent amongst the UFO community regarding consciousness and ufology, and telepathy and psychic phenomena are key fundamental elements within the UFO arena.

Besides the usual witness testimonials and accounts of alien encounters and telepathic communication, the craft involved are also possibly artificial intelligence many thousands of years in advance of where we are now. Documentation of some of these accounts abound throughout the web, as individuals or group sessions use meditative skills before their efforts to see lights or objects in the sky.

Do I think that I used deliberate intent via my consciousness to bring this sight into existence? Possibly. This could explain how I have seen so many strange things in the sky. Is the object actually really there? It is filmed objectively; therefore it must be. Can others also see it at the same time? I expect so, although I am struggling with this because the two rectangular objects over the Melbourne Grand Prix Lake should have startled everyone who was out walking and jogging along the perimeter, but as I drove past from a short distance I did not see evidence of this. I scoured over the internet for many months afterwards, searching for anyone else who may have witnessed the objects, but found nothing.

As for the sighting in this chapter, all I can say is that as I got up off the park bench to continue filming I was aware that in the distance some 43 yards (40 m) away a council worker jumped out of his truck and looked up in the sky towards where I was aiming my camera, but judging by the way he was moving his head all over the place he may not have seen it. Sure, everyone's eyesight is different, which could explain him not seeing it; and admittedly, it was not large in the sky. One key thing underlining most of my sightings is how at the time I have always been in a relaxed state of mind, not stressed, angry or agitated.

Uploading this sighting onto a computer makes it fascinating, not so much with the object itself, but with what becomes apparent. Even before any magnification takes place, you can see what appears to be faces within or on the surface of the balloon-looking object. As with most of the unusual balloon-type objects, the tether looks strange. This one is smaller but distinctly thicker; there was a lack of shine or reflection in the overall view of the object, and I would describe it as white with the unaided eye yet yellowish through the camera. That may be a trick of the mind or an actual projection onto the object from another dimension, perhaps.

As the old optical illusion of the "Old Hag - Young Woman" first seen on an anonymous German postcard in 1888 teaches us, you should never assume that others see the world the way that you do. In this illusion some people see a young woman while others see a haggard old woman, and if you are clever you can switch between the two, but you will never be able to see both at once.

I have found the same principle applies with this object, which was so high in the sky. Upon magnification, more than one image appeared. They were mainly heads, and when enhanced by adjustment of the mid-tones they became clearer. In one consecutive section of video and stills, I can see what appears to be, in the first instance, a face like a cat looking down towards the ground. Then if you concentrate at the upper forehead area, another striking creature comes forward. This time it looks like an animal with a wide head staring forward and its tongue slightly hanging from its mouth.

Ambiguous images have been used for many years in the field of psychology, often as research tools for patients.

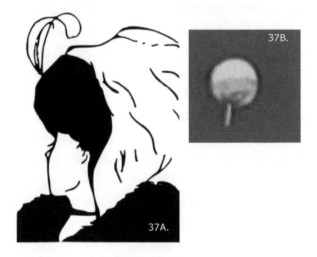

Image 37A: You can only see one at a time: the ambiguous image or reversible optical illusion of a young woman or an old woman. (Wikipedia)
Image 37B: The white balloon-type object clearly shows the head of an "alien" looking down towards the ground with dark eyes. On the other hand, if you look at the top part of the head, a pair of eyes on either side of the head gives the appearance of a wide-headed animal looking ahead, mouth open with tongue protruding.

One important point in all these objects - or most, anyway - is the similarly small common size and the similar height when observed in the sky. Could the reason be that only small objects, less than 13 ft (4 m) in size, can pass through the portal created by CERN LHC? What are they? Are they actual living organisms, or technologically advanced surveillance systems? If I look at the "Golden Man" the impression I have, especially with the five distinct stages over five days, is that in the early stages it's comprised of seemingly separate objects. Then later it mysteriously comes together to make up the whole "Golden Man", even though only in the one profile.

We see this level of organisation throughout nature, from the atomic, to the biological, to the social structures where whole sciences identify and describe structures and processes in which individual parts make up a whole. On the other side of the coin, I very rarely see the small objects such as the yellow-orange orbs, most of the balloon-like objects and the jellyfish, as individual more than once. The internet claims otherwise, where many objects are seen in clumps and groups. (Please refer to the chapter on Cluster "Balloon Formation").

Many witnesses have observed the orange orbs in formation with some very close together. Others have seen strange clumps of balloons flying in formation, where it is obvious they are individual balloon-like objects, yet nothing seems to be holding them together but it happens as if by an unknown force.

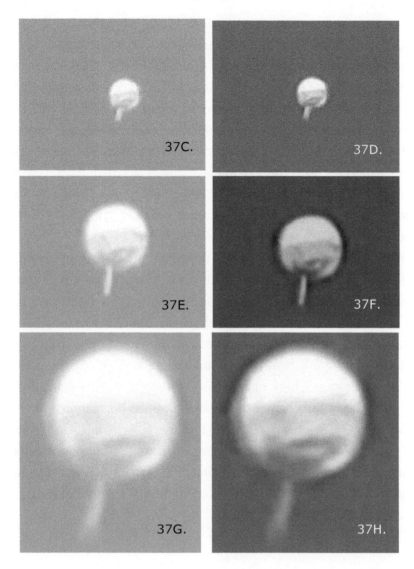

37C.

37D.

37E.

37F.

37G.

37H.

Images 37C-37H: *In the first instance, these three images show the head of an "alien" looking at the ground, until your mind switches to seeing the head of an animal, with eyes on either side of the head looking towards the camera. The three images on the left are normal, while the three on the right have had the mid-tone adjusted to a high degree to enable details to be seen.*
Images 37I-37J: *Image of a different head of a creature looking towards the ground with head tilted; note the dark eyes and long head.*

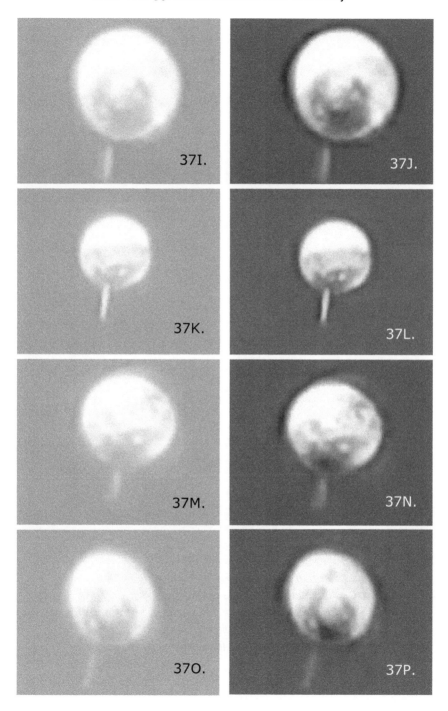

37I.

37J.

37K.

37L.

37M.

37N.

37O.

37P.

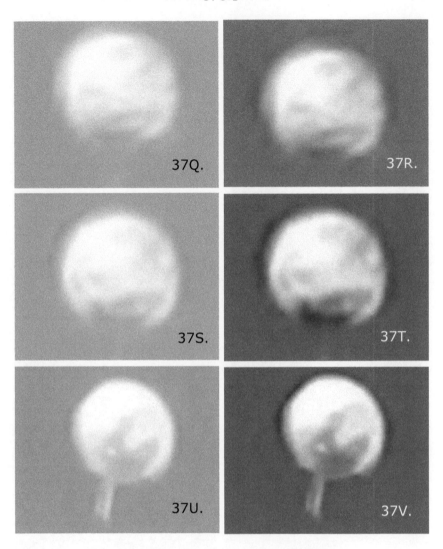

37Q.

37R.

37S.

37T.

37U.

37V.

Images 37K-37L: Ambiguous image of "alien" face.
Images 37M-37N: Image of "alien" eyes open and tongue out...?
Images 37O-37P: Ambiguous image of "alien" with eyes towards the sky;
while second image is like image 38J, looking towards the ground.
Images 37Q-37T: Ambiguous image of "alien".
Images 37U-37V: I will leave this one up to you.

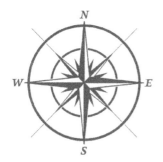

CHAPTER 36

Red Object Concealed Amongst White Balloons

Date: 18 February 2018   Angle: W, 45°

Time: 08:24 am   Direction: W to SE

Height: 6,560 ft. (1.24 mi, 2 km)   Photo: 0

Horizontal Distance: 6,560 ft (1.24 mi, 2 km)

Temperature: 60°F (16°C)   Video: 4 min 16 sec

Camera: Digital Camera 16MP   Wind: NE, 4 mi/h (7 km/h)

Estimated Size of Object: 8.2 ft (2.5 m) Visibility: Partly sunny

Estimated Size of Object: 2.3 ft (0.7 m) – Red Object only

I was determined not to include this sighting within the chapters of possible legitimate sightings, but upon closer examination, I believe that it is a successful candidate and I hope you will too. I must agree that at first it looked like a comical face with ears and a red nose. As I was filming, I thought that it was a bunch of balloons and I was ready to turn the camera off, but something inside me found the red balloon too unusual. The internet is rife with comments about cloaked UFOs using ingenious methods, and some not so ingenious; while others rubbish the notion of balloons as UFOs. I have my own section at the end of this book dedicated to sightings that have almost fooled me into thinking they were from out of this world but only proved to be an earthly balloon, whereas others like the "Bird" formation looked like balloons but behaved very differently.

Either many people publish videos on YouTube intending to deceive, or they understandably believe that what they are showing is a strange conglomerate of balloons when in fact they are not. It is a growing trend to film just about anything in the sky that moves or looks anomalous, and then publish it on YouTube; most are described as morphing, when the object is obviously just a plastic bag caught in the atmosphere as it tumbles and turns. Most people in this situation believe that they have filmed something strange and bizarre, and I do not blame them. But I do not approve of those who deliberately set out to deceive and to humiliate.

I firmly believe that entities do mimic balloons, but it is becoming very difficult to distinguish these from normal balloons. After the publication of this book, I feel sure that this will become even more difficult as even stranger and ingeniously deceptive balloons are constructed and released. Also, in late March 2018 a proposal was been put forward in Perth, Western Australia, for legislation containing a state-wide ban on balloon release. I truly hope that this is enforced around the world. I believe that I have on video balloons that seem to change shape, morphing until they are slightly different, or very different, from when they began. I realise that the glowing tethers are a dead giveaway for standard balloons, although this is not always the case. I realise that the distinct rolling and swaying of a balloon in the breeze is also a dead giveaway, but I soon learned that this is not always the case either. The balloon travelling with the wind is also a dead giveaway, but again it is not always the case. I have seen very prominent sightings that for some reason do also fly with the wind.

Having been bamboozled in the past by the run-of-the-mill, partially deflated foil balloons that glisten against the glaring sun, I have been led to think that I was witnessing a plasma shape-shifting biological entity. We have talked about the dangers to the environment of the latex and foil balloon fragments that litter the world's oceans and coastlines.

As this chapter will discuss, at times entities do mimic balloons to disguise themselves. It feels a little humorous to think that if these are indeed interdimensional creatures, objects, beings, or surveillance drones, then they could surely have made cleverer use of advanced knowledge, used such as invisibility and cloaking. Being conspicuous could, perhaps, be their wish; and as previously mentioned, I have presupposed that something unusual would be seen and my request was instantly granted. At other times, I have felt something was out there and again instantly a yellow-orange orb has materialised. Strange cloud formations are also a favourite with conspiracy theorists, as a method for objects to cloak themselves. Another important point is that most good sightings I have found seem to result in normal looking balloons at the same vicinity anyway, complicating the matter further. Are these normal looking balloons made of the same rubber and latex?

We all know what a red balloon looks like, and magnifying this chapter's object on my computer confirmed that it was something unique, at least for me. I have never seen anything like it, even though you can see on the video that it behaves like a bunch of balloons (such as the red balloons with the tethers), swaying with the light wind.

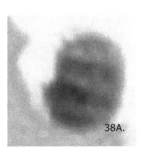 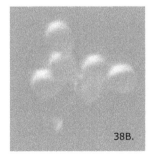

Image 38A: Close-up of the red object below the "nose" area of the bunch of white balloons. Notice the waffle-like squares.

Image 38B: A picture of a bunch of normal red party balloons with string/ tether below it. Bunches of red balloons like these were seen and photographed immediately following sighting of a red H-Shape craft, but could not be filmed.

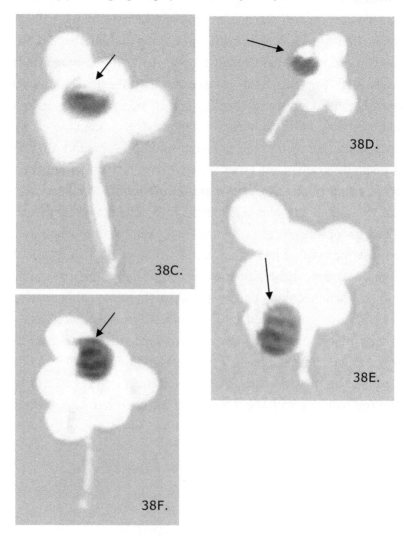

Images 38C-38F: The strange red object is in front of the five or six white balloons. The black arrows indicate a bright red dome on the surface, which seems to be a significant feature of this object, besides the tether.

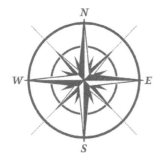

CHAPTER 37

Biological Entity (Balloon-Like)

Date: 26 February 2018   Angle: E, 75°

Time: 7:02 pm   Direction: E to NE

Height: 9,842 ft (1.86 mi, 3 km)   Photo: 0

Horizontal Distance: 6,560 ft (1.24 mi, 2 km)

Temperature: 73°F (24°C)   Video: 8 min 43 sec

Camera: Digital Camera 16MP   Wind: S, 13.6 mi/h (22 km/h)

Estimated Size of Object: 6.3 ft (1.94 m) Visibility: Sunny

This sighting appeared to me to be biological more than anything else. It looks similar to the balloon-like object sighted on 13 February 2018, but with differences as follows: there do not appear to be any faces on the surface, and it looks more pinkish than the white-orange colour previously seen. The bizarre entity was drifting through the sky heading towards the north-east with the wind (S at 22 km/h) – this was evident as the object and tether rolled and swayed. It certainly does look like a standard balloon in the first instance, but I had a feeling within me that it was more biological than not.

The uncontrollable movement of the object gave the impression that it was at the mercy of the wind. I actually do not find this "deflating", because even though I identified the direction and speed of the wind, I have quickly learnt that this no longer is significant because some objects go with the wind and some do not. Depending on the height of the object, the prevailing winds at these altitudes may not correspond to the wind direction and speed published by the Bureau of Meteorology. This will be acknowledged by visual verification from comparing the direction of the clouds to the published wind direction.

With regard to the concept of the CERN LHC and the developed portals through which objects are entering and exiting, we need to ascertain whether this is a living, breathing organism entering our reality from there. Will the reactivation of the CERN LHC in 2018 allow this interdimensional organism trapped in this reality to escape when the portals re-open once again?

Even physicists believe that such biological entities exist, and they suggest that they live in outer space and are capable of surviving in the extreme temperatures that the deep vacuum of space has to offer. They believe they have formed from organic elements and compounds in space, and could be the earliest lifeforms to develop. If the belief holds true that these are biological in nature and come from our very own solar system, then I would expect to see a lot more of them consistently throughout the year. On the basis that these sightings pick up in frequency during CERN's LHC activation dates, then it is my belief that there will be an incursion of these entities via the created portals.

At times I still struggle with the questions of what these objects are made of and what they do during their stay in our world, however long or brief. This round "balloon" with tether has a clearly defined shape, but I have seen other amorphous objects which do not have a clear form or shape. The belief is that these are just atmospheric life forms residing in the upper atmosphere, not unlike the possibly one million mostly unseen and undiscovered creatures of the deep. If this were the case, one would expect that witness testimonials would have recorded their accounts worldwide through the centuries.

Two books written in 1959 and 1978 by the same author claimed to have photographed otherwise invisible amoeba-like entities, using infrared film and special techniques devised by him. Carl Sagan the famed astronomer, astrophysicist, astrobiologist, and many others in his field, have discussed and written about the possibility that balloon-like creatures could adapt to harsh atmospheric environments, such as is found on Jupiter the gas giant. At some stage it may be revealed whether these balloon-like and jellyfish-like creatures are interdimensional and travel via portals to our reality, or whether they are simply from outer space, which is teeming with such entities.

As I have said many times, I have only been seeing these objects since 2012. One or two astronauts have anonymously talked about seeing energetic plasma-like life forms in the vacuum of space. Reports have been written about the discovery of microscopic biological entities within the stratosphere, at an altitude of 22-27 km. The experiments conducted in July 2013 used a balloon sampler to capture these microbes. The report goes on to state the plausibility that these biological entities came from outer space.

Why do I believe that the object I saw is a living biological entity? Well, as I always go with my first impressions through the lens of the camera, it was partly because of the light pink colour, but also due the overall nature of the object. It reminded me of the skin of the pink salamander.

Caucasians have a small amount of melanin in the epidermis of the skin which gives their skin the pink-yellow appearance. The pink colouration comes from the blood in the capillaries, while the yellow appearance comes from the collagen in the dermis. The main difference between the epidermis and dermis skin layers is that the epidermis, the outer layer of skin, does not contain blood vessels but is nourished via the dermis, which is composed of connective tissue.

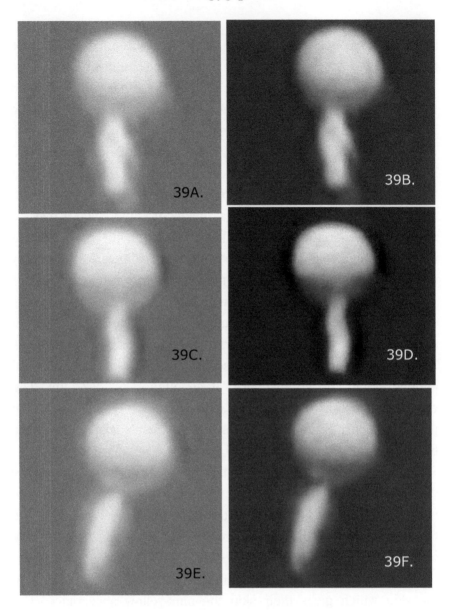

Images 39A-39F: The strange pink, balloon-like object blows around in the wind. The three images on the left are normal, while the three on the right have had the mid-tone adjusted to a high degree to enable details to be seen.

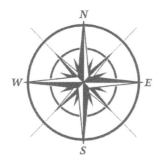

CHAPTER 38

UFO Disclosure
UFO data collection

In December 2017 we were finally told what we were all waiting for, that a highly secretive government operation called the Advanced Aerospace Threat Identification Program, initially based at the Pentagon, and had a key role in investigating reports of mysterious objects in the sky. Established in 2007 it investigated sightings of UFOs, especially by members of the U.S. armed forces.

Apparently, the AATIP objective was to assess the national security risks these objects might present, and to consider the possibility of reverse engineering them. The program's funding was cut off in 2012, but by the end of that year it had spent a total of around $22 million.

It is very hard to believe that this kind of program ever ceased or even declined since the late 40s especially in America. I refuse to also believe that such a laughable amount of $22 million was set aside for such an important study. The existence of the program was made public and claimed that unfunded investigations are still ongoing. The footage released worldwide shows what is claimed to be a flying white object with "no flight surfaces, no apparent type of thrust mechanism, something that is hovering and something that is demonstrating extreme manoeuvrability.

Apparently, it was made public due to the excessive secrecy surrounding the then program and the ridicule present towards its personnel from the Pentagon which hindered their work. Again, it is very difficult to believe that such highly secretive information was ever allowed to be made public, however the footage that was released lacks any real detail especially with such advanced high definition cameras available on these types of jets.

As mentioned earlier in this book archival programs such as Project Bluebook within the military and defence concluded that the objects whether were considered, real or not, posed no threat whatsoever to national security. We are now told that the UFO interest by the public was the perfect cover to allow its secretive aviation projects, when witnessed by the public, to be set aside as just another unexplained UFO sighting.

It is not only the United States who have been trying to understand these aerial mysteries. Since World War II, several countries have set up offices or agencies to collect data on UFO sightings, including Australia, Brazil, Canada, Chile, France, New Zealand, Spain, Sweden, and the United Kingdom. Most of the UFO studies were under the Ministries of defence as was the well-known Nick Pope in Britain from 1991 to 1994.

Some UFO investigators when asked if there will ever be UFO disclosure do not think so. We have been constantly teased by NASAs potential Alien or UFO announcement with internet headlines such as "Is NASA about to announce discovery of ALIEN LIFE in just over an hour?" and "World on brink of being told aliens EXIST" after NASA "hints at announcement". What eventually is announced is something as basic as "NASA Confirms Evidence That Liquid Water Flows on Today's Mars".

I also do not believe that the United States will announce Alien and UFO disclosure anytime soon, but I would believe leaders from other countries such as the Russian President Vladimir Putin might. No US President will admit that Aliens exist as it is claimed that it would "breach the US Constitution" and risk the "collapse of the global economy unless the ultimate aim is to finalise the introduction of the One World Government". Other suggestions have been on the impact it will have on the world's religion as well as the civil unrest around the world that will be the result, especially with the fact that we had been lied to all these years.

The December 2017 official release by the Pentagon of two separate videos of seemingly UFOs filmed by two US Navy pilots off the coast of San Diego in 2004 were the latest media release on the subject at the time of writing this book. Some are of the belief that the US Government had officially released the footage because there would be an imminent disclosure from the government that aliens have been visiting earth for decades and it has been kept a closely guarded secret. So, we all thought something huge was about to be revealed only to be disappointed again especially when it was revealed that the former Pentagon UFO official who was personally responsible for releasing the videos had done so after resigning, and not by an official department of the government.

…and then there is Project Blue Beam which is thought to be a top-secret American project which will use holographic and other technologies to project images onto the sky via chemically bound compounds such as sodium oxide in the Earth's lower atmosphere. The images could be of an attacking alien spacecraft or images of war between alien UFOs and Earths jet aircraft. It is also thought to potentially manipulate the followers of religions for the purpose of introducing a One World Religion designed to suit the Global Elites purposes.

I have a problem with this because we should decide on one and only one path that will be thrust upon us. Either incremental disclosure by the US government (I doubt it) or by a foreign Government which may also result in a partial of full US disclosure, or Project Blue Beam may be revealed in in all its glory.

There are many people pushing government officials for that mind-blowing moment where the announcement of the existence of UFOs and extra-terrestrials amongst us is finally addressed after decades. Even past presidents such as Ronald Reagan and Jimmy Carter who have witnessed UFO sightings themselves have tried without success. Even Bill Clintons success at releasing declassified military records, even though most were not UFO related, was a step in the right direction.

I surely hope books like this will help revive the push for disclosure.

"....to know that honesty is the
1st chapter in the book of wisdom." -
Thomas Jefferson

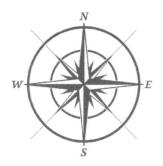

CHAPTER 39

Mistaking Objects For UFOs

When I started to take this subject seriously, I had not realised how difficult it would be to differentiate unnatural phenomena from the natural. In the early days, I was falling into the trap of mistaking normal stars for aerial phenomena, especially low in the sky.

Bright stars can scintillate furiously when low in the sky, and at one stage I mistakenly thought I was witnessing a UFO low in the southern sky because it flashed so much with every colour imaginable.

I remember how I started filming and after five minutes or so, I gave in to the notion that it was only a star. The atmosphere is to blame, as starlight passes through variations in density and humidity as it makes its way to our eye. These variations perform like a lens in the sky, focusing its own image of the star. If you bring the wind into the mix, the quantity and positions of all the individual images produced by the "lens" are constantly changing, and this produces the twinkling effect which in scientific terms is called refraction.

The biggest hurdle I face even now is misinterpreting balloons as UFOs. Metallic balloons with shiny tethers reflecting in the sun are easily mistaken for UFOs. It is frustrating when some of the footage on YouTube clearly shows a plastic bag blowing in the wind or a "happy birthday" balloon with a string below it. These are seldom redacted and removed, so the cringeworthy videos and photographs remain, seemingly with intention, forever.

I will be the first to say that one or two of the sightings in this book may unintentionally fall in this category of misinterpretation. On the other side of the coin, some in this chapter could probably be in fact real aerial anomalies.

Is this a deflated balloon?

Date: 10 December 2016   Angle: E, 85°

Time: 5:46 pm   Direction: S to N

Height: 3,280 ft (0.62 mi, 1 km)   Photo: 0

Horizontal Distance: 0 ft (0 mi, 0 km)

Temperature: 64°F (18°C)   Video: 00 min 34 sec

Camera: Digital Camera 16MP   Wind: SE, 14.9 mi/h (24 km/h)

Estimated Size of Object: 0.9 ft (0.29 m) Visibility: Passing clouds

I saw this at the last minute before it flew over my roof. It looked very unusual at the time, due to its vertical nature and dark underside. At one point it folds over, indicating it is possibly a piece of plastic or deflated latex balloon. Images 41A-41D:

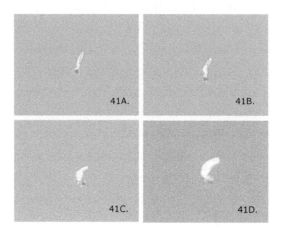

41A.

41B.

41C.

41D.

Is this a plastic bag?

Date: 25 December 2016   Angle: S, 45°

Time: 06:02 pm   Direction: S to SW

Height: 3,280 ft (0.62 mi, 1 km)   Photo: 0

Horizontal Distance: 3,280 ft (0.62 mi, 1 km)

Temperature: 97°F (36°C)   Video: 1 min 53 sec

Camera: Digital Camera 16MP   Wind: N, 18.6 mi/h (30 km/h)

Estimated Size of Object: 0.6 ft (0.18 m) Visibility: Sunny

The erratic behaviour of this object in the wind instantly identifies it as a plastic bag, although anything is possible in this world. Images 41E-41H:

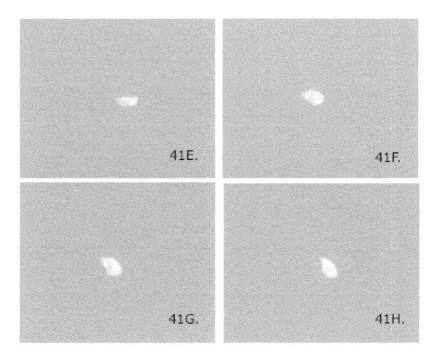

41E.

41F.

41G.

41H.

Is this a blue object hiding amongst a bunch of balloons?

Date: 15 January 2017   Angle: S, 75°

Time: 6:03 pm   Direction: S to N

Height: 3,280 ft (0.62 mi, 2 km)   Photo: 0

Horizontal Distance: 3,280 ft (0.62 mi, 2 km)

Temperature: 66°F (19°C)   Video: 4 min 39 sec

Camera: Digital Camera 16MP   Wind: S, 16 mi/h (26 km/h)

Estimated Size of Object: 3.2 ft (1.0 m)   Visibility: Passing clouds

From a distance this object appeared to be glowing, but when viewed through the camera it just looked like a normal bunch of green and white balloons. When it is been further scrutinised on the computer, one bluish balloon stands out. All the balloons seem connected to each other except this bluish one, but I cannot be certain. Images 41I-41L:

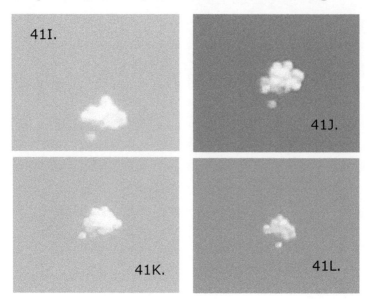

A piece of cardboard flying

Date: 18 October 2017   Angle: S, 45°

Time: 6:03 pm   Direction: S to W

Height: 2,624 ft (874 yds, 800 m)   Photo: 0

Horizontal Distance: 1,640 ft (546 yds, 500 m)

Temperature: 84°F (29°C)   Video: 0 min 09 sec

Camera: Digital Camera 16MP   Wind: NNE, 21 mi/h (35 km/h)

Estimated Size of Object: 1 ft (0.3 m) Visibility: Sunny

How easily photos like this, along with the inherent videos, can make their way to the internet under the banner of rectangular shaped UFO. Images 41M-41P:

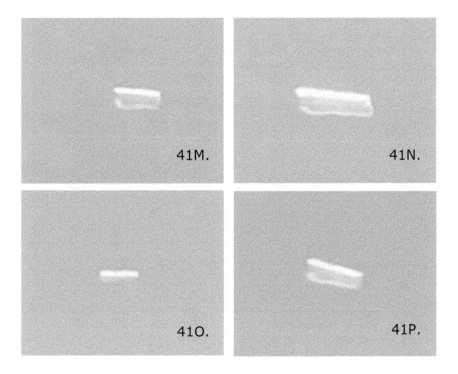

41M.

41N.

41O.

41P.

A five-pointed balloon

Date: 5 November 2017   Angle: W, 45°

Time: 03:21 pm   Direction: SW to NW

Height: 2,624 ft (874 yds, 800 m)   Photo: 0

Horizontal Distance: 2,624 ft (874 yds, 800 m)

Temperature: 62°F (17°C)   Video: 1 min 06 sec

Camera: Digital Camera 16MP   Wind: S, 16 mi/h (26 km/h)

Estimated Size of Object: 1.3 ft (0.4 m) Visibility: Sunny

This one fooled me until I examined it on the computer. Images 41I-41L:

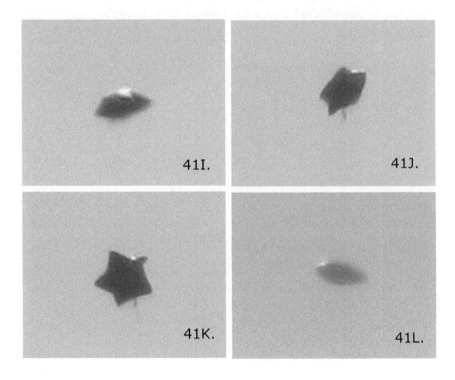

41I.

41J.

41K.

41L.

Four balloons appear as multiple orbs

Date: 13 November 2017   Angle: NE, 85°

Time: 5:01 pm   Direction: NE to W

Height: 9,842 ft. (1.86 mi, 3 km)   Photo: 0

Horizontal Distance: 2,624 ft (874 yds, 800 m)

Temperature: 89°F (32°C)   Video: 5 min 30 sec

Camera: Digital Camera 16MP   Wind: NNW, 21 mi/h (35 km/h)

Estimated Size of Object: 1.6 ft (0.5 m) Visibility: Passing clouds

This one fooled me as well, until uploading and zooming on the computer immediately revealed the string connecting the four balloons. This proves how the direction of the wind as detailed by the Bureau of Meteorology is not necessarily in the same direction at a considerable height. Images 41M-P:

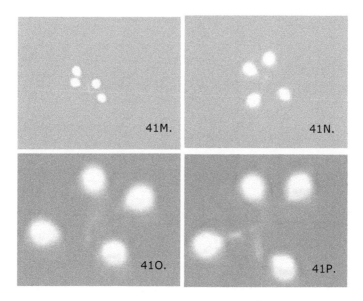

Silver (gold) letter "O"-shaped balloon

Date: 19 November 2017   Angle: W, 75°

Time: 10:01 am   Direction: W to SW

Height: 2,624 ft (874 yds, 800 m)   Photo: 0

Horizontal Distance: 2,624 ft (874 yds, 800 m)

Temperature: 75°F (24°C)   Video: 10 min 27 sec

Camera: Digital Camera 16MP   Wind: S, 13.6 mi/h (22 km/h)

Estimated Size of Object: 2.6 ft (0.8 m)   Visibility: Partly sunny

As you can see by the length of the video taken, this balloon easily fooled me. It was a very sunny day and even though I was not 100 percent sure, I kept filming so I could analyse it later. Within minutes I was certain it was a balloon.

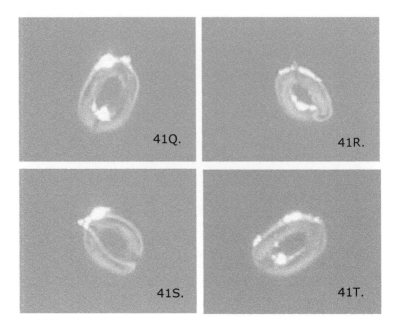

41Q.

41R.

41S.

41T.

Dark metallic flat disc balloon

Date: 15 December 2017   Angle: W, 75°

Time: 2:46 pm   Direction: W to SE

Height: 2,624 ft (874 yds, 800 m)   Photo: 0

Horizontal Distance: 3,280 ft (0.62 mi, 1 km)

Temperature: 77°F (25°C)   Video: 13 min 30 sec

Camera: Digital Camera 16MP   Wind: S, 13.6 mi/h (22 km/h)

Estimated Size of Object: 1.5 ft (0.46 m) Visibility: Sunny

The reflection off the sun was peculiar at first. This object seemed to be in a fixed position for some time, even with a moderate breeze. It disappeared for a while, only to re-appear in the south-east.

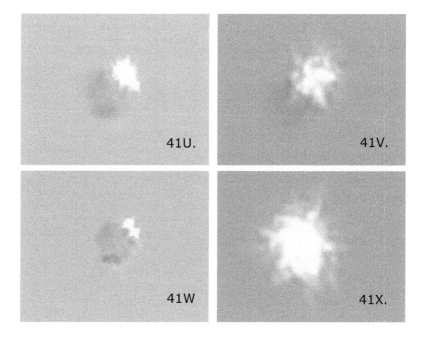

41U.

41V.

41W

41X.

Four metallic balloons spell "BIRD"

Date: 4 February 2018   Angle: W, 75°

Time: 9:09 am   Direction: W to E

Height: 9,842 ft (3,280 yds, 3000 m)   Photo: 0

Horizontal Distance: 3,280 ft (1,093 yd., 1000 m)

Temperature: 64°F (18°C)   Video: 17 min 0 sec

Camera: Digital Camera 16MP   Wind: WSW, 9 mi/h (15 km/h)

Estimated Size of Object: 6.8 ft (2.1 m) Visibility: Passing clouds

This was a very strange sighting, beyond comprehension even if they were normal balloons. Yes, they look like normal balloons, but their behaviour turned out to be odd. Initially they were seen in the west as a group of separate balloons. I hadn't noticed that they were made up of four letters, B-I-R-D, until I uploaded them on my computer. The B and I rotated clockwise between 4 and 3 seconds each, while the R rotated counter-clockwise in over 3 seconds. The D unfortunately was out of focus, so I was unable to see much detail.

   B – average rotation time, 4.17 seconds, clockwise
   I – average v 2.99 seconds, clockwise
   R – average 3.14 seconds, counter-clockwise
   D – inconclusive

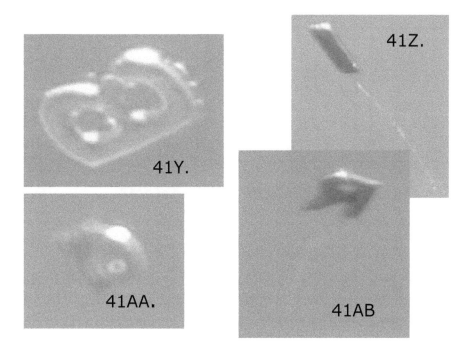

41Z.

41Y.

41AA.

41AB

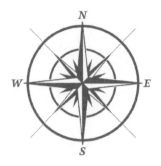

CHAPTER 40

Super Blood Moon Eclipse of 2018

Well, this is where my journey ends for now. As it started, so it ends. There is a very special reason for including the spectacular eclipse of 2018. Not only was it a Total Lunar Eclipse and Super Blue Blood Moon (a rare event last seen in 1866), but I had the privilege of seeing it with my mother. I woke my mother on 31 January 2018 at 11:15 pm to come and see the eclipse, as it was about to start.

Before she went to bed, she was excited about this event and I promised I would wake her. As she got up and put on her robe, I could see the enthusiasm in her face. She walked out the front door and looked up to see the beautiful full moon in all its glory. It reminded me of that day over 50 years ago when my mother woke me up to observe our own heavenly display, The Great Comet of 1965. So it ends as it started.

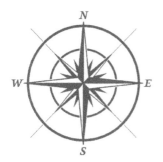

CHAPTER 41

UFO 1 The Book - The End

Like a father entertained by his children in the backyard, I stand and sit transfixed by the sky. It has become my labour of love, whether I am in Australia at home, at work, holidaying interstate or overseas. I look up at every opportunity, and close members of my family celebrate with understanding as I upload and project the spoils of my day on my laptop.

Wherever possible, I preserve the images and photos on the original SD camera card and micro SD cards for my mobile phones. I also religiously copy to two external hard drives, and I always carry with me copies on USB sticks. This is how obsessed I have become, although I remain remarkably unaffected, as I still get up to go to work and follow my normal routine, giving 100 % in everything I do.

After every sighting, I place my imagination out to pasture as I sit beneath the garret waiting for its return with possible answers to my questions about what I have seen. I learned quick smart that I cannot openly discuss such things with just anyone - not even with my extended family - due to their complex nature. In fact, it was a very long time before I had the courage to show my mother the Golden Man, because of the religious impact I thought it might have. But my mother has taken it with a pinch of salt. In my experience, religion is that it can be very emotional at times and it is comforting to know it is there in time of need. I may get teary-eyed as it stirs my heart, knowing that it pulls me into the physical as well during times of prominent sightings. As the priest blesses me, I will still light candles, cross myself, and fast.

The unification of humanity regardless of religion should be the goal - not the mindless violent path this world is moving toward.

For thine is the kingdom and the power and the glory, forever.
Matthew 6:13

For Yours is the kingdom and the power and the glory of the Father and the Son and the Holy Spirit, now and forever and to the ages of ages.

Peace be with you all.

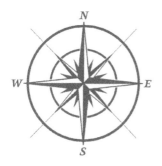

CHAPTER 42

Coming in UFO 2

As this book finally goes to print, I have summarised the observed sightings, just for the month of March 2018, that will be included in the next volume:

- Incredible communications from another dimension.
- Be amazed as thin flat objects are coming within 50 feet, floating in the air trying to attract my attention.
- You will be astonished to see images displayed in the sky, more real than any hologram. As it moves higher in the sky, one object cleverly displays for me real-life animals, cycling repetitively through images of large fish swimming and small- to medium-sized marsupials. One image seamlessly moulds into the other and this shot zooms back to provide perspective with street power cables and poles in the foreground.
- The Golden Man returns once more, this time aimlessly rotating head over tail, no longer in a vertical position but almost as if it is lying down, tether missing, with a sense of lifelessness.
- As at end of March, the yellow-orange orbs and mirrors in the sky are yet to return since last sighted in December 2017 and early February 2018.

Where one door shuts, another opens.
Don Quixote 1609 (Book I, Chapter XXI)

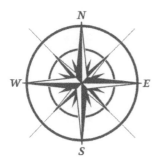

CHAPTER 43

The Calculations- Estimated Size of Object

Chapter 4 - Here Come the Glowing Orbs

The Pythagorean Theorem to calculate distance from me is

$a^2 + b^2 = c^2$ or (vertical distance)^2 + (horizontal distance)^2 = (distance from camera)

(1,000 m)^2 + (1,000 m)^2

(1,000,000) + (1,000,000) = $\sqrt{2,000,000}$ = 1,414 m (distance from camera)

10MP Digital Camera

Sensor size = 7.176 mm x 5.319 mm

Average = 6.25 mm (0.00625 m)

Size on image = 1 mm (0.001 m)

Vertical height of screen = 150 mm (0.15 m)

% of screen taken by object = 0.67

% of above compare with sensor size = 0.041 mm (0.000041 m)

35-420 mm (focal length used ~ 35 mm) = 0.035 m

To calculate size of object (m) = ((0.000041 x 1,414)/ (0.035))

= 5.2 ft (1.6 m)

Chapter 7- The Glyfada, Athens (Greece) Red Orb

The Pythagorean Theorem to calculate distance from me is

$a^2 + b^2 = c^2$ or (vertical distance)^2 + (horizontal distance)^2 = (distance from camera)

(300 m)^2 + (1,000 m)^2

(90,000) + (1,000,000) = $\sqrt{1,090,000}$ = 1,044 m (distance from camera)

CHAPTER 43: The Calculations- Estimated Size of Object

10MP Digital Camera

Sensor size = 4 mm x 4 mm

Average = 4 mm (0.004 m)

Size on image = 1 mm (0.001 m)

Vertical height of screen = 150 mm (0.15 m)

% of screen taken by object = 0.67

% of above compare with sensor size = 0.026 mm (0.000026 m)

35-420 mm (focal length used ~ 35 mm) = 0.035 m

To calculate size of object (m) = ((0.000026 x 1,044) / (0.035))

= 2.6 ft (0.8 m)

Chapter 9 - Ring Shape and Morphing S-Shape

The Pythagorean Theorem to calculate distance from me is

$a^2 + b^2 = c^2$ or (vertical distance)^2 + (horizontal distance)^2 = (distance from camera)

(4,000 m)^2 + (1,000 m)^2

(16,000,000) + (1,000,000) = $\sqrt{17,000,000}$ = 4,123 m (distance from camera)

20MP Digital Camera + Skywatcher Telescope

Sensor size = 6.2 mm x 4.6 mm

Average = 5.4 mm (0.0054 m)

Size on image = 8 mm (0.008 m)

Vertical height of screen = 150 mm (0.15 m)

% of screen taken by object = 5.3

% of above compare with sensor size = 0.028 mm (0.00029 m)

1,000 mm (focal length used ~ 1,000 mm) = 1 m

To calculate size of object (m) = ((0.00029 x 4,123) / (1))

= 3.87 ft (1.18 m)

Chapter 10 - Bright Yellow-Orange Orb 1

The Pythagorean Theorem to calculate distance from me is

$a^2 + b^2 = c^2$ or (vertical distance)^2 + (horizontal distance)^2 = (distance from camera)

(3,000 m)^2 + (2,000 m)^2

(9,000,000) + (9,000,000) = $\sqrt{13,000,000}$ = 3,605 m (distance from camera)

16MP Digital Camera

Sensor size = 6.2 mm x 4.6 mm

Average = 5.4 mm (0.0054 m)

% of screen taken by object = 5.33

% of above compare with Sensor size = 0.288 mm (0.00029 m)

1,000 mm (focal length used ~ 1,000 mm) = 1 m

To calculate size of object (m) = ((0.00029 x 3,605) / (1))

= 3.3 ft (1.0 m)

Chapter 11 - Bright Yellow-Orange (White) Orb 2

The Pythagorean Theorem to calculate distance from me is

$a^2 + b^2 = c^2$ or (vertical distance.) ^{2} + (horizontal distance) ^{2} = (distance from camera)

(3,000 m) ^{2} + (1,000 m) ^{2}

(9,000,000) + (1,000,000) = $\sqrt{10,000,000}$ = 3,162 m (distance from camera)

16MP Digital Camera

Sensor size = 6.2 mm x 4.6 mm

Average = 5.4 mm (0.0054 m)

Size on image = 8 mm (0.008 m)

Vertical height of screen = 150 mm (0.15 m)

% of screen taken by object = 5.33

% of above compare with sensor size = 0.288 mm (0.00029 m)

1,000 mm (focal length used ~ 1,000 mm) = 1 m

To calculate size of object (m) = ((0.00029 x 3,162) / (1))

= 2.9 ft (0.9 m)

Chapter 12 - Bright Yellow-Orange Orb 3

The Pythagorean Theorem to calculate distance from me is

$a^2 + b^2 = c^2$ or (vertical distance) ^{2} + (horizontal distance) ^{2} = (distance from camera)

(3,000 m) ^{2} + (1,000 m) ^{2}

(9,000,000) + (1,000,000) = $\sqrt{10,000,000}$ = 3,162 m (distance from camera)

16MP Digital Camera

Sensor size = 6.2 mm x 4.6 mm

Average = 5.4 mm (0.0054 m)

Size on image = 10 mm (0.01 m)

Vertical height of screen = 150 mm (0.15 m)

% of screen taken by object = 6.66

% of above compare with sensor size = 0.36 mm (0.00036 m)

1,000 mm (focal length used ~ 1,000 mm) = 1 m

To calculate size of object (m) = ((0.00036 x 3,162) / (1))

= 3.6 ft (1.1 m))

Chapter 13 - Precursor - "The Golden Man" 1

The Pythagorean Theorem to calculate distance from me is

$a^2 + b^2 = c^2$ or (vertical distance) ^{2} + (horizontal distance) ^{2} = (distance from camera)

(3,000 m) ^{2} + (1,000 m) ^{2}

(9,000,000) + (1,000,000) = $\sqrt{10,000,000}$ = 3,162 m (distance from camera)

16MP Digital Camera

Sensor size = 6.2 mm x 4.6 mm

Average = 5.4 mm (0.0054 m)

Size on image = 17 mm (0.0017 m)

Vertical height of screen = 150 mm (0.15 m)

% of screen taken by object =11.33

% of above compare with sensor size = 0.612 mm (0.00061 m)

1,000 mm (focal length used ~ 1,000 mm) = 1 m

To calculate size of object (m) = ((0.00061 x 3,162) / (1))

= 6.2 ft (1.9 m)

Chapter 15 - Precursor - "The Golden Man" 2

The Pythagorean Theorem to calculate distance from me is

$a^2 + b^2 = c^2$ or (vertical distance) ^{2} + (horizontal distance) ^{2} = (distance from camera)

(3,000 m) ^{2} + (1,000 m) ^{2}

(9,000,000) + (1,000,000) = $\sqrt{10,000,000}$ = 3,162 m (distance from camera)

16MP Digital Camera

Sensor size = 6.2 mm x 4.6 mm

Average = 5.4 mm (0.0054 m)

Size on image = 25 mm (0.025 m)

Vertical height of screen = 150 mm (0.15 m)

% of screen taken by object =16.66

% of above compare with sensor size = 0.9 mm (0.0009 m)

1,000 mm (focal length used ~ 1,000 mm) = 1 m

To calculate size of object (m) = ((0.0009 x 3,162) / (1))

= 9 ft (2.8 m)

Chapter 16 - HAQSR - High Altitude Quantum Singularity Reactor?

The Pythagorean Theorem to calculate distance from me is

$a^2 + b^2 = c^2$ or (vertical distance) ^{2} + (horizontal distance) ^{2} = (distance from camera)

(4,000 m) ^{2} + (1,000 m) ^{2}

(16,000,000) + (1,000,000) = √ 17,000,000 = 4,123 m (distance from camera)

20MP Digital Camera + Skywatcher Telescope

Sensor size = 6.2 mm x 4.6 mm

Average = 5.4 mm (0.0054 m)

Size on image = 6 mm (0.006 m)

Vertical height of screen = 150 mm (0.15 m)

% of screen taken by object = 4

% of above compare with sensor size = 0.216 mm (0.00022 m)

400 mm (focal length used ~ 400 mm) = 0.4 m

To calculate size of object (m) = ((0.00022 x 4,123) / (0.4))

= 7.2 ft (2.2 m)

Chapter 17 - Precursor - "The Golden Man" 3

The Pythagorean Theorem to calculate distance from me is

$a^2 + b^2 = c^2$ or (vertical distance) ^{2} + (horizontal distance) ^{2} = (distance from camera)

(3,000 m) ^{2} + (2,000 m) ^{2}

(9,000,000) + (4,000,000) = √ 13,000,000 = 3,605 m (distance from camera)

16MP Digital Camera

Sensor size = 6.2 mm x 4.6 mm

Average = 5.4 mm (0.0054 m)

Size on image = 21 mm (0.021 m)

Vertical height of screen = 150 mm (0.15 m)

% of screen taken by object = 14

% of above compare with sensor size = 0.756 mm (0.00076 m)

1,000 mm (focal length used ~ 1,000 mm) = 1 m

To calculate size of object (m) = ((0.00076 x 3,605) / (1))

= 8.8 ft (2.7 m)

Chapter 18 - Cluster Balloon Formation

The Pythagorean Theorem to calculate distance from me is

$a^2 + b^2 = c^2$ or (vertical distance) ^{2} + (horizontal distance) ^{2} = (distance from camera)

$(4,000$ m$)$ ^{2} + $(2,000$ m$)$ ^{2}

$(16,000,000) + (4,000,000) = \sqrt{20,000,000} = 4,472$ m (distance from camera)

16MP Digital Camera

Sensor size = 6.2 mm x 4.6 mm

Average = 5.4 mm (0.0054 m)

Size on image = 40 mm (0.04 m)

Vertical height of screen = 150 mm (0.15 m)

% of screen taken by object = 26.67

% of above compare with sensor size = 1.44 mm (0.0014 m)

1,000 mm (focal length used ~ 1,000 mm) = 1 m

To calculate size of object (m) = ((0.0014 x 4,472) / (1))

= 21 ft (6.4 m)

Chapter 19 - The Golden Man

The Pythagorean Theorem to calculate distance from me is

$a^2 + b^2 = c^2$ or (vertical distance) ^{2} + (horizontal distance) ^{2} = (distance from camera)

$(3,000$ m$)$ ^{2} + $(1,000$ m$)$ ^{2}

$(9,000,000) + (1,000,000) = \sqrt{10,000,000} = 3,162$ m (distance from camera)

16MP Digital Camera

Sensor size = 6.2 mm x 4.6 mm

Average = 5.4 mm (0.0054 m)

Size on image = 35 mm (0.035 m)

Vertical height of screen = 150 mm (0.15 m)

% of screen taken by object = 23.33

% of above compare with sensor size = 1.26 mm (0.00126 m)

2,000 mm (focal length used ~ 2,000 mm) = 2 m (due to 100% zoom)

To calculate size of object (m) = ((0.00126 x 3,162) / (2))

= 6.52 ft (1.99 m)

Chapter 20 - Multiple Orbs in Formation

The Pythagorean Theorem to calculate distance from me is

$a^2 + b^2 = c^2$ or (vertical distance)^2 + (horizontal distance.)^2 = (distance from camera)

(4,000 m)^2 + (1,000 m)^2

(16,000,000) + (1,000,000) = √ 17,000,000 = 4,123 m (distance from camera)

16MP Digital Camera

Sensor size = 6.2 mm x 4.6 mm

Average = 5.4 mm (0.0054 m)

Size on image = 20 mm (0.02 m)

Vertical height of screen = 150 mm (0.15 m)

% of screen taken by object = 13.33

% of above compare with sensor size = 0.72 mm (0.00072 m)

2,000 mm (focal length used ~ 2,000 mm) = 2 m (due to 100% zoom)

To calculate size of object (m) = ((0.00072 x 4,123) / (2))

= 4.9 ft (1.5 m)

Chapter 22 - Vertical Blue – Plasma 1 and the Cartoon Characters

The Pythagorean Theorem to calculate distance from me is

$a^2 + b^2 = c^2$ or (vertical distance)^2 + (horizontal distance)^2 = (distance from camera)

(4,000 m.)^2 + (3,000 m)^2

(16,000,000) + (9,000,000) = √ 25,000,000 = 5,000 m (distance from camera)

16MP Digital Camera

Sensor size = 6.2 mm x 4.6 mm

Average = 5.4 mm (0.0054 m)

Size on image = 40 mm (0.004 m)

Vertical height of screen = 150 mm (0.15 m)

% of screen taken by object = 26.66

% of above compare with sensor size = 1.44 mm (0.00144 m)

2,000 mm (focal length used ~ 2,000 mm) = 2 m (due to 100% zoom)

To calculate size of object (m) = ((0.00144 x 5,000) / (2))

= 2.9 ft (0.9 m)

Chapter 23 - Vertical Blue – Plasma 2 and the Cycles of Life

The Pythagorean Theorem to calculate distance from me is

$a^2 + b^2 = c^2$ or (vertical distance)^2 + (horizontal distance)^2 = (distance from camera)

$(4,000 \text{ m})^2 + (3,000 \text{ m})^2$

(16,000,000) + (9,000,000) = $\sqrt{25,000,000}$ = 5,000 m (distance from camera)

16MP Digital Camera

Sensor size = 6.2 mm x 4.6 mm

Average = 5.4 mm (0.0054 m)

Size on image = 15 mm (0.015 m)

Vertical height of screen = 150 mm (0.15 m)

% of screen taken by object = 10

% of above compare with sensor size = 0.54 mm (0.00054 m)

2,000 mm (focal length used ~ 2,000 mm) = 2 m (due to 100% zoom)

To calculate size of object (m) = ((0.00054 x 5,000) / (2))

= 4.4 ft (1.35 m)

Chapter 26 - Unmarked Airplane 1

The Pythagorean Theorem to calculate distance from me is

$a^2 + b^2 = c^2$ or (vertical distance)^2 + (horizontal distance)^2 = (distance from camera)

$(2,000 \text{ m})^2 + (2,000 \text{ m})^2$

(16,000,000) + (4,000,000) = $\sqrt{20,000,000}$ = 4,472 m (distance from camera)

16MP Digital Camera

Sensor size = 6.2 mm x 4.6 mm

Average = 5.4 mm (0.0054 m)

Size on image = 15 mm (0.015 m)

Vertical height of screen = 150 mm (0.15 m)

% of screen taken by object = 10

% of above compare with sensor size = 0.54 mm (0.00054 m)

2,000 mm (focal length used ~ 2,000 mm) = 2 m (due to 100% zoom)

To calculate size of Black Balloon (m) = ((0.00054 x 4,472) / (2))

= 3.9 ft (1.2 m)

Chapter 24 - Bright Yellow-Orange Orb 4

The Pythagorean Theorem to calculate distance from me is

$a^2 + b^2 = c^2$ or $(\text{vertical distance})^2 + (\text{horizontal distance})^2 = (\text{distance from camera})$

$(3{,}000 \text{ m})^2 + (0 \text{ m})^2$ - directly overhead

$(9{,}000{,}000) + (0) = \sqrt{9{,}000{,}000} = 3{,}000 \text{ m}$ (distance from camera)

16MP Digital Camera

Sensor size = 6.2 mm x 4.6 mm

Average = 5.4 mm (0.0054 m)

Size on image = 8 mm (0.008 m)

Vertical height of screen = 150 mm (0.15 m)

% of screen taken by object = 5.33

% of above compare with sensor size = 0.288 mm (0.00029 m)

1,000 mm (focal length used ~ 1,000 mm) = 1 m

To calculate size of object (m) = ((0.00029 x 3,000) / (1))

= 2.6 ft (0.8 m)

Chapter 25- Bright Yellow-Orange Orb 5

The Pythagorean Theorem to calculate distance from me is

$a^2 + b^2 = c^2$ or $(\text{vertical distance})^2 + (\text{horizontal distance})^2 = (\text{distance from camera})$

$(3{,}000 \text{ m})^2 + (2{,}000 \text{ m})^2$

$(9{,}000{,}000) + (4{,}000{,}000) = \sqrt{13{,}000{,}000} = 3{,}605 \text{ m}$ (distance From camera)

16MP Digital Camera

Sensor size = 6.2 mm x 4.6 mm

Average = 5.4 mm (0.0054 m)

Size on image = 5 mm (0.005 m)

Vertical height of screen = 150 mm (0.15 m)

% of screen taken by object = 3.33

% of above compare with sensor size = 0.18 mm (0.00018 m)

1,000 mm (focal length used ~ 1,000 mm) = 1 m

To calculate size of object (m) = ((0.00018 x 3,605) / (1))

= 1.9 ft (0.6 m)

Chapter 26 - The Return of the Golden Man

The Pythagorean Theorem to calculate distance from me is

$a^2 + b^2 = c^2$ or (vertical distance) ^{2} + (horizontal distance) ^{2} = (distance from camera)

(3,000 m) ^{2} + (2,000 m) ^{2}

(9,000,000) + (4,000,000) = $\sqrt{13,000,000}$ = 3,605 m (distance from camera)

16MP Digital Camera

Sensor size = 6.2 mm x 4.6 mm

Average = 5.4 mm (0.0054 m)

Size on image = 30 mm (0.03 m)

Vertical height of screen = 150 mm (0.15 m)

% of screen taken by object = 20

% of above compare with sensor size = 1.08 mm (0.00108 m)

2,000 mm (focal length used ~ 2,000 mm) = 2 m (due to 100% zoom)

To calculate size of object (m) = ((0.00108 x 3,605) / (2))

= 6.2 ft (1.9 m)

Chapter 28 - H-Shape Blue

The Pythagorean Theorem to calculate distance from me is

$a^2 + b^2 = c^2$ or (vertical distance) ^{2} + (horizontal distance) ^{2} = (distance from camera)

(3,000 m) ^{2} + (2,000 m) ^{2}

(9,000,000) + (4,000,000) = $\sqrt{13,000,000}$ = 3,605 m (distance from camera)

16MP Digital Camera

Sensor size = 6.2 mm x 4.6 mm

Average = 5.4 mm (0.0054 m)

Size on image = 10 mm (0.01 m)

Vertical height of screen = 150 mm (0.15 m)

% of screen taken by object = 6.67

% of above compare with sensor size = 0.36 mm (0.00036 m)

1,000 mm (focal length used ~ 1,000 mm) = 1 m

To calculate size of object (m) = ((0.00036 x 3,605) / (1))

= 4.2 ft (1.3 m)

Chapter 29 - The Hooded Man

The Pythagorean Theorem to calculate distance from me is

$a^2 + b^2 = c^2$ or (vertical distance) ^{2} + (horizontal distance) ^{2} = (distance from camera)

$(5,000 \text{ m})^2 + (2,000 \text{ m})^2$

(25,000,000) + (4,000,000) = $\sqrt{29,000,000}$ = 5,385 m (distance from camera)

16MP Digital Camera

Sensor size = 6.2 mm x 4.6 mm

Average = 5.4 mm (0.0054 m)

Size on image = 30 mm (0.01 m)

Vertical height of screen = 150 mm (0.15 m)

% of screen taken by object = 20

% of above compare with sensor size = 1.08 mm (0.00108 m)

2,000 mm (focal length used ~ 2,000 mm) = 2 m (due to 100% zoom)

To calculate size of object (m) = ((0.00108 x 5,385) / (2))

= 9.5 ft (2.9 m)

Chapter 33 - White-Yellow-Orange Orb 1, 2018, and the Portal Entry Above NZ

The Pythagorean Theorem to calculate distance from me is

$a^2 + b^2 = c^2$ or (vertical distance) ^{2} + (horizontal distance) ^{2} = (distance from camera)

$(3,000 \text{ m})^2 + (2,000 \text{ m})^2$

(9,000,000) + (4,000,000) = $\sqrt{13,000,000}$ = 3,605 m (distance from camera)

16MP Digital Camera

Sensor size = 6.2 mm x 4.6 mm

Average = 5.4 mm (0.0054 m)

Size on image = 5 mm (0.05 m)

Vertical height of screen = 150 mm (0.15 m)

% of screen taken by object = 3.33

% of above compare with sensor size = 0.18 mm (0.00018 m)

1,000 mm (focal length used ~ 1,000 mm) = 1 m

To calculate size of object (m) = ((0.00018 x 3,605) / (1))

= 2 ft (0.6 m)

Chapter 34 - Yellow-Orange Orb 2, 2018

The Pythagorean Theorem to calculate distance from me is

$a^2 + b^2 = c^2$ or (vertical distance)^2 + (horizontal distance)^2 = (distance from camera)

$(2,000 \text{ m})^2 + (2,000 \text{ m})^2$

$(4,000,000) + (4,000,000) = \sqrt{8,000,000} = 2,828$ m (distance from camera)

16MP Digital Camera

Sensor size = 6.2 mm x 4.6 mm

Average = 5.4 mm (0.0054 m)

Size on image = 5 mm (0.005 m)

Vertical height of screen = 150 mm (0.15 m)

% of screen taken by object = 3.33

% of above compare with sensor size = 0.18 mm (0.00018 m)

1,000 mm (focal length used ~ 1,000 mm) = 1 m

To calculate size of object (m) = ((0.00018 x 2,828) / (1))

= 1.6 ft (0.5 m)

Chapter 35 - Alien/Demonic Face in the Sky

The Pythagorean Theorem to calculate distance from me is

$a^2 + b^2 = c^2$ or (vertical distance)^2 + (horizontal distance)^2 = (distance from camera)

$(3,000 \text{ m})^2 + (2,000 \text{ m})^2$

$(9,000,000) + (4,000,000) = \sqrt{13,000,000} = 3,605$ m (distance from camera)

16MP Digital Camera

Sensor size = 6.2 mm x 4.6 mm

Average = 5.4 mm (0.0054 m)

Size on image = 25 mm (0.025 m)

Vertical height of screen = 150 mm (0.15 m)

% of screen taken by object = 16.67

% of above compare with sensor size = 0.9 mm (0.0009 m)

1,000 mm (focal length used ~ 1,000 mm) = 1 m

To calculate size of object (m) = ((0.0009 x 3,605) / (1))

= 10.4 ft (3.2 m)

Chapter 36 - Red Object Concealed Amongst White Balloons

The Pythagorean Theorem to calculate distance from me is

$a^2 + b^2 = c^2$ or (vertical distance) ^{2} + (horizontal distance) ^{2} = (distance from camera)

(2000 m) ^{2} + (2,000 m) ^{2}

(4,000,000) + (4,000,000) = √ 8,000,000 = 2,828 m (distance from camera)

16MP Digital Camera

Sensor size = 6.2 mm x 4.6 mm

Average = 5.4 mm (0.0054 m)

Size on image = 50 mm (0.05 m)

Vertical height of screen = 150 mm (0.15 m)

% of screen taken by object = 33.33

% of above compare with sensor size = 1.8 mm (0.0018 m)

2,000 mm (focal length used ~ 2,000 mm) = 2 m (due to 100% zoom)

To calculate size of object (m) = ((0.0018 x 2,828) / (2))

= 2.3 ft (0.7 m)

Chapter 37 - Biological Entity (balloon-like)

The Pythagorean Theorem to calculate distance from me is

$a^2 + b^2 = c^2$ or (vertical distance) ^{2} + (horizontal distance) ^{2} = (distance from camera)

(3,000 m) ^{2} + (2,000 m) ^{2}

(9,000,000) + (4,000,000) = √ 13,000,000 = 3,605 m (distance from camera)

16MP Digital Camera

Sensor size = 6.2 mm x 4.6 mm

Average = 5.4 mm (0.0054 m)

Size on image = 15 mm (0.015 m)

Vertical height of screen = 150 mm (0.15 m)

% of screen taken by object = 10

% of above compare with sensor size = 0.54 mm (0.00054 m)

1,000 mm (focal length used ~ 1,000 mm) = 1 m

To calculate size of object (m) = ((0.00054 x 3,605) / (1))

= 6.3 ft (1.94 m)

_____

Milton Keynes UK
Ingram Content Group UK Ltd.
UKHW040804291223
435170UK00001B/134

9 781923 156265